A FOURTEEN-UNIT COURSEBOOK

Thomas W. McKeown
Carol M. Cram

Clear Communications Press

This book includes material previously published in *Write To Win* by Thomas W. McKeown (North Vancouver: Clear Communications Press, 1987).

Printed in Canada

Published by:
Clear Communication Press
1818 Greenock Place
North Vancouver, BC
V7J 2Z7

Canadian Cataloguing in Publication Data
McKeown, Tom.
Better business writing

ISBN 0-969-3134-1-1

1. English language – Business English.
2. Commercial correspondence. 3. Business report writing. I. Cram, Carol M. (Carol Marie), 1956-
II. Title.
PE1115.M34 1990 808'.06665 C90-091510-2

For the graduates of the
Written Power seminars – who
wanted more.
TWM

For my mother, who taught me
the power of language.
CMC

Table of Contents

Table of Contents

Introduction

What is Better Business Writing?

Better Business Writing teaches you how to acquire excellent writing skills in fourteen weeks – the length of most single semester courses. As you work through the material in *Better Business Writing*, you can test your progress by completing the hundreds of exercises provided. These exercises will teach you everything you need to succeed as a business writer. You may even enjoy the process!

Benefits

Better Business Writing will help you:

1 Write excellent business letters.

2 Gain confidence in your writing ability.

3 Complete business reports and academic essays faster.

4 Improve your style through self-marked exercises.

5 Attain correctness in grammar, punctuation, and spelling.

What's New in *Better Business Writing*?

Better Business Writing gives you a step-by-step method to accomplish your goal of writing effectively. Check your progress by correcting exercises with the Answer Keys. Some review exercises do not include an Answer Key: your instructor may wish to test you on these exercises, or you can use *Better Business Writing* as a self-paced correspondence program by also ordering the *Better Business Writing Answer Key*. If you've taken a writing course, you can use *Better Business Writing* to refresh and update your understanding.

Practice Makes Perfect

You will sharpen your editing skills by completing the exercises in *Better Business Writing* and identifying the elements that distinguish well-written letters and reports. Use the exercises in *Better Business Writing* to practise correcting mistakes before you submit the final draft to your professor or manager. You will find the book ideally suited to self-paced learning.

A Note to Instructors

You can use *Better Business Writing* as your course text for Business Writing, Adult Basic Education, English Grammar, or English as a Second Language. The fourteen Units of *Better Business Writing* have been arranged to correspond to the fourteen weeks of a college or university semester.

Notice that some Units (for example, One and Three) contain more information than others (for example, Two and Thirteen). You may wish to devote two weeks to Unit One, and then cover Unit Two in one short session. How you schedule the presentation of material will depend on what particular skills you wish to emphasize.

Your students will learn a great deal by marking their own results with the Answer Keys provided. You can then test your students on the Review Exercises at the end of each unit and mark their work with the help of the *Better Business Writing Answer Key*. Units Seven and Fourteen contain review exercises suitable for your mid-term and Final examinations. We've set the course up so that you can combine the material in *Better Business Writing* with the *Answer Key* to save you countless hours of preparation time.

If you wish to use the *Better Business Writing Answer Key* to help you mark the Review Exercises, you may obtain it free of charge if you teach a college or university course. Alternatively, you can order the *Answer Key* as a textbook in itself for students who wish to pursue a self-study course. Some students learn faster when they have immediate access to answers.

A Special Thanks

We wish to extend a special thanks to Colin Dutson, who patiently edited the book and to William Messenger, who provided valuable advice. In addition, we gratefully thank our spouses, Rosalind McKeown and Gregg Simpson, for their unwavering support. Finally, I'd like to acknowledge my late mother-in-law, Ferne Weight, for her constant encouragement – CMC.

UNIT ONE

How To Write A Clear Sentence

Unit One shows you how to write sentences that will communicate your thoughts clearly. Here's what you'll learn:

1. Definition of a Sentence
2. The Reader's Viewpoint
3. Recognizing Subject/Object Nouns
4. Recognizing Linking/Action Verbs
5. The Red Ferrari: Using the Active Voice
6. The Yellow Hammock: Avoiding the Passive Voice
7. The Clear Picture: Being Specific
8. The Power Sentence: Summary and Review

As you learn each concept, improve your level of understanding by completing the relevant exercises. Then check your answers with the Answer Key. When you've mastered the Power Sentence, go on to the Review Exercises.

Introduction

To write simply is as difficult as to be good.
– *W. Somerset Maugham*

Clarity comes *first* in good business writing. You may think of good ideas, but until you capture them clearly on paper you cannot communicate them to other people.

Translating abstract thoughts into clear, concrete words takes practice. Some people may seem to write clearly without effort. You may think you have to spend more time revising for clarity than other people. Don't be misled: all clear writing requires hard work.

In Unit One you will learn the powerful techniques all good writers use to communicate. Once you understand these key techniques, you will communicate your written ideas to others more quickly and effectively.

The first step in learning to write well involves understanding how to write a clear sentence. In order to write clear sentences you will need to know the following terms:

1 Noun (Subject and Object nouns)
2 Verb (Action and Linking verbs)
3 The Active Voice
4 The Passive Voice (Regular and Divine)

Learning these terms poses a challenge. But once you learn *first* how to distinguish them and *second* how to apply them, you'll be well on your way to writing crisp memos and clear letters.

1. *Definition of a Sentence*

The sentence represents the hammer in your writing kit – the indispensible tool. Every letter or report you write, no matter how long, consists of individual sentences which your readers encounter one at a time. The quality of each sentence determines the overall quality of your writing. Before defining the inner qualities that turn an ordinary sentence into a *Power Sentence*, let's consider length.

Sentence Length >

Sentences run anywhere from two words ("Jim succeeded") to hundreds (think of typical legal documents). In general, your sentences should *average* fifteen words, some having as few as two words, others as many as thirty. Why use so few words in business writing? Because that's all most readers can absorb quickly. Practise counting the words in every message you write, and then trying to compress your ideas.

2. *The Reader's Viewpoint*

Let's examine how a sentence works from the reader's viewpoint, so that you can understand why you should limit the length of your sentences.

The period at the end of a sentence signals the end of a complete thought. But what activity do *readers* engage in when they encounter a period? Readers don't just put their minds in neutral, but actively *think about* the meaning of the sentence and its connection to previous ones.

For example, you will not simply *absorb* the meaning of this sentence when you come to the period, you will think about it, perhaps *judge* it. If you disagree with the content, you may let it slide out of your mind; if the form of the sentence confuses you, you may stop trying to understand the message.

If you write sentences that are too long, your readers may respond by tuning you out. Busy readers will not hold a lengthy sentence in their memories long enough to accept or reject it. They prefer fairly short sentences which permit them to identify meaning quickly. In literary writing, sentences are often much longer and more complex because their intention is to move the reader to reflection, rather than action. Other differences appear in point form below. Don't make the mistake of following literary models. Remember the business writing motto: "Short is beautiful".

Table Showing Differences between Literary and Business English

Literary Writing	*Business Writing*
Designed to be read many times before revealing full meaning	Reveals full meaning on a single reading
Long sentences	Short sentences
Unusual words	Familiar words
Colourful phrases	Plain meaning
Variety encouraged	Consistency expected
Imagery and symbolism	Numbers and charts
Long, complex sentences	Short, clear sentences
Impossible to read quickly	Easy to read quickly
Ambiguity acceptable	Clarity essential
Leads the reader to REFLECT	*Leads the reader to* ACT

How Many Ideas Should I Pack Into a Sentence?

As a rough guide, 80% of your sentences should contain *one main idea*. That leaves 15% of your sentences to convey two main ideas and 5% to convey three ideas or more. These three-idea sentences often appear in the form of a list, which readers can follow easily.

It takes less time to learn to write nobly than to learn to write lightly and straightforwardly.
– *F.W. Nietzsche*

Since 80% of your sentences should convey only one main idea, writing them represents your most critical task. Let's look at how to write these "one-main-idea" sentences so as to maximize their impact on the reader. We call the perfectly written "one-main-idea" sentence the *Power Sentence*.

The *Power Sentence* contains one main thought, an active verb, and specific words as follows:

Three-Step Checklist for Writing a Power Sentence

1 **Specific Subject:**
noun, noun phrase or pronoun

2 **Specific Action Verb:**
(not a linking or passive verb)

3 **Specific Object:**
noun, noun phrase or pronoun

If you use the Power Sentence structure to communicate your meaning, your writing will be strong, precise, and *effective*. To understand how to write a Power Sentence, you need to start by mastering a number of definitions.

First, we'll define nouns and verbs. Next, we'll arrange them within the sentence to form the Active Voice. After that, we'll show how to recognize the Passive Voice – in order to avoid it. Then we'll learn how to choose specific words. As you progress through these concepts in Unit One, you'll complete several exercises to test your understanding. At the end of Unit One, try the Review Exercises, and then go on to Unit Two to find out how to assemble Power Sentences into Power Paragraphs.

Time for a cup of tea?

3. *Recognizing Subject/Object Nouns*

The word noun comes from the Latin word "nomen" which means name. A noun, therefore, refers to words which denote or name an item that can be classified into one of the five following categories:

Noun Classifications

	Noun Category	*Example*
1.	Person	Jane Smith, Bill Jones, Ms. Abrams
2.	Place	Vancouver, Tokyo, Paris
3.	Thing	pen, book, procedure, map, outline, computer
4.	Quality or Feeling	love, justice, anger, time
5.	Verb-noun (gerund)	jogging, eating, sleeping, writing, feeling

We use two other parts of speech in the same way as nouns: pronouns and noun phrases. Pronouns are words which, as the meaning of the Latin prefix "*pro*" suggests, stand *for* nouns in a sentence: *she, he, me, us, it, they*, etc. In Unit Three you will learn more about how to use pronouns correctly. Noun phrases are groups of two or more words which together stand for a noun such as *The Director of Corrections* or *The Personnel Committee.*

Both pronouns and noun phrases perform the same function as nouns: they identify the *doers* and the *receivers* of the actions in a sentence:

> **She** [pronoun identifying the "doer"]
> **influences** [verb]
> **department policy** [noun phrase identifying the "receiver"].

Depending on its function in a particular sentence, a noun, pronoun, or noun phrase may act as either a *doer* (a "subject") or a *receiver* (an "object"). To write Power Sentences, you must be able to distinguish subject nouns from object nouns, so we will now explain how to make this distinction.

Subject Nouns >

Nouns within a sentence function in different ways, and take on different descriptive names with different functions. The term "subject noun", for example, has a special meaning in grammar. It does not necessarily refer to the noun which comes first in the sentence. Instead, it refers to the noun which *performs the action* described by the verb in the sentence:

> *The manager* approved my report.

Here the "manager" is the "doer" because he or she performs the action: "approved". As a result, "manager" represents the subject noun of the sentence.

Object Nouns >

"Object noun" refers to the noun which receives the action performed by the subject noun:

> The manager approved *my report.*

Here the object noun ("my report") receives the action "approved". As a general rule, the "receiver" of the action (the object) should come *after* the verb in the sentence. Notice that you *could* place the receiver of the action (the report) in front of the verb. "*My report* was approved by the manager." Grammatically, "my report" becomes the *apparent* subject of this sentence. However, the words "my report" do not perform any action. To make the sentence into a Power Sentence, you must drag the "doer" of the action (the manager) back up to its strongest position – at the beginning of the sentence.

Remember the Power Sentence structure:

Subject (the "doer" of the action):
    The manager
    Verb:
        approved
        Object (the "receiver" of the action):
            my report.

If you place the receiver of the action ("my report") at the beginning of the sentence and the doer of the action ("the manager") at the end of the sentence, you end up with the undesirable Passive Voice, which we will examine later.

EXERCISE 1

Recognizing Subject Nouns and Object Nouns

Underline the true subject nouns (the "doers" of the action) and double underline the object nouns (the "reccivers" of the action) in the following sentences.

1. The memo set forth seven purchase options.
2. After several years of neglect, he organized his budget.
3. My letter was cut in half by the hard-nosed editor.
4. Tests were conducted by Bill on the three-blade propeller.
5. The analysis of results was presented by the field engineer.

Check your answers with the Answer Key at the end of this section. Review the preceding definitions if your answers are not correct. If you scored 100%, pat yourself on the back and go on to try the Review Exercises.

4. *Recognizing Linking/Action Verbs*

Now that you have learned to recognize the two main classes of nouns, subjects and objects, you are ready to classify verbs. Verbs divide into two categories: Action verbs and Linking verbs. Power sentences use Action verbs rather than Linking verbs, so we will now define each type.

Linking Verbs >

The most common linking verb is some form of the verb "to be":

Sharon *is* an above average worker.
The hot tub samples *are* contaminated.
The Department *is* of medium size.
The Managers *are* well qualified.
The complaint *was* valid.
The officials *were* forward-looking.
The report *will be* several pages long.

Notice that the linking verb can occur in any tense: past (was, were), present (is, are), or future (will be).

Although most people find it easier to write with linking verbs instead of action verbs, linking verbs weaken the impact of your writing because they *link* the subject of a sentence with the noun or adjective that follows: Harry *is* a driver. Notice that the words "Harry" and "driver" represent the same person; the sentence links complementary ideas together, and therefore does not give the reader much information.

Action Verbs >

Action verbs, unlike linking verbs, express an action of the body (*clamber*, *waddle*, *slide*) or the mind (*deny*, *judge*, *approve*). For this reason, they energize writing. The action verb tells your reader what the subject noun *does:*

Ho-Lee *evaluated* the computer software.
Susan *rewrote* the report.
Parminder *distributed* the affidavits.
The guard *slumbered.*

Transitive & Intransitive Verbs

You also need to understand the different ways in which an action verb can function in a sentence. For example, some action verbs (called transitive verbs) carry the action of the verb across from the doer (the subject) to the receiver (the object):

Sandra [subject]
played [action verb: transitive]
soccer [object].

In this sentence, the action verb "played" functions as a transitive verb because it carries the subject (Sandra) to the receiver (soccer). As a result, the sentence is a Power Sentence: Subject/Action Verb/Object.

However, you cannot simply insert an action verb into a sentence and hope it becomes a Power Sentence. An action verb may not carry the action from the doer (subject) to the receiver (object) because the receiver is not a noun, noun phrase, or pronoun. When an action verb does not carry across an action from subject to object, we call it an intransitive verb. For example:

Sandra [subject]
played [action verb: intransitive]
quietly [adverb].

Study the following pairs of sentences to determine when a verb acts as a transitive verb and when it acts as an intransitive verb.

Transitive:	Claudia **wrote** ten pages of her report.
Intransitive:	Claudia **wrote** all morning.
Transitive:	They always **buy** their groceries in a hurry.
Intransitive:	They always **buy** in a hurry.
Transitive:	Our rose bush **covered** the fence in one summer.
Intransitive:	Our rose bush **grew** quickly.

If you use the Subject/Action Verb/Object format, you will avoid the weaker intransitive verb structure. Therefore, make sure your subject noun works with the verb to affect an object noun:

Janice [subject noun]
cultivated [verb: transitive because it's followed by an object]
her tomatoes [object noun].

Changing Linking to Action Verbs >

To replace a linking verb with an action verb, you need to rethink what you want to tell your reader. For example, you can rewrite the sentence we looked at earlier: "Harry *is* a driver" as "Harry *drives* an MGB". Similarly, you can rewrite "Lin *is* a student of psychology" as "Lin *studies* psychology". This sentence conveys more energy in fewer words than the version with the linking verb. Use of the action verb shows a dynamic relationship between Lin and psychology.

In mathematical terms, you might think of a linking verb as a plus sign (+) that adds together two complementary ideas ("I *am* Tarzan"), and an action verb as a multiplication sign (X) that powerfully transmits energy between two *different* entities ("Tarzan *fights* crocodiles"). Action verbs compress thought more effectively than linking verbs do – they have a higher octane rating!

Let's look at another example:

> He *is* [linking verb] inclined to disagree with his manager.

Substitute an action verb for is:

> He often *disagrees* [action verb] with his manager.

You can also change linking verbs in the future tense:

> Her budget presentation *will be* [linking verb] half an hour in length.

Choose an action verb instead of *will be*:

> Her budget presentation will *require* [action verb] half an hour.

Macro Hint

You can improve your writing more quickly by increasing your ratio of action verbs to linking verbs than by any other technique. Try it!

EXERCISE 2

Changing Linking Verbs to Action Verbs

Underline the Linking Verbs. Rewrite the sentences, replacing the Linking Verbs with Action Verbs. Notice that you may need to change the order of the nouns in some sentences to use an Action Verb.

1. The second memo is sixteen pages longer than the first one.
2. The President and the executive committee are in agreement.

3. The lieutenant will be an effective leader of the men.
4. Jim is unhappy with the Personnel Committee's decision.
5. This layout will be satisfactory to the staff.

Check your answers with the Answer Key at the end of this section. Once you learn how to change linking to action verbs you will have overcome the greatest challenge most writers face. So far so good? If you're eager for more practice, tackle the Review Exercises at the end of this unit.

5. *The Red Ferrari: Using the Active Voice*

If you could have any car you wanted to drive for one evening, which car would you choose – a brand new red Ferrari or a rusty old Datsun? Most of us would choose the Ferrari because of its speed, sleek design, and efficient handling. In writing, you can choose between the energetic Active Voice (the Red Ferrari) or the sluggish Passive Voice (the Yellow Hammock). If you wish to convey meaning as quickly and efficiently as possible, you need to learn how to use the active voice.

Now that you can identify the subject, object, and action verb, you are ready to place them in the most powerful sentence order: Subject-Action Verb-Object.

This order identifies the Active Voice. All you have learned to this point has equipped you to write sentences in this active voice pattern. Purpose? To ensure the clearest expression of your thinking.

Before going further, be particularly careful not to confuse the terms "Action Verb" and "Active Voice". As explained above, we call words that express actions Action Verbs. On the other hand, the term "Active Voice" refers to sentences that follow the subject-noun, action verb, object-noun pattern (S - V - O). That is, sentences in the Active Voice use transitive verbs that transmit energy from a subject noun to an object noun.

The Regular Active Voice (S–V–O) >

To write a sentence in the active voice, ensure that the subject noun comes in front of the action verb. Do you know how to locate the subject noun of your sentences, in order to put it before your verb? Take this passive voice sentence for example:

The Chairman was elected by the committee.

To change this passive voice sentence into an active voice sentence, follow these three steps:

1	Locate the root or stem of the verb "was elected": *elect*
2	Ask yourself: "*Who or what elects?*"
3	The answer to Question 2 *always* provides the true subject of your sentence: *committee.*

Once you determine the subject of the above sentence, simply place the subject noun before the verb:

The *committee* elected the Chairman.

Notice that the verb form changes too, and that the word "by" disappears. Good riddance!

Now try the same procedure with this passive voice sentence:

The question was answered by the manager.

Remember the checklist:

1 Simplify the verb phrase "was answered" (which is in the past tense) to the root or stem of the verb: *answer.*

2 Ask: "*Who or what answers?*"

3 Obviously, the *manager* "answers". Therefore, the true subject of the sentence is "manager".

To rewrite the sentence in the active voice, simply put the subject first:

The *manager* answered the question.

EXERCISE 3

Rewriting in the Active Voice

Using the 3-step procedure outlined above, underline the true subject in each of these sentences; then rewrite each sentence, if necessary, in the Active Voice pattern.

1. The public information office was misled by the letter.
2. The field staff were thrilled by the supervisor's remarks.
3. Bill engineered the satellite tracking antenna.
4. Angela was commended by the Vice-President for her work on the Carter account.
5. After working for the company for twenty years, I was discharged by the new president.

Check your answers with the Answer Key at the end of this section. For more practice, go on to the Review Exercises.

Writing sentences in the active voice (S-V-O) will give your letters more impact and clarity, so...practise, practise, practise.

The Special Active Voice Pattern (V–O) >

One kind of sentence may trick you when you attempt to write in the active voice. For example, what is the subject of this sentence?

> Please send a copy of the report to Mr. Lum.

The verb is "send", but who or what does the sending? The answer is the person for whom the sentence is intended:

> [*You*] please send a copy of the report to Mr. Lum.

The subject in this kind of sentence is "You" understood. The reader instinctively knows that a sentence which begins with a verb has "you" for its subject. Although the subject is not named, it is clear, and obviously comes before the verb. Therefore this Verb-Object sentence pattern follows the Active Voice pattern, just as though the subject was present. Be careful not to confuse the Verb-Object pattern with the Object-Verb pattern that marks the notorious Divine Passive pattern. Read on for information about the Divine Passive.

Summary >

The grammarians are at variance, and the matter is still undecided.

–*Horace*

At this point, you have learned how to identify the subjects, objects, and verbs in your sentences in order to write in the active voice. You have also learned the correct order in which to place your subjects, objects, and verbs. To edit your own writing, you also need to be able to recognize the passive voice when it occurs. Just as the active voice distinguishes the professional writer, so the passive voice characterizes the bureaucratic, foggy-minded buck-passer.

6. *The Yellow Hammock: Avoiding the Passive Voice*

Business writing should lead the reader to act. It cannot do this effectively if you structure your sentences in a way that makes your readers feel as though they were swinging lazily in a yellow hammock.

To avoid the passive voice, you need to recognize its two forms: the Regular Passive and the Divine Passive. We'll examine each in detail.

The Regular Passive (O–V–S) >

The Regular Passive sentence puts the "doer" of the action (the subject) *after* the "receiver" of the action (the object). For example, in the sentence "Ariel was promoted by Frank", the noun "Ariel" receives the action initiated by "Frank". Therefore, "Ariel" should be the object noun. Since this word comes before the verb, the sentence follows the Regular Passive pattern.

The passive drains energy from your sentences. Rewrite the sentence to read:

> Frank promoted Ariel.

Notice that this active voice sentence requires only three words, while the passive voice sentence requires five words.

Why do Intelligent People Often Write in the Passive Voice

Many relatively intelligent and sophisticated thinkers use the passive voice far too often. Why? The answer may be that although we *think* in the active voice (Frank promoted Ariel), when we come to *write* our thoughts, we recall the last word that we actually thought (Ariel) first; then we recall the verb (was promoted by); finally, we recall the subject (Frank). This act of recall causes us to write "backwards," in the passive voice: "Ariel was promoted by Frank".

Imagine watching a home video of someone walking out of the house and then diving into the swimming pool. Now imagine what this scene would look like if it was run backwards. It's funny at first, then annoying. Take the time to rewind the tape, then run it forward. If you use the active voice, your readers will understand you more easily.

The greater part of this world's troubles are due to questions of grammar.
-Montaigne

You will most likely fall into the passive voice when you deal with complex thoughts, rather than simple actions. For example:

> The impeachment (receiver of the action) was conducted (verb), after many delays and a great deal of argument, by the Senate Committee (doer of the action: true subject).

You can easily rewrite this sentence in the active voice by taking the true subject (Senate Committee) and placing it at the beginning of the sentence:

> The Senate Committee conducted the impeachment after many delays and a great deal of argument.

Exercise particular caution with your sentence structure when you formulate sophisticated concepts – such as legal agreements.

The Divine Passive (O–V)

Both the Active Voice and the Regular Passive Voice sentences contain a true subject noun, either before or after the verb. Sometimes, however, a sentence contains no "doer" of the action at all. This form of sentence follows the "Divine Passive" structure. Take this sentence, for example:

> The specimens were analyzed.

Since the writer provides no "doer" to perform the action described by the verb, the reader can only assume that an unseen person or force must have performed the analysis.

The Chief Drawback of the Divine Passive

The qualifier "Divine" in the phrase "Divine Passive" ironically implies that the "doer" in the sentence must be in the heavens or sitting on a cloud somewhere! Writers often resort to this form when they want to dodge responsibility for an action by maintaining anonymity.

For example:

> Your application for vacation leave has not been approved.

Does this mean that no manager in the company denied your application?

How about:

> A decision has been made not to ratify your nomination for the position.

Does this mean no influential person opposed your nomination?

Here's another one:

> Another person has been selected for the position.

Does this mean the person signing the letter to you did not have a hand in, or support, the decision? Of course this might be the case; nevertheless, the reader will very likely draw the opposite conclusion (whether correct or not!). Therefore, such grammatical refuges – or subterfuges – are pointlessly evasive. The reader will likely assume that the person who signed the letter has taken the action, or supports it.

I have often wished that there was a language in which it would be impossible to tell a lie.
– *G.C. Lichtenberg*

Let's look at another example:

> Your lease has been cancelled.

Cancelled by whom? Why? Struggling with the disquieting fact that an anonymous authority is directing a negative power in your direction, you may want to know which person to challenge, or in which direction to assert your rights.

On the other hand, providing your reader with a clear subject in sentences signals your willingness to accept responsibility. For example:

> *We* have cancelled your lease because of non-payment of rent.

Or:

> Since *you* have not paid your rent, *your* lease has lapsed.

Turning the Divine Passive into the Active Voice

But how do you turn a tricky phrase like the following one from the Divine Passive into the active voice?

> Your application for vacation leave has been denied.

First, you have to notice that no "doer" of the action is present, and then provide one. Remember your three-step "How to Find the Subject Noun" Checklist:

1. Find the root or stem of the verb phrase: "has been denied": deny.
2. Ask, "Who or what denies?"
3. Answer: no-one or nothing is doing the action.

The vacation leave does not deny itself, so it can't be the subject. The subject is missing. The reader must guess who performed the action, and this causes unnecessary confusion.

If you can't provide a subject, you may have nothing to say – in which case delete the sentence. On the other hand, you may not have thought clearly – in which case stop and think! Then rewrite.

Should the Divine Passive Ever Be Used?

Yes. You can effectively use the Divine Passive to convey *welcome* news:

> Your application has been accepted.
> Your film has been nominated for an award.
> You have been elected to the Board.

Here your readers will see your anonymity as the mark of modesty rather than cowardice.

The Divine Passive is also sometimes appropriate when the subject-noun is irrelevant or unknown – that is, where you are obviously not attempting to avoid responsibility for an action:

> My purse was stolen on the bus.

However, even here you could effectively write:

> *Someone* on the bus stole my purse.

Aside from these two exceptions, however, strive to shake the majority of your sentences out of the comfortable yellow hammock which the passive voice provides.

EXERCISE 4

Changing the Passive to the Active Voice

Circle the true subject nouns (the "doers" of the action) in the following sentences, where present. Underline the objects (the "receivers" of the action). Double-underline the verbs. Provide a true subject noun if needed, and use action verbs to rewrite all the sentences in subject-verb-object order.

1. Labour peace has been sought.
2. A way will be found to master this material.
3. Susan is considered to be a successful negotiator.
4. One was struck by the clock.
5. The data was collected on August 2nd.

Check your versions against the Answer Key. If you scored 100%, you have a good grasp of the Active Voice and a significant segment of English grammar. Go on to try the Review Exercises.

7. *The Precise Goods: Being Specific*

Once you know how to use the active voice (S-V-O order), and action verbs, you have accomplished two-thirds of the journey toward writing effective sentences. The final one-third involves *being specific*. When you add this quality of specificity to the active voice and the use of action verbs, you will have attained the ability to write the *Power Sentence.*

Recognizing Umbrella Verbs >

Check your sentence for specific words, beginning with your choice of verb. For example, in the sentence "The manager handles reports", the action verb "handles" does not convey a clear picture. It could mean "reviews", "approves", "shreds", "burns", "drafts", "writes", or many other specific activities.

Generalized verbs like "handles" are "umbrella words," under which huddle multitudes of specific meanings. In using these vague words, the writer might as well say to the reader, "Guess what I mean!" The bewildered reader irritably concludes that such writers either do not know what they mean themselves or cannot be bothered to be clear. Perhaps they even intend to conceal their meaning from their readers! Such a lack of consideration alienates readers – not a good idea. Instead, peer under the umbrella and select the most appropriate specific word from those sheltering there.

Refer to the section on Strength in Unit Ten – Develop Your Style for more information on choosing specific verbs.

Recognizing Umbrella Nouns >

Also avoid choosing "umbrella" subject nouns and object nouns. For example, write "the quarterly report" instead of "the report" or "the Selection Board" instead of "the appropriate authorities". When you take the trouble to locate the specific word for the exact meaning you wish to convey, you save your reader time and energy.

8. *The Power Sentence: Summary and Review*

Three-Step Checklist for Writing a Power Sentence

Let's put all the bits of advice from Unit One together and see how they affect your attitude to the following sentence:

The report was handled by the executive member.

The *Power Sentence* checklist shows you how to edit this sentence in three steps. Here it is again:

1. Put the sentence in Subject-Verb-Object order.
2. Choose an action verb.
3. Choose a specific subject and object.

When you check the sentence against these three steps, you will notice that it displays three shortcomings: the passive voice order; a vague, umbrella verb; and umbrella nouns. Use the three steps to improve the sentence:

S-V-O
1 The executive member handled the report.

Action Verb
2 The executive member *approved* the report.

Specific Nouns
3 Our *vice-president* approved my *annual budget forecast.*

Your own revision might differ in your choice of specific words, but if you made the same *kinds* of changes, you help your reader by making your sentences clear and concise.

EXERCISE 5

Writing the Power Sentence

Turn the following passive voice sentences into Power Sentences. Follow the format provided for the first sentence.

1. The course was talked about by the people concerned.

   Notice that the subject, verb, and object are all umbrella words. Provide specific replacements to successfully rewrite the sentence.

	S	V	O
1	______	______	______
2	______	______	______
		action verb	
3	______	______	______
	specific subject	*specific verb*	*specific object*

2. Most of the company's assets were sold by the bank.
3. Your qualifications were not considered acceptable for this position.
4. The presentation was given by the speaker.
5. The article was published by the newspaper.

Check your answers against the Answer Key. Notice that the Power Sentence Checklist keeps you from waffling and ensures that you have something specific to tell your reader.

If you can now recognize and write *Power Sentences*, congratulations! For more practice, try the Review Exercises.

Answer Key

EXERCISE 1
Recognizing Subject- and Object-Nouns

Underline the true subject nouns (the "doers" of the action) and double underline the object nouns (the "receivers" of the action) in the following sentences.

1. The memo set forth seven purchase options.
2. After several years of neglect, he organized his budget.
3. My letter was cut in half by the hard-nosed editor.
4. Tests were conducted by Bill on the three-blade propeller.
5. The analysis of results was presented by the field engineer.

EXERCISE 2
Changing Linking Verbs to Action Verbs

Underline the Linking Verbs. Rewrite the sentences, replacing the Linking Verbs with Action Verbs. Notice that you may need to change the order of the nouns in some sentences to use an Action Verb.

1. The second memo is sixteen pages longer than the first one.

   The second memo contains sixteen pages more than the first one.

2. The President and the executive committee are in agreement.

   The President agrees with the executive committee.
   or
   The President and executive committee agree.

3. The lieutenant will be an effective leader of the men.

   The lieutenant will lead the men effectively.

4. Jim is unhappy with the Personnel Committee's decision.

   The Personnel Committee's decision upset Jim.

5. This layout will be satisfactory to the staff.

   This layout will satisfy (or, *please*) *the staff.*

EXERCISE 3
Rewriting in the Active Voice

Using the 3-step procedure outlined above, underline the grammatical subject in each of these sentences; then rewrite each sentence, if necessary, in the Active Voice pattern.

1. The public information office was misled by the letter.

   The letter misled the public information officer.

2. The field staff were thrilled by the supervisor's remarks.

The supervisor's remarks thrilled the field staff.

3. Bill engineered the satellite tracking antenna.

[*This sentence is already in the Active Voice.*]

4. Angela was commended by the Vice-President for her work on the Carter account.

The Vice-President commended Angela for her work on the Carter account.

5. After working for the company for twenty years, I was discharged by the new president.

The new president discharged me after I had worked for the company for twenty years.

EXERCISE 4
Changing the Passive to the Active Voice

Circle the true subject nouns in the following sentences, where present. Underline the objects. Double-underline the verbs. Provide a true subject noun if needed, and use action verbs to rewrite all the sentences in subject-verb-object order.

1. Labour peace has been sought.

No true subject present (Divine Passive).
[*The contractor*] sought labour peace.

2. A way will be found to master this material.

No true subject present.
[*They*] *will find a way to master this material.*

3. Susan is considered to be a successful negotiator.

No true subject present.
[*We*] *consider Susan a successful negotiator.*

4. One was struck by the clock.

True Subject: clock.
The clock struck one.

5. The data was collected on August 2nd.

No true subject present
[*The Field Staff*] *collected the data on August 2nd.*

EXERCISE 5
Writing the Power Sentence

S-V-O

Action Verb

Specifics

Turn the following passive voice sentences into Power Sentences. Follow the format provided for the first sentence.

1. The course was talked about by the people concerned.

1 *The people concerned talked about the seminar.*

2 *The people concerned approved of the seminar.*

3 *The secretaries approved of the Written Power seminar.*

2. Most of the company's assets were sold by the bank.

The Northwest Bank liquidated 82% of Trenton Inc.'s assets.

3. Your qualifications were not considered acceptable to this position.

The position of Financial Analyst requires a person with a minimum of five years' experience at the executive level.

Note: This sentence *implies* rejection by stating what the position requires, rather than vaguely stating that the applicant lacks the necessary qualifications. Refer to Unit Six - How to Structure Letters Effectively for more examples of how to write a rejection in the active voice that does not personally attack the applicant.

4. The presentation was given by the speaker.

Ms. Jansen, an expert on financial planning, presented her analysis of Mason Inc.'s Annual Report.

5. The article was published by the newspaper.

The Morning Star *published Joan Smith's article on corporate recycling in its June 24th issue.*

Your answers will differ from the examples provided. However, if your sentences use Subject-Verb-Object order and contain specific subjects, objects, and action verbs, you will have successfully written the Power Sentence.

Review Exercises

Test your understanding of Unit One with the following exercises. Refer to the *Better Business Writing Answer Key* or your instructor for the correct responses.

EXERCISE 1

Recognizing Subject and Object Nouns

Underline the true subject nouns (doers of the action), and double underline the object nouns (receivers of the action) in the following sentences.

1. The financial statements for Stetson Inc. were analyzed by the accountant.
2. We will sell our subsidiary companies in two years.
3. Mr. White's report contained several errors.
4. The company fired all of its employees.
5. George Marvin received a pay increase after he had worked 15 weeks.
6. A new Personnel Manager has been hired by the company.
7. The Vice-President asked me to handle the Chadwick account.
8. The new Director of Programming started his career as a radio announcer.
9. Before we can rent this car, we must make sure it is insured.
10. Several programs were run by Joanne at the seminar.

EXERCISE 2

Changing Linking Verbs to Action Verbs

Underline the Linking Verbs. Rewrite the sentences, replacing the Linking Verbs with Action Verbs. Notice that you may need to change the order of the nouns in some sentences to use an Action Verb.

1. With a word processor, you are free to shift text around.
2. The Chief Executive Officer is quick to adopt new methods.

3. Janice is an efficient computer programmer.
4. Alex is responsible for investigating all accidents that occur on company premises.
5. A comprehensive management training program is useful for all employees.
6. The assessment team were in a meeting at the Pacific Hotel.
7. Each employee is ready for work by 9 a.m.
8. Alice was well qualified for the position of Credit Manager.
9. The air is cold and wet.
10. The courier was late bringing the new contracts.

EXERCISE 3

Rewriting in the Active Voice

Using the 3-step procedure outlined in the section on the Active Voice, underline the true subject in each of these sentences; then rewrite each sentence, if necessary, in the Active Voice pattern.

1. A copy of the report is sent by the client.
2. Disciplinary action is taken by the supervisor after thoroughly investigating the incident.
3. Administrative staff are authorized by the company to ensure that employees conform to the company's dress code.
4. Two probationary reviews are written by the manager for each employee.
5. Andrea was dismayed by Mr. Aiken's poor reaction to her presentation.
6. You will be presented with a free sample from our company.
7. New employees will be advised by the Department Head regarding the location of their lockers.
8. Six employees were honored with a long service recognition ceremony.
9. A trip to Japan was received by Joe Morgan for his outstanding sales record last year.

10. All overtime hours must be confirmed by the employee's Department Head.

EXERCISE 4

Changing the Passive to the Active Voice

Circle the true subject nouns in the following sentences, where present. Underline the objects. Double-underline the verbs. Provide a subject noun if needed, and use action verbs to rewrite all the sentences in subject-verb-object order.

1. Sam weighed the alternatives and made a decision.
2. Grievances are handled in accordance with the step approach method.
3. Every effort will be made to handle problems as they arise.
4. The safety rules are designed to ensure employees avoid accidents.
5. Employees are advised by management not to bring excessive amounts of money or valuables to the workplace.
6. Vacation times are allocated in accordance with each employee's years of service to the company.
7. There is nothing to be done about our high absentee rate.
8. You were asked to submit the report no later than 3 p.m. on Tuesday, December 22.
9. Sick leave is payable only when a regular full or part-time employee is absent from work as a result of an illness or non-work related injury.
10. Requests for credit information regarding company employees are received in writing.

EXERCISE 5

Writing the Power Sentence

Turn the following passive voice sentences into Power Sentences. Note that you may have to supply a true subject for those sentences written in the Divine Passive. Follow the format provided for the first sentence.

1. You are requested to submit your application to the Personnel Manager.

Notice that the subject, verb, and object are all umbrella words. Provide specific replacements to rewrite the sentence.

	S	V	O
1	______	______	______
2	______	______	______
		action verb	
3	______	______	______
	specific subject	*specific verb*	*specific object*

2. Your concern about our product will be addressed by the Customer Relations Department.

3. The fax machine was fixed by the technician.

4. This problem was not resolved to our satisfaction by the personnel concerned.

5. The correct form must be filled in completely by people who want funding.

6. The suite of offices was obtained by the big consortium.

7. Your request for a refund has been granted by our company.

8. You are required to submit your tax returns for the past three years to the accounting firm.

9. Last week the lawyer's client was found innocent of the crime by the judge.

10. The new employee is well liked by all his colleagues.

Check your sentences to make sure you have included specific subjects, verbs, and objects and then refer to the *Better Business Writing Answer Key* for suggested responses.

How To Structure Paragraphs

How are you doing so far? Unit One contains the most difficult and most important material in this entire book. Once you understand how to write a Power Sentence, you command a skill that gives you a distinct advantage over most business writers. Just eliminating linking verbs will energize your writing and compress your ideas.

In Unit Two you get a bit of a breather from all those nouns and verbs you contended with in Unit One. You will return to grammar in Unit Three, but for now you can concentrate on learning how to write the following components of Power Paragraphs:

1. Bridging Paragraphs
2. Developed Paragraphs
3. Transitional Markers.

At the end of this section, you will review the concepts you've learned in Units One and Two to prepare you for the material in Unit Three – How To Connect Thoughts.

Introduction

Just as a sentence describes a transfer of energy from a subject noun to an object noun, a paragraph links sentences together into a sequence of combined energies that have a central core of meaning. The word "paragraph" comes from the Greek *para*, meaning beside, plus *graphos*, meaning mark. Originally the word referred to a short stroke placed within the tightly crabbed script of a papyrus manuscript to mark the beginning of a new thought.

Now that paper is less expensive, we indent the first line of a new paragraph to alert readers to a change of thought. Just as a period at the end of a sentence provides your readers with time to reflect upon your sentence, so a visual break of white space between paragraphs gives readers proportionately more time to weigh the central meaning of a number of sentences.

You commonly use two types of paragraph in business and technical writing: bridging paragraphs and developed paragraphs.

1. *Bridging Paragraphs*

Bridging paragraphs provide transitions into and out of memos and letters, and are shorter than developed paragraphs. Often, bridging paragraphs contain only one sentence. You see them most frequently as the first and last paragraphs in memos or letters.

Generally, you use a bridging paragraph to introduce or to end a topic. You may also find a bridging paragraph useful in a long letter to give your readers a break from a steady diet of long, developed paragraphs. But be careful not to string too many bridging paragraphs together or your thought will strike the reader as sporadic and lightweight.

Examples of Bridging Paragraphs

You can use the following examples of bridging paragraphs to give you ideas on how to start and finish your own letters.

Opening paragraph in a response to an inquiry:

> Thank you for your letter of July 9, asking for details of our tenant protection policy.

Opening paragraph in a Royal Bank *Monthly Letter:*

> The basic skill in every profession and in most businesses is the ability to organize and express ideas in writing and in speaking.

Concluding paragraph in a Public Service letter:

> If I can be of further assistance, please call me at (202) 414-6657.

EXERCISE 1

Writing Bridging Paragraphs

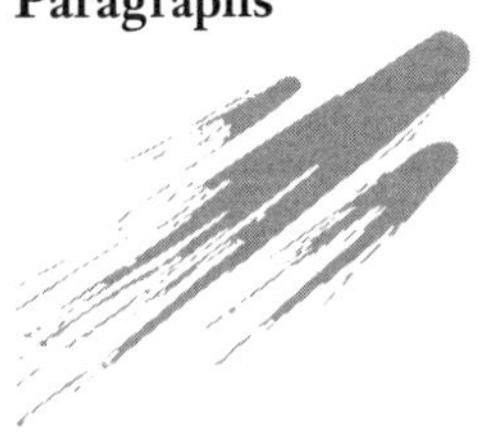

Write a bridging paragraph of one or two sentences for each of the situations provided. Supply details such as names and dates as required. Here's an example:

Situation: Thank customer (Alan Smith) for his order of 30 office chairs, and make delivery appointment for April 9.

Bridging Paragraph: Thank you, Mr. Smith, for placing your order for 30 chairs with The Department Store. We will deliver the chairs on April 9.

1. Opening: Confirm receipt of an order for 800 envelopes.
2. Closing: Wish a client luck with a new business.
3. Opening: Apply for a job as a Financial Advisor with the Western Credit Union.
4. Opening: State that a customer's account is overdue.
5. Closing: Confirm an appointment for September 22 at 3:30 p.m.

Check your paragraphs with the Answer Key.

2. *Developed Paragraphs*

The developed paragraph develops meaning to a fuller extent than the bridging paragraph. When the developed paragraph is specific, coherent, unified, and uses Power Sentences, we call it the *Power Paragraph.*

Developed paragraphs usually consist of four or five sentences. First comes the *key sentence* which establishes the core idea developed by the rest of the sentences in the paragraph. Next come three or four sentences, each of which adds an illustration or example to support the key sentence. Finally, the concluding sentence sums up the idea of the paragraph as a whole. If you keep this pattern in mind, you will write well-developed, *power paragraphs.*

Analyze how the following two paragraphs conform to the above pattern:

Paragraph 1

Key Sentence

Illustrations

Spending too little time organizing your writing can cost you money. Suppose you write a memo to 1,000 people, perhaps your employees or agents. You take one hour to block out the memo; your readers take an average of five minutes to read and understand it. On the other hand, suppose you were to spend two hours in composing the memo or letter, writing it so simply and briefly that your readers could absorb it in only four minutes. You would

Concluding Sentence

spend 60 extra minutes and your readers together would save 1,000 minutes. Taking a little longer to write clearly, you would have saved time and money, while encouraging friendly feeling.
– Adapted from the Royal Bank *Monthly Letter.*

Paragraph 2

Key Sentence

Illustrations

Concluding Sentence

In large organizations, such as government agencies, you may find your superiors disagree on how much detail you should include in reports. You may try to please your immediate boss by including as much detail as possible. She may be pleased, but the next one up the line says, "Too much detail burdens the reader. The Assistant will never approve this." You spend a day removing the details, and the next boss up says, "Conclusions are unsupported by details." Such disagreements lie behind many cases of premature balding in young civil servants.
– Adapted from International Writing Institute's *Put It in Writing.*

Such perfectly structured paragraphs too rarely occur. Usually one or more of the elements is left out or shifts position, marring the paragraph's coherence. Often, irrelevant ideas intrude to destroy the paragraph's *unity.* However, if you master the skill of building coherent and unified paragraphs, you will soon be in high demand as a writer.

EXERCISE 2

Writing the Developed Power Paragraph

The following sentences relate to one theme: how to reduce stress before an exam. However, these sentences are not in an effective order. Rearrange and rewrite the sentences to make a Developed Power Paragraph.

Get a good night's rest before the exam and then eat a nutritious breakfast. Last minute "cramming" will only increase stress; complete your study schedule well in advance. You can reduce the stress associated with writing an exam in several ways. Exercise regularly. Try not to over-estimate the number of hours you actually have available for studying. By applying these few simple techniques to reduce stress, you maximize your chances of succeeding in an exam situation. Use the last day before the exam to read over your notes slowly and calmly. Make a study schedule that lists all the topics you will encounter on the exam and then allot a number of hours to each topic, keeping in mind realistic goals.

3. *Transitional Markers*

Just as signposts show the destination you will reach by taking certain roads while driving, so certain words or phrases tell your reader the direction your thought will take within the paragraph. Usually, these words or phrases, called Transitional Markers, occur at the beginning of a paragraph, and also at the beginning of sentences that take new directions within the paragraph. Here is a sample list, grouped according to the type of thought they introduce.

List of Transitional Markers

Thought type	*Transitional Marker*
Addition	again, also, finally, first, second, third, furthermore, in addition, last, likewise, next, too, then
Example	for example, for instance, in other words, specifically, such as, that is, to illustrate
Concession	after all, at the same time, even though, of course
Comparison	likewise, similarly, in turn, in a like manner, by the same token
Contrast	on the other hand, at the same time, but, on the contrary, nevertheless, still, yet, whereas, however
Cause/Effect	consequently, hence, in short, otherwise, since, so, then, therefore, thus, accordingly, as a result
Time	when, after, as soon as, at that time, before, now, later, meanwhile, presently, soon, while
Summary	in conclusion, in short, in essence, on the whole, in brief, to sum up

In an unusually long developed paragraph such as the following one, see how the Transitional Markers (printed in italics) act like signposts to help keep you on the right track and to ensure coherence:

Example of Transitional Markers used to Establish Coherence

> Memos and letters share certain qualities, but differ in important ways. The memo must speak clearly and concisely. *Likewise*, the letter will accomplish more if it makes its point quickly. *Both* types of communication strive for unity and coherence; *that is*, every sentence follows logically from the one before it. *In turn*, each sentence leads naturally into the one following. The two forms differ, *on the other hand*, in that the memo usually takes up half a page or less, uses an informal tone, and reaches internal correspondents, *whereas* the letter usually runs from one to two pages, uses a more formal tone, and communicates with those outside the organization. *Of course*, both forms perform important tasks in different ways. *In essence*, choose the one which suits your current audience.

The markers are of the following categories (in order): *comparison*, *example*, *comparison*, *contrast*, *contrast*, *concession*, *summary*.

EXERCISE 3

Underline the transitional markers in the following paragraph and then determine the correct category for each marker.

Transitional Expressions

You may find the mere thought of delegating responsibility for certain tasks difficult to imagine. After all, you've sweated over your own business, nurtured it along for months or years, and only you know how to do it right. But what do you do when your business starts to grow? At the same time, the number of hours available in a day will not grow. To meet the needs of your business you therefore have to learn how to trust other people to work for you. Start off slowly. Delegate tasks such as answering the phone or typing sales letters, and concentrate on those tasks that demand your special expertise. You can also consider contracting work out to other professionals. For example, you could weigh the time you spend doing your bookkeeping against the cost of hiring a bookkeeper. Chances are you will find that the time you save more than compensates for the money you spend. Remember the well-worn advice: you have to spend money to make money, and then spend some of that money to take a portion of the work your business generates off your tired shoulders.

Refer to the Answer Key for the correct responses.

Coherence and Unity

Transitional markers provide your chief tool in establishing *coherence*. Coherence means that each sentence connects easily and logically with the preceding one. Therefore, practise using a variety of transitional markers in your paragraphs to dovetail your sentences and guide your reader easily along your paths of thought.

In addition to coherence, strive for *unity* in your paragraphs. Unity requires that all sentences illustrate or support the major thought expressed by the key sentence.

Here's an example of a unified paragraph:

Example of a Unified Paragraph

> In English, word order is crucial. Phrases can be arranged and rearranged like putty, turning nouns into verbs, verbs into nouns, nouns into adjectives. One can, as the *Encyclopedia Brittanica* observes, plan a table or table a plan, book a place or place a book, lift a thumb or thumb a lift.
>
> – U.S. *News & World Report*

In the above paragraph, the topic is word order, and every sentence and detail refers directly to this topic, thereby providing the paragraph with the quality of unity.

When you write Power Paragraphs that contain the qualities of coherence and unity, you will make yourself easily understood, and your reader will respect and appreciate your style.

4. *Review: Units One and Two*

You have studied how to achieve clarity through Power Sentences, and coherence and unity through Power Paragraphs. If you now can recognize the nouns in a sentence, and know which is the subject and which is the object; if you can also distinguish between linking and action verbs; if you can replace generalized nouns and verbs with specific ones; if you can construct ideas in the form of developed paragraphs using clear transitional markers – then you will soon be indispensable to your organization.

Writing is easy; all you do is sit staring at a blank sheet of paper until the drops of blood form on your forehead.
– *Gene Fowler*

While good writers know many additional grammatical techniques, the ability to write a clear sentence and a clear paragraph stands at the top of the list in terms of importance to the writer and the reader.

In Unit Three, you will learn how to use correct grammar to connect your thoughts and in Unit Four, you will learn how to avoid the most common errors of mechanics. You don't want to go to all the trouble of writing a good *Power Sentence*, only to slip in a pronoun agreement error or misspell a word. In Units Five to Nine you will leave grammar behind and look at how to write from the reader's point of view, and then progress to a discussion of how to develop your style in Unit Ten. Finally, Units Eleven to Thirteen discuss how to organize and research major writing projects such as reports, and how to use word processing features to write and format your documents.

The skills discussed in the following Units depend upon your ability to be clear in your individual sentences and paragraphs. Therefore, the time you have invested in studying the principles explained here in Units One and Two will pay you handsome dividends as you study the rest of this book and throughout your career. I hope your headache has vanished, or at least grown less intense, and that you feel your mugs of tea and coffee have been well invested. Now on to Unit Three: *How to Connect Thoughts.*

Answer Key

EXERCISE 1
Bridging Paragraphs

Write a bridging paragraph of one or two sentences for each of the situations provided. Supply details such as names and dates as required.

1. *Opening:* Confirm receipt of an order for 800 envelopes.

Thank you for your order of 800 envelopes.

2. *Closing:* Wish a client luck with a new business.

Good luck with the opening of your new restaurant, Ms. Peterson. I know it will be a success.

3. *Opening:* Apply for a job as a Financial Advisor with the Western Credit Union.

I wish to apply for the position of Financial Advisor with the Western Credit Union. My resume is enclosed.

4. *Opening:* State that a customer's account is overdue.

We have not yet received payment of your account for $428.99.

5. *Closing:* Confirm an appointment for September 22 at 3:30 p.m.

I look forward to meeting with you on September 22 at 3:30 p.m. in your office.

You can see how bridging paragraphs should be short and to the point with an efficient and friendly tone. For more practice, go on to the Review Exercises.

EXERCISE 2
The Power Paragraph

Put the sentences in a logical order to write a developed Power Paragraph. Check your finished paragraph against the following:

Key Sentence

Illustrations

Concluding Sentence

You can reduce the stress associated with writing an exam in several ways. Try not to over-estimate the number of hours you actually have available for studying. Make a study schedule that lists all the topics you will encounter on the exam and then allot a number of hours to each topic, keeping in mind realistic goals. Last minute "cramming" will only increase stress; complete your study schedule well in advance. Exercise regularly. Use the last day before the exam to read over your notes slowly and calmly. Get a good night's rest before the exam and then eat a nutritious breakfast. By applying these few simple techniques to reduce stress, you maximize your chances of succeeding in an exam situation.

EXERCISE 3
Recognizing Transitional Markers

Underline the transitional markers in the following paragraph and then determine the correct category for each marker.

You may find the mere thought of delegating responsibility for certain tasks difficult to imagine. After all, you've sweated over your own business, nurtured it along for months or years, and only you know how to do it right. But what do you do when your business starts to grow? At the same time, the number of hours available in a day will not grow. To meet the needs of your business you therefore have to learn how to trust other people to work for you. Start off slowly. Delegate tasks such as answering the phone or typing sales letters, and concentrate on those tasks that demand your special expertise. You can also consider contracting work out to other professionals. For example, you could weigh the time you spend doing your bookkeeping against the cost of hiring a bookkeeper. Chances are you will find that the time you save more than compensates for the money you spend. Remember the well-worn advice: you have to spend money to make money, and then spend some of that money to take a portion of the work your business generates off your tired shoulders.

after all:	concession
but:	contrast
at the same time:	contrast
therefore:	cause/effect
also:	addition
for example:	example
then:	cause/effect

How To Connect Thoughts

In Unit One you learned to write the Power Sentence, to use the Active Voice, and to use specific nouns and verbs, and in Unit Two you learned to write the Power Paragraph. If you understand these concepts, you have already minimized your chances of making many common writing errors. Now you may require a refresher on how to use the rules of grammar to connect your thoughts clearly and correctly.

In Unit Three you will focus on the following elements:

1. Pronouns
2. Subject–Verb Agreement
3. Point of View
4. Parallelism
5. Coordination and Subordination

Once you feel comfortable with your ability to connect words and phrases correctly, you can go on to learn about correct mechanics in Unit Four – How To Build Credibility.

Introduction

Grammar is a piano I play by ear. All I know about grammar is its power.
– *Joan Didion*

Before you plunge into Unit Three, cheer yourself up with the thought that grammar may be mysterious at first, but it need not remain so for long. Once you understand some of the most critical grammar rules, you will know how to communicate thoughts to your reader pleasantly and efficiently.

To help you remember the various grammar rules covered in Units Three and Four, you will periodically see the terms "*Micro Rule*" and **"Macro Rule"**. While every grammar rule has validity, some rules require more attention than others. If your study time is limited, concentrate particularly on the "Macro Rules" and go back to the "Micro Rules" when you want to get all the details right.

1. Pronouns

To use pronouns correctly, you must first understand how a pronoun *functions* in a sentence. You may already know that you use a pronoun to either stand for or take the place of a noun. To ensure that you always use pronouns correctly, you should also recognize that pronouns come in a variety of forms. Grammar texts go into a great deal of detail about these various forms, but you can survive quite nicely if you only know the following most frequently used types of pronouns:

Personal Pronouns refer directly to a person or object: I, me; he, him; she, her; them, they; we, us; you.

Possessive Personal Pronouns refer to the relationship between the pronoun and the object it possesses: my, mine, his, hers, theirs, ours.

Indefinite Pronouns take the place of a personal pronoun to refer to general persons or objects: one, it, many, several, anyone, anybody, everyone, both, each, few, nobody, someone, etc.

Demonstrative Pronouns emphasize the object or people referred to: that, this, those, these. Problems occur when these demonstrative pronouns do not refer to anything. For example: "These tasted great."

The Antecedent

The tricky part about using a pronoun in a sentence occurs when you have to make sure the pronoun *refers* to the correct noun. Grammar experts use the term *antecedent* to identify the noun occurring earlier in the sentence that the pronoun refers to or stands for. Even if you dread the thought of learning grammatical terms, try to make an exception for the term antecedent. Once you understand how pronouns interact with their antecedents you can use them both with confidence.

Pronoun–Antecedent Agreement

You will avoid "slipping in" pronouns that do not function as you intend them to if you recognize that a pronoun should agree with its antecedent in person, number and gender:

Person refers to the voice you use:

First person:	I, we
Second person:	you
Third person:	he, she, they, the people, the committee, etc.

Number refers to how many objects or persons the pronoun stands for:

Singular:	I, he, she, his, hers, etc.
Plural:	we, they, their, etc.

Gender refers to the sex of the pronoun:

Masculine:	he, his
Feminine:	she, her
Neuter:	they, them, it, one.

Here's an example of pronouns that agree with their antecedents:

> John's report needs to be faxed to Ms. Jones so that *she* can give it *her* approval.

Note that the pronouns "she" and "her" refer to the proper noun "Ms. Jones" and agree with it in number (singular) and gender (feminine). Look at the difference an incorrect use of pronouns makes to this sentence:

> John's report needs to be faxed to Ms. Jones so that *he* can give it *their* approval.

Because the pronouns "he" and "their" do not agree with the antecedent Ms. Jones, the sentence makes very little sense. The reader would anxiously look first for a male antecedent to agree with "he" and then for a plural antecedent to agree with "their". What confusion!

Find the pronoun agreement errors in the following slightly more difficult sentence:

> With the skills Patrick acquired after five years of university, he joined the civil service where they quickly advanced to a top position.

"They" could either be changed to "he" or eliminated, along with the word "where" so the sentence would read:

> With the skills Patrick acquired after five years of university, he joined the civil service and quickly advanced to a top position.

This version provides more punch by not repeating the pronoun "he". When you use pronouns, either make sure they refer to the correct antecedent, or rephrase your sentences to reduce the number of pronouns you need.

Antecedents Joined by Conjunctions

A *conjunction* links words or concepts together in a sentence. You must take special care when you join two antecedents with the conjunctions "and", "or", or "nor", and then follow them with a pronoun.

And

Many people get confused when they start a sentence with two antecedents joined by "and". For example:

> The doctor *and* the nurse took good care of _______ patients.

What pronoun would you use to indicate that the doctor and the nurse *both* care for the patients? Because the conjunction "and" joins the two antecedents (doctor and nurse), you use a *plural* pronoun. The sentence then reads:

> The doctor and the nurse took good care of *their* patients.

Rule

Two or more singular antecedents joined by "and" = plural pronoun.

Or/Nor

The opposite occurs when "or" or "nor" joins two singular antecedents. For example:

> *Either* the photocopier *or* the mainframe needs _______ parts serviced at least once a day.

Insert the *singular* pronoun "its" in the blank space, NOT the plural pronoun "their".

Choose the correct pronoun for this sentence:

> Neither Ms. Adams nor Gladys Smith could finish _____ work on time.

Did you choose the pronoun "her"? Well done!

Rule

Two singular antecedents joined by "or" or "nor" = singular pronoun.

What do you do about two *plural* antecedents joined by "or" or "nor"? I'm sure you've guessed: use a plural pronoun. For example:

> Either the secretaries or the clerical workers could volunteer *their* time to organize the staff baseball game.

Rule

Two plural antecedents joined by "or" or "nor" = plural pronoun.

But what about those annoying times when one of your antecedents is plural and the other is singular? Use the pronoun that agrees with the antecedent closest to it. For example:

> Neither the employees nor the supervisor could find _______ schedule.

In this sentence, the singular antecedent "supervisor" comes closest to the pronoun; therefore, the pronoun should be singular:

> Neither the employees nor the supervisor could find *his* schedule.

What happens if you don't know the gender of the supervisor? Switch the order of the antecedents around:

> Neither the supervisor nor the employees could find *their* schedules.

In addition to avoiding the problem of gender, this type of construction projects a clearer, more concise message – the goal of all good business writing.

Pronoun Agreement with Indefinite Pronouns

As defined above, *indefinite pronouns* consist of the words you use to indicate general persons or things. For example: each, everything, some, none, few, several, all, much, etc.

Often an indefinite pronoun acts as the antecedent for a personal pronoun used later in the sentence. For example:

> *Each* of the boys asked for *his* money back.

The indefinite pronoun "each" agrees with the singular personal pronoun "his". To determine which personal pronoun agrees with the indefinite pronoun it refers to, you must first decide if the indefinite pronoun specifies a singular object/person or a plural object/person.

The indefinite pronouns which take singular pronouns include every, all, each, one, either, another, everything, everyone (most of the time), and much:

> *Everything* was placed in *its* proper place.

Rule

Indefinite pronouns that refer to a unit = singular pronoun.

The indefinite pronouns which take plural pronouns include "several," "both," "few," "many," and "some":

Several staff members volunteered *their* services.

Micro Rule

Indefinite pronouns that refer to a variable unit = plural pronoun.

Occasionally, you may encounter a problem with the indefinite pronouns "everyone" or "everybody". In such a case, look at the *context* of the sentence to determine if the pronoun should be singular or plural. For example:

Everyone should stand up for *his* or *her* rights.

Or:

After everybody at the seminar took a workbook, Joanne asked *them* to write a brief description of *their* management experience.

Micro Rule

Choose the correct pronoun depending upon whether the indefinite pronoun stands for a unit or for the individuals in the unit.

Pronoun Agreement with Collective Nouns

Collective nouns such as "company," "committee," "management," "team," and "audience" generally take singular pronouns. For example:

The Education Committee decided to change **its** name to the Training Committee.

However, if in the context of the sentence the collective noun refers to a group of individuals rather than a unit, use a plural pronoun. For example:

The committee moved *their* chairs to another part of the conference hall where *they* listened to the president's speech on effective time management.

Rule

Collective noun as a unit = singular pronoun.

Collective noun as a group of individuals = plural pronoun.

EXERCISE 1

Pronoun Agreement

Underline the incorrectly used pronouns in the following sentences and then replace all linking verbs with action verbs and rewrite the sentences so that each pronoun agrees with its antecedent in person, number, and gender. If possible, you may wish to rephrase some of the sentences to avoid using pronouns or to avoid sexist connotations (refer to Gender Neutral Language in Unit Six). Note also that in some cases you may have to change the form of the verb to agree with the correct pronoun.

1. Several committee members wished to withdraw its support for the new sales program.
2. Neither Allison nor her sister could determine the correct way to phrase their letter of resignation from the company.
3. Her children should not be allowed to accompany his mother to work because it makes too much noise and distracts the other employees.
4. The company ensures all records relating to their legal position are kept in the locked file cabinet reserved for confidential information.
5. All the men in the company attended the meeting, each with their own opinion about what they should do about the strike.

Check your answers with the Answer Key and then try the Review Exercises.

Pronoun Reference >

Now that you know how to make pronouns agree with their antecedents, you need to ensure your pronouns *refer* to the correct antecedent. You don't want to make life difficult for your readers by obliging them to search high and low to find the antecedent your pronoun refers to. For example:

> Buy the new printer at the local computer outlet and make sure it is a good one.

The pronoun "it" should refer to the antecedent "printer". However, you could just as easily think that "it" refers to the "local computer outlet" because the noun "outlet" comes closest to the pronoun "it". As a result, you don't know if the printer should be good or if the outlet should be good. To avoid such confusion, eliminate the pronoun "it" so your reader cannot misinterpret your meaning:

> Make sure you buy a good printer at the local computer store.

Here's another example:

> Mr. Dahl told Sam that *he* needed some time off to prepare *his* records so *he* could help *him* take the summer inventory.

Look at all the pronouns that could refer either to Mr. Dahl or to Sam. The poor reader doesn't know who needs the time off and who wants to help whom take the summer inventory. The severe lack of clear pronoun references makes this sentence virtually incomprehensible. To rewrite it, you have to know exactly what you want to say:

> Mr. Dahl told Sam to take some time off to prepare his records so he could help take the summer inventory.

Now the pronouns "his" and "he" can refer only to Sam. Notice that the pronoun "him" referring to Mr. Dahl can easily be omitted without seriously altering the meaning of the sentence.

Micro Rule

Check to make sure each pronoun you use refers to its correct antecedent.

Demonstrative Pronouns

Another common error that results from faulty pronoun reference occurs when writers blithely use the demonstrative pronoun "this" to refer to something said in a previous sentence. For example:

> She presented her report on the possible locations for a new shopping mall to the Board of Directors. Although *this* was generally well received, the Board criticized it on several minor points.

In the second sentence, "this" should refer to the report. Unfortunately, the reader must search back through most of the preceding sentence to find the antecedent "report" and may well be way-laid by "shopping mall". Misunderstanding results – a bad sign. You can either avoid using "this" by incorporating the second sentence into the first sentence, or by following "this" with a specific noun such as "report". Compare two possible revisions:

> Although the Board of Directors was generally pleased with her report on the possible locations for a new shopping mall, some members required clarification on several minor points.

Or:

> She presented her report on the possible locations for a new shopping mall to the Board of Directors. Although it generally received this report favorably, the Board found several minor points to criticize.

To reduce your chances of using the demonstrative pronouns that, this, these, etc. incorrectly, try to get out of the habit of starting a sentence with "this" or "these" unless you follow it with a specific noun. For example:

> Martin disagreed with how the sales team handled the account. *This* led to his being asked to leave the company.

What does "this" refer to? Presumably, the writer means to imply that "this" refers to the fact that Martin disagreed with how the sales team handled the account. But why leave the meaning open to misinterpretation? Rephrase the sentence to eliminate "this":

> When Martin disagreed with how the sales team handled the account, he was asked to leave the company.

Micro Rule

Follow "this" or "these" with a noun.

No Antecedent

When you write too quickly or find yourself under too much pressure, you may leave out an antecedent altogether. You know what you want to say, but forget that your reader should not be forced to find an implicit meaning – that is, a meaning that you do not clearly state. Here's an example of a sentence that includes a pronoun but no antecedent:

> In response to your letter of November 22 about the application, I need more information about *their* financial situation.

The pronoun "their" does not refer to anything. The reader must assume that the request came from some unidentified group. Provide background information and substitute a specific noun for the pronoun "their":

> In response to your letter of November 22 regarding the application for a loan extension made by Mannix Inc., please send me additional information about the company's financial situation.

The use of "it is" can confuse readers when "it" does not refer to an antecedent. Too often, sentences begin with "it is..." because the writer is thinking with his or her pen rather than taking the time to make sure that "it" refers to something concrete. For example:

> *It is* the goal of our company to maximize revenue and minimize expenses.

The pronoun "it" used as a subject refers to nothing and adds nothing. Avoid starting sentences with "it is" by using the Power Sentence format:

> Our company aims to maximize revenue and minimize expenses.

Micro Rule

Don't let a pronoun do all the work by itself – give it an antecedent.

You will probably spend a fair amount of your revision time clarifying your pronoun references. However, the time spent will pay important dividends by ensuring that your reader always knows exactly what you mean. In business writing particularly, you never want to make your readers work so hard to decipher your meaning that they give up trying to understand what you want them to do.

EXERCISE 2

Pronoun Reference

Underline the pronouns in the following sentences and then replace all linking verbs with action verbs and rewrite the sentences to remove any ambiguous pronoun references. Remember to avoid sexist connotations.

1. We need a full time secretary so that she can have more time to organize the paperwork and do their clerical work such as telephoning and making appointments.
2. There are no costs involved for this service because it is a function of the manager's job.
3. Several pension plans are available for staff members who have satisfied their criteria of ten years of continuous employment.
4. You have had many unexplained absences this past month and I feel this has led to a decrease in sales in your department.
5. The western provinces should separate from the eastern provinces and form their own nation.

Check your answers with the Answer Key and then try the Review Exercises.

2. *Subject–Verb Agreement*

Just as a pronoun must agree with its antecedent in person, gender, and number, so must the number of a verb agree with its subject. You cannot write "the shark eat the fish" because the plural form of the verb "eat" does not agree with the singular subject "shark". Similarly, you cannot write "the sharks eats the fish" because the singular form of the verb "eats" does not match the plural subject "sharks". You will probably have no difficulty with such straightforward Subject/Verb/Object sentences simply because a lack of agreement between the subject and verb *sounds* wrong.

Words That Intrude >

You may encounter difficulties when the subject of your sentence does not immediately follow your verb. Luckily, the work you did in Unit One on finding the true subject of a sentence will help you avoid getting waylaid by extra words that come between your subject and verb. For example, a singular subject may be followed by plural words which seem to demand a plural verb. Determine the subject-verb agreement error in the following sentence:

> Each of the salesmen are committed to making this the best year ever.

What is the subject of this sentence? Salesmen? If "salesmen" were the subject, the verb phrase "are committed" would be correct because "salesmen" is a plural noun and should match the plural verb "are". Look again and ask "who or what commits?" *Each* of the salesman "commits". The subject is therefore "each", which needs a singular verb. To correct this sentence, you would write:

> Each of the salesman *is* committed to making this the best year ever.

Now we have a grammatically correct sentence, even though it sounds rather dull. Why not get rid of the linking verb "is" and make the sentence a *Power Sentence:*

> Each of the ten salesmen at Allen Bros. will try to sell $10,000 worth of merchandise this year and so exceed last year's gross sales of $80,000.

Look at another example:

> The financial statement in the large filing cabinet next to the washrooms (require/requires) a new title page.

You could well look to the noun closest to the verb: "washrooms", which is plural. If so, you would choose "require" for the verb. But remember that the subject of the sentence must be the noun that the verb relates directly to. Therefore, the thing that requires a new title page must be the financial statement, not "washrooms". The sentence should read:

> The financial statement in the large filing cabinet next to the washrooms requires a new title page.

Macro Rules

Plural Subject = Plural Verb:
The companies manufacture...

Singular Subject = Singular Verb:
The company manufactures...

Dangerous Linking Verbs >

Note that most Subject/Verb Agreement errors occur when *linking* verbs are used. If you concentrate on using the Subject/Action Verb/Object sentence format (the *Power Sentence*), you will minimize your chances of making Subject/Verb Agreement errors. For example:

> The Senior Accountant, as well as her colleagues on the auditing job, (was/were) frustrated by the client's total disregard for the tax laws.

If you substitute an action verb for the passive "was frustrated" the subject/verb agreement problem disappears:

> The client's total disregard for the tax laws *frustrated* both the Senior Accountant and her colleagues on the auditing job.

Super Macro Rule

Replace linking verbs with action verbs wherever possible.

Subject Follows Verb >

Subject–Verb Agreement problems may also occur if you discard the Subject/Action Verb/Object order in favor of the weaker Linking Verb/Subject order. For example:

> Also destroyed in the fire (was/were) twenty pages of her report.

Your first impulse may be to choose "was" because it follows the singular noun "fire". But "fire" does not function as the subject of the sentence. To avoid choosing the incorrect verb form, you have to turn the sentence around: "The fire destroyed twenty pages of her report." You can see that the Verb/Subject order can cause more problems than it is worth.

Micro Rule

Avoid the Verb/Subject order.

Compound Subjects >

Two different rules apply regarding compound subjects, depending on whether the subjects are joined by "and" or "neither/nor", "or", "either/or", etc.

Compound Subjects Joined by "And"

For example:

> A good laser printer with several fonts and a computer with a hard drive cost several thousand dollars.

Micro Rule

Two singular subjects joined by "and" take a plural verb.

An exception to this rule occurs when the two subjects represent a unit or are very closely related. For example:

> Gin and tonic is a popular cocktail.

Compound Subjects Joined by "Or"

To decide which verb to choose when you have two compound subjects joined by or, look to the subject *closest* to the verb. For example:

> Neither the report nor the letters *were* typed in time to send to the printer.

Micro Rule

Find the subject closest to the verb and then use a plural verb for a plural subject and a singular verb for a singular subject.

Collective Nouns >

You use the same rules to decide what *verb* agrees with a collective noun as you used to decide what *pronoun* agrees with a collective noun. Look first at the context of the sentence. For example:

Collective Noun refers to a unit:

> The panel revokes its decision.

Collective Noun refers to the individuals in the unit:

> The panel shuffle their feet, whisper among themselves, and pay no attention to the speaker.

Micro Rule

Collective noun stands for a unit = singular verb.

Collective noun stands for the individuals in the unit = plural verb.

EXERCISE 3

Subject–Verb Agreement

Underline the verbs in the following sentences and then replace all linking verbs with action verbs. Rewrite the sentences so that the subjects and verbs agree.

1. The expense of hiring two new secretaries for our clients are justified by an estimated 30% increase in sales.
2. The amount of paperwork, as well as numerous other clerical duties, currently performed by our salespeople take up too much of their time and prevents them from concentrating on sales.
3. Your failure to assume responsibility for the Smith contracts have resulted in a sharp decrease in the company's revenue.
4. Several smaller sessions with the workers and their immediate supervisors, in addition to one whole day session, was used to consolidate the transfer.
5. As the vice president and I understand, there have been a number of unexplained gaps in our inventory levels.

Check your answers with the Answer Key and then try the Review Exercises.

3. *Shifting Point of View*

Few readers want to put up with a writer who shifts too often from present to past tense, active to passive voice, or third to second person. Consider how needlessly the following sentence irritates:

> One avoids taking taxis to work because you will find that it cost a great deal and sometimes taxis are hard to find.

Ouch! This sentence starts in the third person, present tense ("one avoids..."), shifts to second person, future tense followed closely by past tense ("You will find that it cost...") and then finishes off in the present tense ("taxis are hard to find"). Would you give such a writer your willing attention, much less an important contract? Not very likely!

Use a *consistent* voice, tense and person reference in each sentence and from one sentence to the next. For example, if you start a memo by writing in the second person "you", avoid switching to the impersonal "one" halfway down the page. Such shifts in point of view annoy readers and can ultimately obscure your meaning.

Active to Passive Voice > If you start a sentence in the active voice, do not shift to the passive voice. For example:

> The Vice-President handed me my cheque and I was also given an award for my outstanding sales record.

Use of the active voice makes the first part of this sentence clear and vigorous: "the Vice-President handed me my cheque". In the second half of the sentence, no one actually does the giving. "I was given". Who gave "me" something? The vice-president? Probably – but the use of the passive voice makes it sound as if some unknown being, whom we mortals can only guess at, gave the award. Rewrite the sentence as follows:

> The Vice-President handed me my cheque and also gave me an award for my outstanding sales record.

You already know that the passive voice enervates sentences. If you combine the passive voice with the active voice in the same sentence, you will sound as if you are not thinking clearly – a situation you want to avoid in business! Here's another example:

> All staff members must attend the meeting so that decisions can be made regarding the Fairview project.

To revise this sentence, maintain the active voice throughout:

> All staff members must attend the meeting to make some decisions regarding the Fairview project.

Macro Rule **Use the Active Voice.**

Shifting Tenses

Tenses refer to *time:* past, present, and future. For example:

Past tense:	I went to the office.
Present tense:	I go to the office.
Future tense:	I will go to the office.

If you shift tenses in a sentence, you may give your reader the impression that you lack a sense of direction. For example:

> I *went* (past tense) into the meeting and *find* (present tense) that the overhead projector *does* not (present tense) work.

Because this sentence started in the past tense, it should continue in the past tense:

> I *went* into the meeting and *found* that the overhead projector *did* not work.

Micro Rule

Stick with one tense.

Shifting Persons

If you always keep your reader firmly in mind, you will decrease any tendency to hop back and forth between the second person (you) and the third person (one, he/she, their). In formal writing, stick to the *third person;* in less formal writing (such as a business letter) use the *second person* to speak directly to your reader. Whatever you do, avoid mixing second and third person together as in the following sentence:

> *You* should always use correct grammar and punctuation in your letters because *businesspeople* need to create a good impression.

The revised version of this sentence eliminates the third person "businesspeople":

> *You* should always use correct grammar and punctuation in your letters because *you* need to create a good impression.

To lessen your chances of mixing up person references, try to avoid using the formal "one". For example:

> *One* will find that *you* cannot communicate effectively with a client unless *one* speaks clearly and correctly.

Some writers feel that use of the formal "one" makes their writing sound intellectual or distant. Unfortunately, very few writers can sustain the use of "one" without occasionally lapsing into the second person. Revise your writing to eliminate the use of one:

> *You* will find that *you* cannot communicate effectively with a client unless *you* speak clearly and correctly.

Micro Rule

Avoid using "one" altogether.

Macro Rule

Prefer "I" and "you" over "we" and "the client" in all business writing.

EXERCISE 4

Point of View

Replace all linking verbs with action verbs and correct the point of view errors in the following sentences.

1. To start your own business, individuals need a good grounding in basic accounting skills.
2. One's ability to present him or herself accurately and professionally will help one earn their chance to prove him or herself.
3. The Payroll Department gave me a new benefits package and I was also told to pick up my cheque on the last working day of each month.
4. Staff members do not know what roles they are to play in this organization and these roles also were not defined by management.
5. If business is the active trading of one's value for another's, then it becomes quite evident that business is an integral part of your life and has many implications in the country's economy and our daily lives.

Check your answers with the Answer Key and then try the Review Exercises.

4. *Parallelism*

Imagine a power boat skimming across the water. Now imagine this boat pulling three water skiers, each holding on to a separate tow rope. If one of the water skiers catches a tip and goes under, the symmetrical balance set up by the three skiers is destroyed. Think of the core idea in a sentence as a power boat, and three phrases used to modify this core idea as three skiiers who must remain parallel to each other. If one of the phrases uses a grammatical form different to the form used by the other two phrases, the sentence loses its symmetry because the modifying phrases do not parallel each other.

Look at how a lack of parallelism in this sentence jars the reader:

> We compared notes on sales results, year-end reports, and efficiency.

The core idea in the sentence is "we compared notes". Three phrases modify or describe this core idea: sales results, year-end reports, and efficiency. However, while "sales results" and "year-end reports" use an adjective-noun form, "efficiency" lacks an adjective. To make this sentence parallel, supply an adjective to modify "efficiency" so that all three phrases use an adjective-noun construction.

> We compared notes on sales results, year-end reports, and *staff* efficiency.

Verb Phrases

More complicated problems occur when you combine adjectives with verb phrases to describe a subject. For example:

> The two new supervisors were efficient, friendly, liked to chat, wanted to increase the sales team and sold $60,000 worth of products.

In this sentence, the linking verb "were" cannot precede the phrase "liked to chat" because you cannot logically write "the supervisors were liked to chat". The last two phrases should describe the supervisors; however, when combined with the verb "were", the meaning of the two phrases changes completely: the supervisors were wanted to increase the sales team and the supervisors were sold $60,000 worth of products. The supervisors no longer act; they become receivers of another person's actions.

You could revise this sentence in at least two ways. First, you could use a semi-colon to separate the descriptive terms from the verb phrases. For example:

> The two new supervisors were efficient and friendly; they liked to chat, wanted to increase the sales team and sold $60,000 worth of products.

Second, you could make efficient and friendly directly modify the noun "supervisors". For example:

> The two efficient and friendly new supervisors liked to chat, wanted to increase the sales team, and sold $60,000 worth of products.

Micro Rule

Make sure each descriptive phrase uses the same verb form.

Articles, Pronouns, and Prepositions >

A lack of parallelism often occurs when a writer leaves out certain descriptive words such as articles, pronouns, and prepositions in a list of items. For example:

> Allison acquired several new pieces of equipment for the office: one fax machine, three laser printers, chairs, and two desks.

To maintain the parallel structure set up by the words "one," "three," and "two," you must assign a number to the chairs. For example:

> Allison acquired several new pieces of equipment for the office: one fax machine, three laser printers, ten chairs, and two desks.

The following sentence needs an additional word:

> The company directed its employees to comply with all safety rules, to arrive at work on time and maintain the confidentiality of the company's files.

The word "to" should be inserted before "maintain" to make all parts of this sentence parallel:

> The company directed its employees to comply with all safety rules, to arrive at work on time and to maintain the confidentiality of the company's files.

Micro Rule

Use consistent articles, pronouns and adjective/noun combinations to maintain parallelism.

***Mixed Constructions* >**

Another common error in parallel structure occurs when writers use a mixed construction; that is, when they fail to grammatically *balance* the two halves of a compound sentence. For example:

> If you've just started a business, you'll need to familiarize yourself with many aspects of the bookkeeping process in addition to learning to work with your employees.

Notice how the independent clause "you'll need to familiarize yourself with many aspects of the bookkeeping process" does not match the subordinate clause in the second half of the sentence "in addition to learning to work with your employees." The reason these two clauses do not match is because "you'll need" functions as a straight subject-verb construction while "in addition to learning" lacks a subject and does not use the same type of verb form (future tense). Correct this sentence by making both halves independent clauses joined by "and":

> If you've just started a business, you will need to familiarize yourself with many aspects of the bookkeeping process and learn to work with your employees.

Now the two clauses both start with the same type of construction: "need to familiarize" and "learn to work". Here's another example:

> Typing is faster than to write by hand.

Make this sentence parallel in construction by changing "to write" to "writing":

> Typing is faster than writing by hand.

Micro Rule

Avoid mixed constructions – balance the second half of your sentence with the first half.

Using "That" >

Watch how you use the word "that" in sentences with more than one verb. For example:

> The Board of Directors informed the president that his appointment was terminated and he should leave the company as soon as possible.

In this sentence, the Board of Directors informs the president about two things: that his appointment was terminated and that he should leave. Without the second "that", the sentence lacks parallel structure and sounds awkward. The sentence should read:

> The Board of Directors informed the president that his appointment was terminated and that he should leave the company as soon as possible.

Micro Rule

If you start the first clause with "that", start the second clause with "that".

EXERCISE 5

Parallelism

Replace all linking verbs with action verbs and rewrite the following sentences to eliminate errors in parallel structure.

1. I finally realized that my frequent absences from the office were preventing me from getting a pay raise, a promotion, and learning new procedures.
2. The Purchasing Agent requisitioned a new computer, box of paper, and a set of file folders.
3. He was so sure he deserved a promotion and that he needed a new office.
4. Nothing you can say will convince me that you are right in your answer to the question and therefore I am wrong.
5. Only when the office personnel are performing reliably, the paperwork being completed efficiently, and the calls answered promptly, do we have a firm predictable base to manage the store for profit.

Check your answers with the Answer Key and then try the Review Exercises.

5. *Coordination and Subordination*

Heaven forbid that your readers suspect you can't think logically! Unfortunately, you may give such an impression when you include two ideas in a sentence and neglect to show either that they are related or that one idea ranks as more important than the other. To prevent your readers from questioning your ability to think coherently, you must apply the principles of coordination and subordination.

Faulty Coordination

If you wish to show that two or more ideas in a sentence are equally important, you must ensure that the ideas are in fact related. For example:

> The establishment of a new business can revitalize the economy and one small business owner may employ a great many people.

Because the conjunction "and" joins the two ideas in this

sentence, you may well think that both ideas merit equal emphasis. However, the second idea does not necessarily relate to the first idea. Instead, the first idea (that the establishment of a new business can revitalize the economy) merely *implies* a relationship with the second idea (that one small business owner may employ a great many people). That is, the second idea functions as a *specific example* of the general first idea. To revise this sentence, you could either substitute a colon for the "and" or make one part of the sentence subordinate. For example:

> The establishment of a new business can revitalize the economy: one small business owner may employ a great many people.

Or:

> Because one small business owner may employ a great many people, the establishment of a new business can revitalize the economy.

Think of the conjunction "and" as the middle portion of a balance beam scale. The ideas placed at either end of the scale should weigh the same so that the beam portion stays horizontal. When one idea ranks as more important than the other idea, the beam portion tilts. The "and" then loses its power to make the two ideas equal.

Macro Rule

Make sure two ideas joined by "and" deserve equal emphasis.

***Weak Coordination* >**

Weak coordination occurs in sentences which use "and this". For example:

> Marsha's report detailed the new product's advantages, and this was much appreciated by the committee.

The two halves of this sentence may be related, but because the word "this" does not refer to an antecedent, the sentence lacks strength. Revise the sentence so that it expresses only one idea:

> The committee appreciated Marsha's report, which detailed the advantages of the new product.

Look back at the section on demonstrative pronouns and remember the advice about not using "this" unless you follow it with a noun. For example: this idea, this report, etc.

Micro Rule

If you see "this" all by itself, make it work with a noun or substitute a relative pronoun "which".

***Subordination* >**

Not all ideas are created equal. When you combine two ideas in a sentence and need to show that one idea has more importance than the other, you use some form of subordination. To do this, you must be able to recognize independent and dependent clauses. A clause refers to a sequence of words that contains one idea. A clause may be independent (it has a subject and a verb and can stand alone as a complete sentence) or dependent (it may have a subject and a verb but it cannot stand alone as a complete sentence). For example:

> While we waited for the train, we noticed three strange men watching us.

This sentence contains two clauses that express a single idea or action: waiting for the train and noticing the strange men. The first clause, "While we waited for the train" cannot stand alone even though it includes a subject (we) and a verb (waited). The clause cannot stand alone because it includes the word "while". This word *diminishes* the power of the "we waited" construction by making it conditional; that is, the clause does not express a complete thought. If you write "while we waited for the train" as a complete sentence, you leave your reader in limbo because the word "while" leads him or her to expect more action. What were we doing "while we waited"? Because the clause "while we waited for the train" cannot stand alone as a complete sentence, you refer to it as a dependent clause.

Micro Rule

A dependent clause needs help before it earns the right to be a complete sentence.

The clause "we noticed three strange men watching us" can stand alone as a complete sentence. It does not need the first clause ("while we waited for the train") to complete it. You refer to the second clause as an independent clause.

Micro Rule

An independent clause contains a subject and a verb and so has already earned the right to be a complete sentence.

To subordinate one idea to another, you must make the subordinate idea into a dependent clause to show that it depends upon the main idea expressed in the independent clause. For example:

> Although we planned to complete the inventory by July, the flood in the stockroom prevented us from even starting the inventory until August.

In this sentence, the subordinate clause begins with "although", which makes it dependent upon the independent clause ("the flood in the stockroom prevented...) for completion.

Errors can occur if you neglect to show how two ideas are related in the same sentence or if you write two separate sentences that would be clearer if joined together.

Two Ideas in One Sentence

You usually want to indicate that one of the ideas in your sentence *depends* upon the other idea for completeness. For example, the ideas in the following sentence do not warrant equal emphasis because one idea logically depends on the other idea:

> Ms. Louis, the present company secretary, cannot possibly find the time to complete all the typing required of her and many letters do not get typed.

The clause "many letters do not get typed" only makes sense when the writer specifies that this activity results from the fact that Ms. Louis cannot complete all her typing. In its present form, the sentence only *implies* a relationship between the two clauses. Show this relationship by subordinating one part of the sentence to the other:

> *Because* Ms. Louis, the company secretary, cannot possibly find the time to complete all the typing required of her, many letters do not get typed.

The addition of "because" makes the first clause into a dependent clause: "Because Ms. Louis, the company secretary, cannot possibly find the time to complete all the typing required of her...". This clause cannot stand alone as a complete sentence. To complete it, you must add the second clause, which remains independent: "a lot of letters do not get typed". Now the sentence makes sense - letters do not get typed *because* Ms. Louis doesn't have enough time.

Think of any sentence with more than one idea as a **cause-effect** unit: one half of the sentence should directly relate to and be dependent upon the other half of the sentence. To make a clause dependent, use a **subordinating conjunction,** that is, words such as: *after*, *although*, *because*, *before*, *if*, *since*, *unless*, *while*. Rewrite the following sentence to subordinate one half to the other:

> Ms. Zbrownski submitted the report and the committee asked for revisions.

Use a subordinating conjunction to show that the action of submitting the report *resulted* in the committee asking for revisions. For example:

> *After* Ms. Zbrownski submitted the report, the committee asked for revisions.

The subordinating conjunction "after" shows the cause-effect relationship between the two actions: submitting the report and asking for revisions. Here's another example:

> You should be compensated for any loss you incurred and I would like to offer you a $20 gift certificate.

The two independent clauses in this sentence probably do relate; however, the writer has failed to make this relationship obvious. You can rewrite the sentence as follows:

> To compensate you for any loss you incurred, I would like to offer you a $20 gift certificate.

Micro Rule

Use a subordinating conjunction to show that one idea depends upon another in a sentence.

Two Separate Sentences

Use subordination to make your writing flow smoothly. Few things annoy readers more than a series of short, monotonously constructed sentences. For example:

> He submitted the report. It compared the IBM computer with the Macintosh computer. He recommended we buy the IBM. We agreed. We need to test the computer. Then we can make a decision.

Imagine how much more pleasing this series of sentences would be to read if the writer had used the occasional subordinating conjunction to tie the ideas together. For example:

> *After* we read his report comparing the IBM computer with the Macintosh, we agreed with his recommendation to buy the IBM; *however*, we need to test the IBM *before* we can make a decision.

This type of sentence uses a more complex type of subordination because it joins two independent clauses ("we agree..." and "we need..." with the conjunction "however" and a semi-colon. While the clause following "however" does not depend upon the first clause, it still ranks as subordinate to it because it logically needs the information provided in the first independent clause. We like his recommendations but we have a provision – we will test the computer first. This type of subordination can very effectively link ideas and avoid unnecessary repetition and monotony.

Here's another example:

> Wellington TV Inc. is a small business. It cannot keep up with the processing of its sales records. The company requires another secretary. This secretary could handle the processing of sales records.

Make one sentence out of these four sentences by using coordinating conjunctions and subordination:

> *Although* Wellington TV Inc. is a small business, it cannot keep up with the processing of sales records; *therefore*, the company requires another secretary to handle this task.

Note how the first sentence becomes a dependent clause starting with "although"; the second sentence becomes an independent clause that states the problem; and the third sentence provides the solution to the problem by becoming an independent clause preceded by the coordinating conjunction "therefore". Go easy on writing such long sentences, however. You want to keep your sentences to in average of 15 words with only the *occasional* foray into the woods of a 30 word sentence.

Micro Rule

Link ideas together to avoid choppiness but don't go overboard.

Use of "As"

Avoid using the word "as" in place of the coordinating conjunction "because". For example:

> We must improve our current sales levels as we are committed to achieving a 30% increase in profits by year-end.

The word "as" could mean either "because" or "while". If the reader decides the "as" means "while", the meaning of the sentence changes: "We must improve our current sales levels *while* we are committed to achieving a 30% increase in profits by year-end."

Micro Rule

Never use "as" to mean "because".

Use of "more"

Avoid using "more" to show a comparison when you do not specify what object or concept you make the comparison to. For example:

> The pay increase was more easily accepted by the employees.

As the reader of this sentence, you would likely want to ask "more than what?" Balance the "more" with a comparison:

> The employees accepted the pay increase more easily than they accepted the cutback in overtime hours.

To prevent your readers from having to ask "more than what?", do not use "more" if you do not also provide a "more than...". Your readers should not have to guess. Here's another example:

> His interest in the project became more intense when he studied the results of the survey.

To avoid the "more than what?" question, you can revise the sentence in two ways:

1. Omit the "more": His interest in the project increased when he studied the results of the survey.
2. Provide a "more than": When he studied the results of the survey, his interest in the project became more intense than it was before.

As you can see, the first option – eliminating the "more" – makes a stronger impact than the second option – specifying a "more than".

Micro Rule

Don't let "more" stand alone.

EXERCISE 6

Coordination and Subordination

Replace all linking verbs with action verbs and rewrite the following sentences to make them logical and grammatically consistent.

1. The entrepreneurial spirit embodies the ideas of diligence and efficiency and the thrills of competition and material gain are stressed.
2. Perhaps just a few staff members are the cause of the growing number of complaints I have received from your department, but this is an extremely important issue which must be dealt with immediately.
3. We need expert advice to introduce modern filing concepts, and then a junior filing clerk should be hired to keep it current.
4. The impact of the current financial slump on our company is more severe as it affects our ability to service our customers.
5. The new printing system is perhaps the most important of all. It is designed to tie all our work together. It will improve efficiency. This will make sure excess copying is not done. Therefore the success of the whole Sales Department will be measured by the use of this Integrated Printing Responsibility System.

Check your answers with the Answer Key and then try the Review Exercises.

6. *How To Connect Thoughts: Review*

In Unit Three you studied how to connect your thoughts clearly and correctly.

First, you analyzed how *pronouns* function in a sentence so that you could avoid making the two most common pronoun errors: lack of agreement and faulty reference. You can now likely spot the error in this sentence:

> All our sweaters are made from a revolutionary new yarn that looks and feels like the real wool our customers demand, but they are actually made with the new SleekSheep acrylic.

The word "they" refers to customers when it should refer to "sweaters". Now that you understand how pronouns work in a sentence, you can confidently rewrite the sentence to eliminate the pronoun reference error:

> We make all our sweaters with the new SleekSheep acrylic yarn that looks and feels like the real wool our customers demand.

I have laboured to refine our language to grammatical purity, and to clear it from colloquial barbarisms, licentious idioms, and irregular combinations.

– *Samuel Johnson*

Second, you learned how to make the *subject of a sentence agree with the verb,* even when extra words intrude between the subject and verb or when you have a compound subject. For example, you know that the following sentence with a compound subject should take a singular verb and NOT a plural verb:

> Neither the salespeople nor Ms. Durham want to leave early.

Because of the "neither/nor" construction, you know that the verb should agree with the subject that immediately precedes it - in this case, Ms. Durham, which is singular. You would rewrite the sentence as follows:

> Neither the salespeople nor Ms. Durham *wants* to leave early.

Third, you learned how to use a consistent *point of view* in your sentences. You know, for example, how to correct the following sentence that mixes the active voice with the passive voice:

> We listened to the speaker for two hours, after which two days were required to make sense of what we learned.

The first clause "we listened to the speaker..." uses the active voice while the second clause "two days were required..." uses the passive voice. Wherever possible, use the active voice throughout as follows:

> We listened to the speaker for two hours and then required two days to make sense of what we learned.

Fourth, you learned how to write sentences in *parallel structure* by making all elements grammatically consistent. You know, for example, that the following sentence jars the reader with its lack of parallel structure:

> Hiring a new Executive Assistant, purchasing a new computer system, and an efficient bookkeeping system should help the company increase its productivity level.

This sentence contains three elements that describe ways to help the company increase its productivity level. However, the grammatical structure of the last element (an efficient bookkeeping system) does not conform to the grammatical structure of the other two elements (*hiring* a new... and *purchasing* a new...). Make each of these elements parallel:

> Hiring a new Executive Assistant, purchasing a new computer system, and *adopting* an efficient bookkeeping system should help the company increase its productivity level.

Fifth, you learned about *coordination* and *subordination* – perhaps the most difficult and yet most important area of grammar. Once you understand how to coordinate ideas or to subordinate one idea to another in your sentences, you can raise your writing to a sophisticated level that still maintains the clarity and precision of the Power Sentence format. For example, you can now spot how a lack of subordination in the following sentence reveals the writer's inability to think coherently:

> Our production costs could be lowered if we purchased desktop publishing software and our word processors could double their current output.

Because the conjunction "and" merely joins the two independent clauses in the above sentence, the relationship between them seems vague. Switch the order of the information around and use a subordinating conjunction to show how the two clauses relate:

> *If* we purchased desktop publishing software, our production costs could be lowered *because* our word processors could double their current output.

Let school-masters puzzle their brain,
With grammar, and nonsense, and learning,
Good liquor, I stoutly maintain,
Gives genius a better discerning.
– *Oliver Goldsmith*

The material presented in Unit Three should provide answers to most of your questions about grammar. However, don't allow yourself to get so worried about writing *correctly* that you prevent yourself from writing at all. Learn to use the Power Sentence format to write quickly and coherently, and then use the rules of grammar to *edit* what you have written.

In Unit Four, we will look at how to build credibility through correct usage, spelling, and punctuation.

Answer Key

EXERCISE 1
Pronoun Agreement

Underline the incorrectly used pronouns in the following sentences and then replace all linking verbs with action verbs and rewrite the sentences so that each pronoun agrees with its antecedent in person, number, and gender. If possible, you may wish to rephrase some of the sentences to avoid using pronouns or to avoid sexist connotations (refer to Gender Neutral Language in Unit Six). Note also that in some cases you may have to change the *form* of the verb to agree with the correct pronoun.

1. Several committee members wished to withdraw <u>its</u> support for the new sales program.

   Several committee members wished to withdraw ***their*** *support for the new sales program.*

2. Neither Allison nor her sister could determine the correct way to phrase <u>their</u> letter of resignation from the company.

   Neither Allison nor her sister could determine the correct way to phrase ***her*** *letter of resignation from the company.*

3. Her children should not be allowed to accompany <u>his</u> mother to work because <u>it</u> makes too much noise and distracts the other employees.

   Her children should not accompany ***their*** *mother to work because* ***they make*** *too much noise and* ***distract*** *the other employees.*

   Note: change the verbs "makes" and "distracts" to agree with "their", and delete "be allowed to".

4. The company ensures all records relating to <u>their</u> legal position are kept in the locked file cabinet reserved for confidential information.

   The company keeps all records relating to ***its*** *legal position in the locked file cabinet reserved for confidential information.*

5. All the men in the company attended the meeting, each with <u>their</u> own opinion about what <u>they</u> should do about the strike.

   All the men in the company attended the meeting, each with ***his*** *own opinion about what* ***he*** *should do about the strike.*

If you correctly identified the pronoun agreement errors in the above sentences, go on to the Review Exercises.

EXERCISE 2
Pronoun Reference

Underline the pronouns in the following sentences and then replace all linking verbs with action verbs and rewrite the sentences to remove any ambiguous pronoun references. Remember to avoid sexist connotations.

1. We need a full time secretary so that she can have more time to organize the paperwork and do their clerical work such as telephoning and making appointments.

   We need a full time secretary to organize the paperwork and to perform clerical work such as telephoning and making appointments.

2. There are no costs involved for this service because it is a function of the manager's job.

   The manager will perform this service as part of his or her job.

   Or:

   Mr. Jackson, the manager, will perform this service as part of his job.

3. Several pension plans are available for staff members who have satisfied their criteria of ten years of continuous employment.

   Staff members who have worked for ten continuous years may qualify for several pension plans.

4. You have had many unexplained absences this past month and I feel this has led to a decrease in sales in your department.

   I feel your many unexplained absences this past month have led to a decrease in your department's sales.

5. The western provinces should separate from the eastern provinces and form their own nation.

   The western provinces should break away from the eastern provinces to form a separate nation.

Note how many of the sentences had to be changed quite considerably to eliminate pronoun reference errors. Concentrate on determining the meaning of the sentence first and then work on rewriting it in a clear and concise manner. For more practice, try the Review Exercises.

EXERCISE 3
Subject–Verb Agreement

Underline the verbs or verb phrases in the following sentences and then replace all linking verbs with action verbs and rewrite the sentences so that the subjects and verbs agree.

1. The expense of hiring two new secretaries for our clients are justified by an estimated 30% increase in sales.

   Correct Verb Phrase: were justified

   Rewrite with Action Verb:
   An estimated 30% increase in sales will justify the expense of hiring two new secretaries for our clients.

2. The amount of paperwork, as well as numerous other clerical duties, currently performed by our salespeople take up too much of their time and prevents them from concentrating on sales.

   The amount of paperwork, as well as numerous other clerical duties, currently performed by our salespeople ***takes*** *up too much of their time and prevents them from concentrating on sales.*

3. Your failure to assume responsibility for the Smith contracts have resulted in a sharp decrease in the company's revenue.

   Your failure to assume responsibility for the Smith contracts ***has resulted*** *in a sharp decrease in the company's revenue.*

4. Several smaller sessions with the workers and their immediate supervisors, in addition to one whole day session, was used to consolidate the transfer.

   Correct Verb Phrase: were used

   Rewrite with Action Verb:
   To consolidate the transfer, we required several smaller sessions with the workers and their immediate supervisors in addition to one whole day session.

5. As the vice president and I understand, there have been a number of unexplained gaps in our inventory levels.

   Correct Verb Phrase: has been

   Rewrite with Action Verb:
   The vice president and I discovered a number of unexplained gaps in our inventory levels.

For more practice, try the Review Exercises.

EXERCISE 4
Point of View

Replace all linking verbs with action verbs and correct the point of view errors in the following sentences.

1. To start your own business, individuals need a good grounding in basic accounting skills.

To start your own business, ***you*** *need a good grounding in basic accounting skills.*

2. One's ability to present him or herself accurately and professionally will help one earn their chance to prove him or herself.

Change to Second Person to avoid wordiness:
Your *ability to present* ***yourself*** *accurately and professionally will help* ***you*** *earn* ***your*** *chance to prove* ***yourself.***

3. The Payroll Department gave me a new benefits package and I was also told to pick up my cheque on the last working day of each month.

Maintain a consistent "voice":
The Payroll Department gave me a new benefits package and told me to pick up my cheque on the last working day of each month.

4. Staff members do not know what roles they are to play in this organization and these roles also were not defined by management.

Staff members do not know what roles they should play in this organization because management has not defined them.

5. If business is the active trading of one's value for another's, then it becomes quite evident that business is an integral part of your life and has many implications in the country's economy and our daily lives.

If business involves the active trading of one person's value for another's, then business acts as an integral part of life and has many implications in the country's economy and the daily lives of individuals.

Note: the above sentence must be completely rewritten to make sense. Make sure your version contains only one tense (present), one voice (active), and one person reference (third).

For more practice, go on to the Review Exercises.

EXERCISE 5
Parallelism

Replace all linking verbs with action verbs and rewrite the following sentences to eliminate errors in parallel structure.

1. I finally realized that my frequent absences from the office were preventing me from getting a pay raise, a promotion, and learning new procedures.

   I finally realized that my frequent absences from the office ***prevented*** *me from getting a pay raise,* ***securing*** *a promotion, and learning new procedures.*

2. The Purchasing Agent requisitioned a new computer, box of paper, and a set of file folders.

   The Purchasing Agent requisitioned a new computer, ***a*** *box of paper, and a set of file folders.*

3. He was so sure he deserved a promotion and that he needed a new office.

   He felt sure ***that*** *he deserved a promotion and that he needed a new office.*

4. Nothing you can say will convince me that you are right in your answer to the question and therefore I am wrong.

   Nothing you can say will convince me that you answered the question correctly and ***that*** *therefore I answered it incorrectly.*

   Note: In this sentence, replace the linking verbs in the vague phrases "you are right" and "I am wrong" with action verbs.

5. Only when the office personnel are performing reliably, the paperwork being completed efficiently, and the calls answered promptly, do we have a firm predictable base to manage the store for profit.

   Only when the office personnel perform reliably, ***complete*** *the paperwork efficiently, and* ***answer*** *the calls promptly, do we have a firm predictable base to manage the store for profit.*

For more practice, go on to the Review Exercises.

EXERCISE 6
Coordination and Subordination

Replace all linking verbs with action verbs and rewrite the following sentences to make them logical and grammatically consistent.

1. The entrepreneurial spirit embodies the ideas of diligence and efficiency and the thrills of competition and material gain are stressed.

   The entrepreneurial spirit embodies the ideas of diligence and efficiency and stresses the thrills of competition and material gain.

2. Perhaps just a few staff members are the cause of the growing number of complaints I have received from your department, but this is an extremely important issue which must be dealt with immediately.

   I must deal immediately with the growing number of complaints I have received from your department, even if responsibility lies with just a few staff members.

   Note: The above sentence takes some thought to rewrite correctly. Determine the most important information and then place it in a coherent order.

3. We need expert advice to introduce modern filing concepts, and then a junior filing clerk should be hired to keep it current.

   We should obtain expert advice on introducing modern filing concepts and then hire a junior filing clerk to keep the filing system current.

4. The impact of the current financial slump on our company is more severe as it affects our ability to service our customers.

   The current financial slump severely affects our ability to service our customers.

   Note: Deleting the "more severe" and using an action verb gives this sentence vigour without changing its essential meaning.

5. The new printing system is perhaps the most important of all. It is designed to tie all our work together. It will improve efficiency. This will make sure excess copying is not done. Therefore the success of the whole Sales Department will be measured by the use of this Integrated Printing Responsibility System.

   Because the Integrated Printing Responsibility System will tie all our work together, improve efficiency, and eliminate excess copying, the success of the whole Sales Department depends upon its use.

For more practice, try the Review Exercises.

Review Exercises

Test your understanding of Unit Three with the following exercises. Refer to the *Better Business Writing Answer Key* or your instructor for the correct responses.

EXERCISE 1

Pronoun Agreement

Underline the incorrectly used pronouns in the following sentences and then replace all linking verbs with action verbs and rewrite the sentences so that each pronoun agrees with its antecedent in person, number, and gender. If possible, you may wish to rephrase some of the sentences to avoid using pronouns or to avoid sexist connotations (see Unit Six). Note also that in some cases you may have to change the form of the verb to agree with the correct pronoun.

1. Her evaluation of the two conferences was not particularly informative because they only included descriptions of the food.
2. These sales letters do not make me want to buy the product because it is full of mistakes.
3. Alex or John will find you the company's latest sales figures so that you can evaluate it.
4. An employee who does not want to work hard at their job should be asked to leave.
5. Everyone should send a letter of complaint to their federal M.P. in order to ensure they understand the magnitude of the problem.
6. Staff members who frequently need to be contacted during his regular shift should make sure they carry a pager at all times.
7. The parking spaces located near the Main Entrance may be used by visitors if they are unoccupied.
8. Staff members may use the Executive Lounge during off-peak hours only when they are empty.
9. You must return your identification badges to the Personnel Department if it is damaged.
10. The secretary and receptionist are responsible for keeping her workstations tidy.

EXERCISE 2

Pronoun Reference

Underline the pronouns in the following sentences and then replace all linking verbs with action verbs and rewrite the sentences to remove any ambiguous pronoun references.

1. It is time consuming to wait for the secretary to finish all of her errrands for the vice-president before doing mine or anybody else's.
2. Each plate is carefully crafted so as to look and feel like the real china most diners prefer, but they are actually made with the new Breaknot plastic.
3. The client was referred to the management consultant by her business associate.
4. Because the company pays employees according to a set scale, it does not reward the creativity or competency of individual employees.
5. Go to stores that specialize in computer software because sales staff at these stores know them.
6. Operators must ensure they record all messages with the necessary details and then drop them into the correct mail slots.
7. If your absences occurred because of personal reasons that could not be taken care of during non-working hours, I would be grateful to hear of them.
8. Working as your own boss is preferable to the anonymity of working in a large corporation even though it is risky and competitive.
9. The dynamic growth of Preston Corporation that we have experienced in the past and wish to keep on experiencing is dealt with in my proposal to make it better.
10. The drop in sales last quarter occurred because the store manager did not obtain sufficient inventory to cover the Christmas rush. This resulted in the reorganization of the corporate head offices.

EXERCISE 3

Subject–Verb Agreement

Underline the verbs in the following sentences and then replace all linking verbs with action verbs and rewrite the sentences so that the subjects and verbs agree.

1. If there is any questions regarding this situation, I would be happy to answer them.
2. Such an improvement would overcome the current system's weaknesses which includes a narrow range of customer service plans and limited access to secretarial, clerical, and reception support.
3. Clients with extremely urgent printing jobs which require the immediate attention of the clerk takes precedence over all other jobs.
4. The demands of the president, in every situation, comes first.
5. Distributed by the secretary was three separate chapters of the book.
6. The number of clients we have acquired and the lowered rent we have recently secured contributes to the 30% rise in profits since January 1 of this year.
7. As a result of our company's growth, the number of business transactions have increased by 20%.
8. The delegation, composed of members from four companies, agree that the proposal should be adopted.
9. Special Extended Assistance, provided now by some companies, offer customers the opportunity to expand their credit limits to $10,000 per year.
10. The time spent on the various tasks amount to 1.5 hours per worker per day.

EXERCISE 4

Point of View

Replace all linking verbs with action verbs and correct the point of view errors in the following sentences.

1. The current trend towards self-employment provides people with the opportunity to increase their freedom in the workplace which means being your own boss lets you pursue your own goals rather than a large corporation's goals.

2. Employees who wish to alter their vacation times because of family concerns, financial difficulties, or urgent work deadlines, may contact your supervisor to discuss scheduling requirements.

3. When he approached me and asked me to invest in his new venture, I agreed that his ideas are good and that I want to continue our partnership.

4. I should not have to alter my plans a second time before some re-scheduling is made to my agenda.

5. If you decide to become a Chartered Accountant, you must prepare yourself for the difficulties many candidates experience when they take the professional examinations.

6. The client told us what he required and then refuses to pay us.

7. We attended the seminar for three days, after which two more days were required to make sense of what we had learned.

8. One should know that they cannot hope to achieve success without first understanding the fundamentals of business practice.

9. It is clear that no amount of practice can ensure you will achieve your goal of becoming a world class musician unless talent is also a factor.

10. We value you as a customer and would hope your requirements are met.

EXERCISE 5

Parallelism

Replace all linking verbs with action verbs and rewrite the following sentences to eliminate errors in parallel structure.

1. The receptionists must be trained to pick up the phone within 3 rings, to never put a caller on hold for more than 2 minutes, and always to ask if the caller still wants to hold.

2. Securing a new job, better people to work with, and reducing your commuting time can help lower your stress level.

3. This notice is to warn you that your unexplained absences from the office have caused a decline in the efficiency of the sales staff, a significant decrease in sales, and inconvenience to our clients.

4. The project began strongly, slowed down after six months and was showing promising growth by the end of the first year.

5. The salary for the new manager is offset by the increase in sales that would result, the motivation that support staff would receive, and the better quality service for customers.

6. These services must be easily accessible, be delivered quickly, and minimize the relocation of clients.

7. Although the profit you earn as a small business owner may be relatively small compared to a large corporation, you are gaining experience from your hard work and you have a feeling of fulfillment.

8. Each of the cards we sell adapts beautifully to framing, includes an envelope, and is available for $3.99.

9. Rick Green carefully presented his proposal, clearly pointed out all its benefits, and making it clear that we benefit from implementing his ideas.

10. The proposed system is designed to encourage increased production, improved accuracy, reduce rejected products, increase recycling efforts, and machinery maintenance upgrading.

EXERCISE 6

Coordination and Subordination

Replace all linking verbs with action verbs and rewrite the following sentences to make them logical and grammatically consistent.

1. I am concerned with the volume of paperwork the sales staff is burdened with and I recommend the company hire a secretary for the sales department.

2. The report was typed. We sent it to the president for approval. He approved the report. He then asked us to make 20 copies of it.

3. I will personally interview all applicants and will as quickly as possible find an applicant who is appropriate for the job.

4. The omissions in your audit report require your immediate attention as the president is considering re-evaluating your work at year-end and possibly hiring another auditor.

5. Your loan agreement for $5,000 states that you must repay the loan within 6 months and we cannot extend it to a year.

6. We gave practical demonstrations of how we make the best of the technology we possess and, at the same time, improving what we have through design modifications.

7. There was nothing we could do about the drop in sales. Head Office didn't give us enough inventory.

8. We will require both Ms. Black and Mr. Chow to work on the project and the amount of the time each needs to spend on the project will depend upon the extent of the research that is required.

9. The franchises operate under the auspices of the Milwaukee Franchise Services and there is one Administrator and one Sales Manager for the whole Milwaukee area.

10. I am confident in your ability to lead our Sales Department; however, your regular presence at work is essential for this position.

UNIT FOUR

How To Build Credibility

You have almost finished the "grammar" part of *Better Business Writing*. Good news? Now all you need to do is quickly review the nitty gritty elements of writing:

1. Usage
2. Spelling
3. Punctuation.

Once you finish Unit Four, you leave grammar behind and study how your use of an effective tone can help you achieve success in your business career.

0 *Introduction*

No matter how beautifully you put together your sentences or how well you choose your words, if you misspell a word or misplace a comma, you invite confusion. Remember your principal goal as a business writer – to elicit action from your readers. If you distract your readers by using a word incorrectly, you may not succeed in influencing them.

Even if you feel confident in your ability to use correct mechanics, scan through the material in Unit Four and try the Review Exercises. You can never be too well prepared.

1. *Usage*

The English language abounds with words and phrases that suffer from abuse. You will see words such as *affect* and *effect* used interchangeably or *it's* used as a possessive as in *The dog ate it's bone* or *good* used instead of *well* as in *He performed good today.* Do not betray a lack of sensitivity to the language or worse, a lack of knowledge, by treating the words you use disrespectfully. Refer to the following list to find some of the words and phrases you may occasionally abuse and read how to use them correctly.

Accept/Except

Use **accept** as a verb meaning to take something: *We accepted his application.*

Use **except** as a verb meaning to make an exception or as a preposition to indicate something that does not conform: *He was excepted (excluded) from the position because he had nothing to offer except (besides) money.*

Micro Hint
To avoid possible confusion, use "exclude" instead of except as a verb meaning to leave out.

Adverse/Averse
Use **adverse** as an adjective to mean detrimental or unlucky: *Because of adverse circumstances, our company went bankrupt.*
Use **averse** as a verb to mean reluctant: *The secretary was averse to working overtime.*

Micro Hint
To avoid sounding pretentious, use "reluctant" or "unwilling" instead of averse.

Affect/Effect
Use **affect** as a verb to mean influence: *The breakdown of the company fax machine affected sales.*
Use **effect** as a noun to mean a result: *The breakdown of the company fax machine had an adverse effect on sales.* You can occasionally use **effect** as a verb to mean bring about: *This policy is effected to ensure all employees conform to established safety rules.*

Micro Hint
Try to avoid using effect as a verb to minimize the chances of making an error and because effect as a verb may sound pretentious.

Allright
Use the correct spelling: **all right** NOT "alright."

Alternate/Alternative
Use **alternate** to mean every other one: *She worked alternate Tuesdays for six months and then switched to alternate Thursdays.*
Use **alternative** to mean a choice: *The company had no alternative but to finance the manufacturing plant.*

Micro Hint
Never use "alternate" when the sense of the sentence involves a choice.

Among/Between
Use **among** as a preposition when three or more persons or things are involved: *We divided the food left over from the company luncheon among the entire staff.*
Use **between** as a preposition when only two persons or things are involved: *The president finally had to choose between going into debt and selling his company.*

Aspect
You can safely delete "aspect" from your vocabulary unless you mean "appearance." Avoid using **aspect** as a jargon term to mean element or reason. For example: *One aspect of this situation is that we must reorganize the filing system.* This sentence communicates little of value because "aspect" means nothing concrete.

Micro Hint

By rephrasing your sentences to avoid using "aspect", you also cut out unnecessary words: *We must reorganize the filing system.*

Choose/Chose

Use **choose** when you make a choice in the present tense and use **chose** when you make a choice in the past tense: *Alice **chose** to work for the bank but the Personnel Manager did not **choose** her from among the applicants.*

Micro Hint

You can't remember as much in the past, so use one "o". You know what's happening in the present, so use two "o's".

Complement/ Compliment

Use **complement** as a noun or verb to mean making something complete: *Her writing skills complemented his verbal skills.* or *Her writing skills provided an effective complement to his verbal skills.*

Use **compliment** as a noun or verb to mean praise: *She complimented him on his excellent speech.*

Macro Hint

If you don't want to mean "praise", you probably want to use complement: *Mr. Birrell complimented (praised) Ms. Hauser on how well her writing skills complemented (made complete) his verbal skills.*

Comprise/Compose

Use **comprise** as a verb to mean include: *The staff comprises workers from three unions.*

Use **compose** as a verb to mean make up: *The staff was composed of workers from three unions.*

Micro Hint

Never use comprise in the passive voice as in *The staff was comprised of workers...* Use compose.

Content/Contented

Use **content** as a noun to mean something that is contained in something else: *The content of the report made good sense.*

Use **contented** as an adjective to describe a state of being: *Our goal is to have a smoothly operating company with contented employees.*

Micro Hint

When the stress is on the *first* syllable, "content" means something contained. When the stress is on the *second* syllable, "content" means satisified.

Criteria/Criterion

The trend toward making "data" a singular noun to take the place of "datum" has not extended to criteria/criterion (see data/datum below).

Use **criteria** as a plural noun: *The criteria for evaluating the students were not specified.*

Use **criterion** as a singular noun: *I suggest that we alter the criterion that governs grievance procedure #216.*

Data/Datum

Technically, **data** is plural while **datum** is singular. However, few writers use "datum" in general business documents. If you choose to use "data" in all cases, just make sure you use it as either singular or plural, not both. For example: *The data were evaluated* OR *The data was evaluated* NOT *After the data* ***were*** *(plural) evaluated, it* ***was*** *(singular) presented to the committee.*

Macro Hint

You are probably safest using "data" as a singular noun in keeping with the current trend toward eliminating the Latin singular form "datum".

Disinterested/ Uninterested

Use **disinterested** to mean objective or neutral: *The committee tried to remain disinterested (neutral) in the outcome of the grievance proceedings.*
Use **uninterested** to mean not interested: *The committee found the presentation uninteresting (boring).*

Disorganized/ Unorganized

Use **disorganized** to mean a lack of organization.

Macro Hint

"Unorganized" is NOT a fully accepted word.

Due to

Avoid beginning sentences with "due" as in: *Due to the fact that it snowed, we were unable to attend the meeting.* Use of "due" in this way sounds awkward and somewhat long-winded. Use "because" instead: *Because it snowed, we were unable to attend the meeting.*

Good/Well

Use **good** as an adjective to describe a noun such as the good report, the good argument, etc.: *He submitted a good report.* You would never say: *He submitted a well report,* right?
Use **well** as an adverb to describe a verb such as perform well, write well, etc.: *He wrote his report well.* You would rather die than say: *He wrote his report good,* wouldn't you?

Macro Hint

Watch out for the verbs "does", "do", "done", etc. NEVER use "good" to modify these verbs. Use "well": *She did very well on the exam.*

Fewer/Less

Use **fewer** to refer to individual numbers or units that can be counted: *Fewer than ten people showed up at the seminar.*
Use **less** to refer to things as quantity or amount, not as number: *It took less money than we anticipated to buy our new car.*

Firstly/Secondly

Use First, Second, etc. to simplify your writing and to avoid ridiculous extremes such as "ninthly" or "tenthly"!

Him/He or Her/She

Use **him** or **her** when modified by a preposition (such as with): *I went to the store with Don and him.*
Use **he** or **she** as the subject of a sentence: *She and Joan went to the meeting.*

I/me

Use **I** as the subject of a sentence: *I needed a raise.*
Use **me** as the direct or indirect object of a sentence: *The vice-president gave me a raise.*
Combining I or me with another person:
As subject: *Jake and **I** voted to cancel the contract.*
As object: *The president gave Donna and **me** a day off.*

Macro Hint 1
You would never say: *The president gave I a day off* **so NEVER write:** *The president gave Donna and I a day off.*

Macro Hint 2
You would never say: *Me wanted a computer* **so NEVER write:** *Alice and me wanted a computer.*

Irregardless

Use "regardless"; irregardless is non-standard.

It's/Its

Use **its** to stand for a possessive: *The dog ran to its kennel.*
Use **it's** as a contraction for "it is": *It's not necessary to complete all four pages of the questionnaire.*
Here's a sentence that uses both "its" and "it's" correctly: *Because **it's** (it is) a prime location, the company far exceeded **its** (possessive) profit expectations.*

Micro Hint
If possible, avoid using "it's" altogether unless you can be sure that the "it" refers back to an antecedent.

Lie/Lay

Use **lie** to mean tell a falsehood: *He lied about his qualifications* or to rest or recline: *I want to lie down.*
Use **lay** to mean the past tense of "lie": *I lay down and closed my eyes* or present tense of an active verb meaning to place on a surface: *I lay paper on the table before I do my drawing.*

Micro Hint
People lie; chickens lay.

Lose/Loose

Lose and Loose mean different things and must not be used interchangeably.
Use **lose** when you cause something to become lost.
Use **loose** when you refer to something lacking in tightness: *If you **lose** your purse, you can always put your **loose** change in your jacket pocket.*

Media

Media is the plural form of medium. However, media now appears frequently as a singular noun or adjective that refers to newspapers, television, and radio, or the people that work in them. Try to avoid using media as a blanket adjective. Be specific: "the television anchor" or "jour-

nalist" rather than the "media spokesperson".
Question: When can a medium appear in the media?
Answer: When she or he is a psychic.

Number/Amount

Use **number** when the persons or objects can be counted: *A number of participants decided to leave early.*
Use **amount** when referring to a quantity of something that cannot be counted or is considered as a whole: *The amount of money required to buy a house increases yearly.*

Oriented/Orientated

Use **oriented** to mean the past tense of "to orient": *The tour guide's detailed map oriented us to our new surroundings.*

Micro Hint

Do NOT use "orientated" – it is old-fashioned and affected.

People/Persons

Use **people** to refer to an unspecified or large number: *The people demanded their rights.*
Use **persons** to refer to a specified or small number: *Only six persons chose to buy our product.*

Macro Hint

Don't overuse "persons" and "people". If possible, use the second person (you) rather than the impersonal "person". For example: *A person should be aware of his or her financial situation* sounds too formal. Humanize your writing: *You should be aware of your financial situation.* The written word comes alive in the **individual** reader.

Prescribe/Proscribe

Use **prescribe** to mean impose or define: *The school prescribed a rigid set of rules.*
Use **proscribe** to mean prohibit or limit: *His movements were severely proscribed by the Court.*

Principal/Principle

Use **principal** as a noun to refer to the head of a school or company or to capital which earns interest and as an adjective to refer to a person or object that is the main or primary component. For example: *The principal on Allison's investment earned 14% more interest than the principal investment held by the principal of her high school.*
Use **principle** as a noun to mean a rule or requirement: *I've based my proposal on the principle that we must invest $15,000 to achieve our goals.*

Micro Hint

If you refer to something other than a person in power or a capital investment, chances are you want to use "principle".

Real/Really

Use **real** to mean authentic NOT as a modifier to emphasize something as in "real nice", "real different", etc.
Use **really** as a modifier to emphasize something: "really

nice", "really different", etc.

Micro Hint

While you should never use "real" as a modifier, you should also think twice about using "really" to emphasize something. "Really" lacks strength: use "incredibly different", "unbelievably different", "absurdly different" – anything but the feeble-minded "really".

Stationary/Stationery

Use **stationary** to mean not moving: *The heavy desk remained stationary even after the earthquake.*

Use **stationery** to refer to letterhead and envelopes used in business. *I paid $350 for new stationery after I moved to a new office.*

Micro Hint

Letters contain "e's" and so does station**e**ry. "Stand still" contains an "a" and so does station**a**ry.

Thank you

Do not write "Thank-you". The hyphenated form is incorrect unless used as a noun: *I wish to add a big thank-you for your help.*

That/Which

Use **that** to introduce a clause that is essential to the meaning of the sentence: *The company that maintains a consistent advertising program has a good chance of soliciting new business.*

Use **which** to introduce a clause that is not essential to the meaning of the sentence; that is, the clause could be enclosed in parenthesis: *XYZ Inc., which maintains a consistent advertising program, made a profit of six million dollars last year.*

Which/Who

Use **which** when referring to things: *The factory, which lacked up-to-date equipment, finally received a Notice of Closure.*

Use **who** when referring to persons: *The factory workers, who were worried about job security, called for a strike.*

Your/You're

Use **your** to indicate a possessive: *Your car is parked in front of my driveway.*

Use **you're** as a short (contracted) version of "you are": *You're (you are) a welcome addition to the company.*

Micro Hint

If you always remember that "you're" means "you are", you won't write: *Your asking me to use you're desk while your on vacation.* Correct the sentence by using "your" to indicate a possessive and "you're" to indicate "you are": *You're asking me to use your desk while you're on vacation.*

EXERCISE 1

Usage

Underline the usage errors in the following sentences and then rewrite the sentences correctly.

1. As a result of averse market trends, our product did not sell real well.
2. Because of the affect the recession had on sales, we had no alternate but to close down our company.
3. Less than twenty people arrived to take part in the festivities.
4. We thought it only fair to divide the profits between our shareholders.
5. Do you really feel the wallpaper compliments the curtains?

Check your answers with the Answer Key and then try the Review Exercises.

2. *Spelling*

Imagine how you would react if you read the following sentence in a letter asking you for a job:

> If the enclosed resume meets with your *aproval,* I hope we can get together to *discus* how I may best *confrom* to your *requirments* for a *comunication specializt.*

Because the writer failed to correct spelling errors, you can't help but think that he or she would apply the same kind of carelessness to a job. By sending the message that poor spelling does not matter, the writer also sends the message that careful attention to detail does not matter.

Student:
How can I improve
my memory?
Professor:
Learn to love
your past.
– Andrea Pontoni

Luckily, help is at hand if you occasionally forget how to spell a word. Most word processing programs and electronic typewriters now include spell checkers that search out and correct your misspelled words and even some of your typographical errors. But what do you do if you find yourself stranded without a computer and expected to produce a hand-written document? You prepare for such an event by writing down the correct spelling of any word which habitually confounds your memory. The act of writing down a correctly spelled word coordinates your eye with your hand. This coordination helps to set the correct spelling in your brain so that the next time you have to write the word, you will be more likely to remember how the word is *supposed* to look.

Good spelling is a visual skill. Study the following list of the most commonly misspelled words and note where your personal difficulties lie.

First, a quick reminder:

> **Prefixes** are letter groups (usually of one syllable) that go at the *beginning* of words. Remember that "pre" means before as in previous, preview, prevent, pre-teen, etc.
> **Suffixes** are letter groups (usually of one syllable) that go at the *end* of words.

abbreviate: two "b's"!

accommodate: think of double occupancy – two "c's" and two "m's".

accumulate: keep the two "c's", but drop an "m".

address: think of the "ad" as a prefix to the word "dress" so that you remember to double the "d".

acquire/acquaint/acquitted: don't forget the "c".

altogether: drop the second "l" in "all". Think of a guy named Al who you'd like to get together with.

argument: when you add the suffix "ment" to argue, drop the "e". In an argument, someone has to lose – let it be the "e".

beginning: think of the suffix as "ning" so that you remember to double the "n".

benefited: do not double the "t" because the root word (benefit) is more than one syllable and is not accented on its last syllable. "Paralleled" is another word that conforms to this rule.

business: pretend "busi" is pronounced "busy" so that you don't double the "s".

changeable: just add the suffix "able" to "change".

committed/commitment: double the "t" for "committed" but NOT for "commitment" – tricky one!

conference: all "e's" – don't add an "a".

conscience: think of two separate words: "con" and "science".

conscious: drop the "ence" from "conscience" and add "ous".

convenient: the "i" has an "e" sound.

criticism: critics hate to be slighted. Give the critic his or her due and then add "ism".

definitely: think of the word "finite" and then add the prefix "de" and the suffix "ly".

desperate: think "er" and "ate". Have you ever been so desperately hungry that you ate a horse?

disagree: agree with the prefix "dis" – no double "s".

explanation: leave out the "i" in explain when you write "explanation". Don't write "explaination"!

ie/ei: use "ei" when you want an "ee" sound as in fiend, believe, and field; a hard "a" sound as in weigh, neighbour, and eight; or an "i" sound as in neither and either. Use "ei" when it is preceded by "c": receive, perceive, conceive.

irrelevant: think of "relevant" and then add the prefix "ir".

maneuver: don't add an "o" – think "eu". A good maneuver doesn't waste time (or use extra letters).

necessary/unnecessary: pronounce "necessary" with a hard "c" as you write: "nekessary" so that you remember to use one "c" and two "s's". For "unnecessary" remember that the "un" prefix is added on – thereby doubling the "n".

procedure: think of the "e" as a short "e" rather than a long "e" to avoid writing "proceedure".

occasionally: think of "occur" to double the "c" rather than the "s".

occur/occurred: add an extra "r" when you put "occur" in the past tense: "occurred". The same rule applies to the past tense of "incur": "incurred".

perform: don't write "preform" when you mean to accomplish something.

prejudice: add the prefix "pre" (meaning to come before) to "judge" and then remove the "ge" and add "ice".

recommend/recommendation: only double the "m".

separate/separately: put an "a" after the "p", NOT an "e", so that if you took out the "a" after the "r", you could write "part". Think of the word "part" when you write "separate" and you can't go wrong.

similar: don't stick in an extra "i" – keep it as simple as it sounds.

stationery: if you refer to letterhead, notepaper, etc., think of the "e" as corresponding to "letters". Use "stationary" to mean not moving or standing still.

EXERCISE 2

Spelling

Underline and then correct the misspelled words in the following letter.

> Dear Mr. Leclair:
>
> Thank you for your letter of Febuary 20 requesting our asistance with your computer programing requirments. Your bussiness is in an excelent position to take full advantageage of the oportunities which instalation of our new programs will permitt.
>
> I've enclosed a pamflet that will provide you with all the aditional information you need. Note how many companies have benefited from the services we ofer.
>
> I fully apreciate your intrest in our services and assure you of the excelent revenus you can expect to reep when you imploy Leclair Paralel Programs to take controll of your oeprations.

Check your answers with the Answer Key and then try the Review Exercises.

3. *Punctuation*

Punctuation marks divide–or link–ideas. Remember that you use punctuation to help increase your reader's understanding of what you have written. If you do not use correct punctuation, your readers may well misinterpret your meaning. For example, notice how a lack of punctuation distorts the meaning of the following sentence:

> Your order for the continuous feed printer paper and software has been delayed.

Without punctuation, this sentence could refer to only two items: paper used for a continuous feed printer and software. However, the original order actually specified three items; therefore, the sentence should read:

> Your order for the continuous feed printer, paper, and software has been delayed.

To understand correct business punctuation, you need to examine the four most useful punctuation marks: the comma, the semi-colon, the colon, and the dash.

Comma >

First Use of the Comma

The comma has four main uses.

Put a comma after a word or phrase which begins a sentence and comes before the words which express the main idea.

The comma could follow a single word or a whole phrase. Single words followed by commas include: "however", "nevertheless", "first", or "sometimes". For example:

> However, we should not use this product in our company.

Commas are used when you have to take a breath, and periods are used when you want to stop and think.
– *Anon*

Phrases which introduce a sentence often begin with words such as "if", "when", "while", "after", etc. For example:

> While I was eating, the sales manager telephoned my client.

If you did not place a comma after "eating", the meaning of this sentence would be comically obscured: "While I was eating the sales manager telephoned my client". You wouldn't want to imply that you made a practice of eating the sales manager!

Here's another example of an introductory phrase followed by a comma:

> After the vice-president circulated the report on time-management techniques, office efficiency improved.

Commas which follow an introductory phrase in a sentence help the readers to distinguish the introductory phrase from the main thought and so avoid confusion.

Second Use of the Comma

Use commas to set off an *Interrupting Construction* within a sentence, or, for a slightly different effect, use parentheses or dashes. To understand this second use of the comma, you need to first define the term Interrupting Construction.

Grammarians define an Interrupting Construction as a group of words inside a sentence which can be removed without changing the meaning of the rest of the sentence. That is, the remaining words contain a subject and a verb, and express a complete thought, regardless of the information in the interrupting construction. For example:

> The annual meeting, which all staff members must attend, will be held on October 23.

Notice that the phrase "which all staff members must attend" acts as an interrupting construction; the sentence could stand without it and still be correct:

> The annual meeting will be held on October 23.

The interrupting construction merely adds extra information to clarify the importance of the meeting.

You can also use **dashes, parentheses,** or **square brackets** to set off an interrupting construction within a sentence.

The Dash

Use dashes to highlight the interrupting information by accentuating it. This use of the dash makes the interrupting construction more important than the rest of the sentence. For example:

> All clients – even those opposed to our philosophy – must be treated with respect.

You may also use dashes for other reasons that will be covered in the section on the dash below.

Parentheses

Use parentheses to make the interrupting construction something like a whisper – that is, less important than the rest of the sentence and more like an aside. For example:

> Credit Unions (sometimes mistaken for Savings & Loan Associations) serve the needs of a particular community.

Square Brackets

Use square brackets to enclose editorial interruptions in a quotation. For example, if you were writing an article quoting someone who misspelled a person's name, you would spell the name correctly inside the square brackets immediately following the misspelled version. For example:

> Dr. Brackendale pointed out in her speech: "Mr. Bunion's [Onion's] proposal has several layers to it."

You also use square brackets when you quote from someone else's writing and must insert a word to make the meaning clearer. For example:

> Mr. Smith's report stated: "The [industrial] community must seriously consider re-cycling its waste materials".

Third Use of the Comma

Use a comma to introduce an informal quotation. For example:

> He then asked me if I had received the June receipts that morning. I remember my reply exactly. I said, "Yes, they came in at 11:05."

Note that an informal quotation usually reports what someone has *said* in conversation. When you write the quotation, "Yes, they came in at 11:05", you must capitalize the first letter of yes because it is the first word in the quotation, even though it was preceded by a comma.

When you use *quotation marks*, remember to use *double quotation marks* to identify the beginning and end of a word-for-word quotation and to use *single quotation marks* to indicate a paraphrase or a quotation within a quotation.

Fourth Use of the Comma

Use a comma between two independent clauses joined by a coordinating conjunction if the subject changes in the second clause. For example:

> He was going to enter the code, but the manager had switched off the override toggle.

In this sentence, "he" is the subject of the first independent clause, while "the manager" is the subject of the second independent clause. Because these two clauses begin with different subjects and are joined by the coordinating conjunction "but," a comma must be inserted.

Note that there are only seven coordinating conjunctions: and, but, or, nor, for, yet, and so. Here's some more examples:

> The Secretary organized the travel arrangements, and the Sales Manager contacted the Conference Facilitator.
>
> Elsa enjoys working with numbers, but George prefers customer relations.

Semi-Colon >

The semi-colon functions mainly to separate two ideas within the same sentence. Of course, you could ask why not just use a period instead of a semi-colon and make two sentences? You use a semi-colon instead of a period in cases where you want to indicate that one action caused another, or both actions occurred at the same time, or the two actions relate closely in some other way. To show such a relationship, you can use the semi-colon in two ways.

First Use of the Semi-Colon

Use a semi-colon to join two independent clauses that are not joined by a coordinating conjunction. Remember the seven coordinating conjunctions: and, but, so, for, nor, or, and yet. Here is a sentence incorrectly punctuated with a comma because it contains no coordinating conjunction and joins two independent clauses:

> The Collections Officer opposed the request, the Customer Relations Supervisor approved it.

The two halves of this sentence cannot be joined by a comma because a comma lacks sufficient strength. To punctuate this sentence correctly, place a semi-colon between the two parts of the sentence:

> The Collections Officer opposed the request; the Customer Relations Supervisor approved it.

Second Use of the Semi-Colon

Use a semicolon between independent clauses joined by a conjunctive adverb. A conjunctive adverb is a word which describes the nature of the relationship between two independent clauses. You may use words such as *accordingly*, *however*, *consequently*, *therefore*, *subsequently*, *nonetheless*, *moreover*, *instead*, and *furthermore* as conjunctive adverbs in a sentence.

For example:

> The Vice-president interceded on behalf of Ajax Supplies; however, the company decided to use a different supplier.

When you use a semi-colon followed by a conjunctive adverb such as "however", you must place a comma after the word "however". Here is another example:

> The personnel manager neglected his duties; consequently, we must hire a new personnel manager.

The Colon >

In general, you use the colon to direct your reader's attention forward. A colon usually occurs near the beginning of a sentence and indicates that something challenging, interesting, or difficult approaches: a list, a complex quotation, a formal statement. You can use the colon in three ways.

First Use of the Colon

Use a colon to introduce a long, formal quotation. For example:

> The Accounts Manual defines an Interest Achiever Account as follows: "The IAA is an account in which interest is paid at increasingly higher rates depending on the daily closing balance."

Note the use of semi-colons to separate the items in the list because each item is more than one word.

Second Use of the Colon

Use a colon to introduce a list. For example:

> Interest rates for these increments are as follows: 9.35%, 9.46%, 10.60%, and 11.43%.

Third Use of the Colon

Use a colon after phrases which include "the following" and "as follows". For example:

> We should proceed with the takeover as follows: appoint an accounts manager, evaluate our financial status, and study alternate locations.

The Dash >

You have already read how to use two dashes to set off an interrupting construction. You can also use one dash to direct the reader's attention backwards – unlike the colon, which directs the reader's attention forward. Usually, therefore, the dash occurs towards the end of a sentence and requires the reader to backtrack in order to fully comprehend the sentence's meaning. For example:

> The proposal to amend flex time had one marked effect – it upset all the staff.

In this example, the words following the dash emphasize or comment on the preceding idea. Here's another example:

> Careful and correct punctuation provides your sentences with one important feature – clarity of thought.

Note that you should not confuse the dash with the hyphen. You use two strokes of the hyphen key to type a dash, whereas you use a hyphen only as an internal word division, as in the word "sub-contractor".

EXERCISE 3

Punctuation

Apply the rules of punctuation specified above to punctuate the following sentences correctly.

1. Whatever I wrote someone corrected my punctuation.
2. The Personnel Manager will advertise the position the vice-president will conduct the interviews.
3. Meet us on the fifth floor not the fourth floor in three hours.
4. The client thanked Ms. Martin Marten for her excellent report.
5. Secondly I would like to discuss how my proposal will increase profits.

Check your answers with the Answer Key and then try the Review Exercises.

Answer Key

EXERCISE 1
Usage

Underline the usage errors in the following sentences and then rewrite the sentences correctly.

1. As a result of averse market trends, our product did not sell real well.

   As a result of ***adverse*** *market trends, our product did not sell* ***very*** *well.*

2. Because of the affect the recession had on sales, we had no alternate but to close down our company.

   Because of the ***effect*** *the recession had on sales, we had no* ***alternative*** *but to close down our company.*

3. Less than twenty people arrived to take part in the festivities.

   Fewer *than twenty people arrived to take part in the festivities.*

4. We thought it only fair to divide the profits between our shareholders.

We thought it only fair to divide the profits ***among*** *our shareholders.*

5. Do you really feel the wallpaper <u>compliments</u> the curtains?

   Do you really feel the wallpaper **complements** the curtains?

EXERCISE 2
Spelling

Underline and correct the misspelled words in the following letter.

Dear Mr. Leclair:

Thank you for your letter of <u>Febuary</u> (*February*) 20 requesting our <u>asistance</u> (*assistance*) with your computer <u>programing</u> (*programming*) <u>requirments</u> (*requirements*). Your <u>bussiness</u> (*business*) is in an <u>excelent</u> (*excellent*) position to take full <u>advantageage</u> (*advantage*) of the <u>oportunities</u> (*opportunities*) which <u>instalation</u> (*installation*) of our new programs will <u>permitt</u> (*permit*).

I've enclosed a <u>pamflet</u> (*pamphlet*) that will provide you with all the <u>aditional</u> (*additional*) information you need. Note how many companies have benefited from the services we <u>ofer</u> (*offer*).

I fully <u>apreciate</u> (*appreciate*) your <u>intrest</u> (*interest*) in our services and assure you of the <u>excelent</u> (*excellent*) <u>revenus</u> (*revenues*) you can expect to <u>reep</u> (*reap*) when you <u>imploy</u> (*employ*) Leclair <u>Paralel</u> (*Parallel*) Programs to take <u>controll</u> (*control*) of your <u>oeprations</u> (*operations*).

EXERCISE 3
Punctuation

Apply the rules of punctuation to correct the following sentences.

1. Whatever I wrote, someone corrected my punctuation.
2. The Personnel Manager will advertise the position; the vice-president will conduct the interviews.
3. Meet us on the fifth floor – not the fourth floor – in three hours.
4. The client thanked Ms. Martin [Marten] for her excellent report.
5. Secondly, I would like to discuss how my proposal will increase profits.

Review Exercises

Test your understanding of Unit Four with the following exercises. Refer to the *Better Business Writing Answer Key* or your instructor for the correct responses.

EXERCISE 1

Usage

Underline and then correct the usage errors in the following sentences.

1. I returned the stationary I ordered as the typesetter had misspelled my name.
2. Good communication skills and a degree in Commerce are the principle requirements for this position.
3. The media spokesperson interviewed me for his radio show.
4. After considering the problem from every aspect, the company decided to lay off half of it's employees.
5. Your someone who would fit real well into our company, especially because of you're proven sales record.
6. I agree with the principal that employees should receive equal pay for work of equal value.
7. Because of his broken leg, his ability to walk was severely prescribed.
8. All persons should agree that the people involved in the fraud case deserve to be fined.
9. I hope you're new dog does as good as it's predecessor at guarding your home.
10. The company was definitely adverse to allowing it's employees extra pay for overtime.

EXERCISE 2

Spelling

Place a tick next to the correctly spelled words and rewrite the incorrectly spelled words in the appropriate spaces below.

1. immediatley ______
2. occurred ______
3. practically ______
4. perseverance ______
5. analysis ______
6. paralel ______
7. eficient ______
8. committed ______
9. committment ______
10. proceedure ______
11. seperately ______
12. improvement ______
13. additional ______
14. maximum ______
15. dismisal ______
16. alcohol ______
17. confidental ______
18. simultaneous ______
19. reorganized ______
20. improvments ______
21. recieve ______
22. prefered ______
23. thier ______
24. expense ______
25. approval ______

EXERCISE 3

Punctuation

Apply the rules of punctuation to punctuate the following sentences correctly.

1. Meet us on the third floor not the mezzanine in two hours.
2. Britnell Construction Inc. well-known for its work on the Ocean Park development specializes in building condominiums.
3. Joe Brown who is the chairperson conducted the meeting very efficiently.
4. Second we decided to market our product only in the western states.
5. While I photocopied the other secretary typed.
6. If your workload is too heavy please contact me, I may be able to help.
7. All of our accounts even those which are not yet due must be paid off immediately.
8. I did not receive the report in time to present it at the meeting yet I still managed to discuss the main issues.
9. The Credit Manager approved my application however he specified that I must repay the loan within one year.
10. Buy the following items a stapler, one box of paper-clips, a roll of tape and two boxes of pens.

How To Understand Your Reader

By now you have a good understanding of how to write clearly and correctly. In Units Five to Thirteen you will turn your attention to learning how to write effectively. Your first step involves cultivating an awareness of your reader – the topic of Unit Five. Here's what you'll learn:

1. The You Attitude
2. The Positive Approach
3. The Human Touch.

You will find the material in Unit Five both challenging and interesting because it deals with people. After working through Unit Five, you will know how to guarantee that the tone of your letters makes a favourable impact on your readers. As a businessperson you need to understand how to relate well to your customers, co-workers, and colleagues. A large part of your success will depend upon your ability to write effectively.

Introduction

You can see the difference between writing that is effective and writing that is only clear and correct if you ask yourself what you think of someone who continually orders you about. They may be perfectly clear in saying: *Send me all vacation leave entitlements in your region* or *Get back to me by Tuesday.* But what about their tone? Most people produce better work when they are *asked* rather than *told* to do something. The effective communicator, therefore, displays sensitivity to the other person's way of looking at things.

Strive to write memos and letters that either *generate* or *retain* good will in your reader. Alternatives to this approach are not attractive. They consist of generating one of the following two attitudes in the reader:

1 ill will
2 bare tolerance.

Caesar is above grammar.
– *Frederick the Great*

"But why should I bother? I'm in control here." True, but although your subordinates may not be in a position to resist decisions you make in your official capacity, you run an unnecessary risk when you write uncaringly, abruptly or officiously. On the other hand, if you promote

good will in all communications, you will benefit later – perhaps in unexpected ways.

Generating good will may seem irrelevant when you are not asking your reader to give you anything immediate or specific in return, such as a refund, a job, or a reference. For example, many memos simply provide a list of information, give instructions, or order supplies. Do you have anything to gain personally by generating good will at all times?

If you think about it carefully, you will see that in fact you *are* asking your reader for something important in situations like this – to accept your information or instructions in a spirit of good will and perhaps to act on them. A reader who receives an abrupt, insensitive memo will be reluctant to co-operate.

Perhaps you will see the results of this friction at some point during your career. A reader may grudgingly carry out your order, request further clarification endlessly, "work to rule," gossip destructively, or complain to superiors or to outside agencies. Even though you may ask nothing specific of your readers, you do depend to some extent on their willingness to give your message an open-minded hearing. A successful tone in communication *depends* on a spirit of good will.

Now that you've thought about the advantages of creating a general climate of good will in your letters, you can consider the three attributes which, when combined, create a tone of good will. Just as learning to write the *Power Sentence* in Unit One required you to recognize three key attributes (the active voice, action verbs, and specific words), so learning how to create an effective tone requires you to attain detailed mastery of three key techniques: the You Attitude, the Positive Approach, and the Human Touch.

To make it easier for you to acquire these key techniques, we'll describe each of them in their turn, and provide examples. We'll then move on to study effective letter structure in Unit Six.

1.

The You Attitude

To write your letters and memos from your reader's point of view, ensure that your sentences frequently begin with your *reader's name*, or the word *"you"*. Cut down on the number of sentences that begin with the words "I" or "We" or the name of your organization. For example, instead of writing "*I* agree with you," write "*You* are correct."

What is the difference? In English, the subject-noun near the beginning of a sentence occupies the place of greatest impact. By putting words which refer to your reader in this privileged position, and by also adopting a polite and considerate tone, you show respect. In a sense, you put the reader's name in bright lights, instead of your own.

Calculating the "You" Attitude >

Calculate the "You" attitude in a letter or memo as follows:

1	Total the number of sentences that begin with the word "we", the word "I", or the name of your organization.
2	Total the number of sentences that begin with the word "you", or your reader's name, or the name of *your reader's* organization.

Do your "you" sentences outnumber "we" sentences by at least three to one? If so, your letters convey a strong "you" attitude.

Of course, the "you" statements must be *positive* ones in order to qualify. Don't write a message such as: "If you had followed our instructions correctly, you wouldn't be in *trouble* now." This sentence certainly does not convey the kind of tone you want to aim for!

Your calculation of the "you" attitude will help you to revise your letters so that you express ideas from your reader's point of view. For example, this sentence lacks the "you" attitude:

> *Our* annual report will undoubtedly supply *you* with the statistics you asked for.

Rewrite the sentence with the "you" attitude:

> *You* will find the statistics you asked for in our annual report.

Readers feel that you have seen things from their perspective when you use the "you" attitude – and you have!

The more you practice the "you" attitude, the better you will be able to see situations from the point of view of your various readers. You will achieve your goal of communicating effectively if you adopt this approach.

Let's analyze a sentence from a typical letter:

> Dear Customer:
>
> It was only after a great deal of thought and effort that *we* were able to come up with this inexpensive overdraft protection plan that we think will benefit *our* new customers, such as yourself.

Only presidents, editors and people with tapeworm have the right to use the editorial "we".

– *Mark Twain*

Can you see how the use of "we" conveys a self-concerned attitude on the part of the writer ("We, we, our")? A simple change of viewpoint leads to this:

> Dear Mr. Inkster:
>
> *You* will find the enclosed overdraft protection plan very economical, offering *you* maximum security.

This "you" version uses the reader's name (where possible), and presents benefits from the *reader*'s point of view. Which version would you rather receive?

EXERCISE 1

You Attitude

Underline the words in the following letter which refer to the writer. Then rewrite the letter with the "you" attitude and check your version against the Answer Key.

> Dear Mr. Winfield:
>
> We are in receipt of your letter requesting permission to franchise our product in Alberta. We always appreciate receiving a letter from agents who wish to handle our soap. We have received more submissions than we can easily handle.
>
> In any case, I am afraid that it is against our policy to sell distributor rights to more than one franchisee in cities of less than 7,000, and as Mr. Hicraft is already open for business in Crow Creek, I regret we cannot authorize another agency.

If we decide to change our marketing policy, we will contact you. We will keep your name on file for six months.

Sincerely,

Derek Jones

You Attitude Examples >

The following paragraph uses the word "you". Does it express the "You Attitude?"

Dear Cardholder:

We are writing to notify you that your account is overdue. You owe us $2,454.67. Our records show that although you have been a cardholder for less than one year, your payments have frequently been received late. This is unacceptable to us.

If you said "NO!", you're correct. As you can see, negative thinking and the "we" attitude predominate, subverting the effect of using the words "you" and "your". Such unenlightened business writing will not assist sales of the company's services in today's competitive marketplace. It might have been better written this way:

Dear Mr. Thompson:

Please note that your outstanding balance of $2,454.67 on your account with us was not paid last month. This has happened three times over the last year. Please make your payments on time in future, so that we will be able to keep your account active.

Here is another example. What do you think?:

THANK YOU for alerting us to your circulation problem. We are checking our records and will make the appropriate adjustment to your subscription immediately.

We sometimes need four to six weeks to integrate changes in the master file, but you will be happy to know that we now have your information correctly on file so that you should receive invoices or renewal notices at the appropriate time.

Your correction will be effective with Issue No. 66. Thank you for your patience.

Sincerely,

Circulation Department

"YES," this letter represents an excellent use of the You

attitude. It builds reader confidence in the company's willingness and ability to serve its clients well. Writing with the You attitude in this way is well worth the effort, and will come with a little practice.

2. *The Positive Approach*

Have you noticed that open-minded people and organizations employ the Positive Approach, as well as the You Attitude? They think, talk, and act as though things were possible. They create interesting directions out of chaos, inspired solutions out of difficulty. They radiate lightness, energy, and humour – as they fulfill their potential.

Closed-minded people and organizations adopt a negative approach. They talk as though things were difficult – or impossible. They doubt, dwell on difficulties, and use rules to guide every action. They refuse to consider the possibility of solving problems, and they radiate arrogance, sarcasm and fear alternately.

Which attitude does your writing style convey to your readers? Which attitude puts your reader into the most receptive mood?

Since you are studying this material in the attempt to improve your ability as a communicator, you are engaged in a positive effort. Therefore, it makes sense that you continue to demonstrate this positive effort in your correspondence by making your tone as positive as possible.

However, the positive attitude is often unnatural. Just as babies have to learn to deal with gravity to stand upright, so we have to deal with negativity to speak positively. Positive attitudes arise from education, not from chance. You can convince yourself of this by recalling typical remarks around the office. What is the ratio of positive to negative comments? In most areas of life, negative thinking dominates. Think of the typical content of TV news programs and daily newspapers.

On the other hand, educated people prize the positive attitude, like gold, for its rarity, beauty, and durability. One popular regional manager, when asked for the theory which accounted for his outstanding success with people, offered this simple phrase: "*A pat on the back is eighteen inches higher than a kick in the pants.*" This vivid advice to act positively illustrates the connection between success and positive thinking.

In order to cultivate this kind of positive attitude, learn to replace negative or even neutral words with positive ones. For example, instead of saying, "Please do not *hesitate* to call me," you could say, "Please feel *free* to call me," or, "Please call me." Similarly, instead of saying, "We *regret* that we cannot continue to provide credit until you send us your *overdue* payment", you could say, "We will be *glad* to provide credit as soon as we *receive* the payment due." Of course, you must use your discretion to avoid effusiveness.

Why Prefer Positive Words?

Psychologists have found that people remember negative thoughts more vividly than positive ones, perhaps because negative thoughts are stored in an ancient, unsophisticated part of the brain (the limbic system). Studies of memory show that major errors or failures (negative thoughts) are five times more easily recalled over a period of three years than pleasant memories or successes (positive thoughts). This may explain why it is five times harder to build a good reputation than to lose it!

Negative Words to Avoid

Try to eliminate the following negative words from your business vocabulary:

argue, argument	fail (failures)
bad	fault
bill (verb)	ate
claim (verb)	reject
complain	sorry
debt	strictly
defect	submit
delay	terrible
difficult (difficulties)	wasted
doubt	wrong
embarrassed	hesitate
error	worthless
careless	problem

Note: The words "no" and "not" are not classified as negative words. You can use them together with positive words to convey unwelcome messages positively. For example: "We are not able to grant your request at this time."

EXERCISE 2

Identifying Negative Words

Underline all the negative words in the following memo. Then rewrite the memo with positive words.

> Some couriers have carelessly sent all their undelivered parcels on to the Halifax depot for storage. This has created several problems.
>
> Therefore, supervisors should eradicate any worthless parcels before forwarding them. The Halifax depot suffers from the general space problems too. We are not a garbage dump.
>
> Do not hesitate to submit further difficulties to this office for inclusion in our list of problem areas within the organization.

Check your answers with the Answer Key.

Choosing Positive Words >

Positive words include "glad," "pleased," "happy," "improvements," "service," "contribution." Use positive words to express unwelcome ideas:

> Our *service* to you *did* not meet the *high standards* we expect of our staff.

Here the use of "not" allows us to use the positive words "meet" and "high standards." Expressed negatively, we might have written:

> Our service *failed* to meet *minimal* standards for treatment of customers.

Readers react more favourably to the positive wording.

Determining Your Negative–Positive Ratio >

Good writers often have a ratio of 0 negative words to 12 positive words. The higher the number of negative words in your letter now, the more challenging this recommendation may seem. However, persevere and your readers will appreciate the difference. Just don't overdo it!

Tone Evaluation Procedure

1 Refer to a letter you have written and multiply the negative words by two.

2 Multiply the number of positive words in the same letter by one.

These totals provide your Negative/Positive word ratio.

What should your ratio be? Use the following Guide to interpret the tone of your writing.

Tone Interpretation Guide

	Negative Words	*Positive Words*
Excellent	0	10+
Good	2	6
Unsatisfactory	6	5
Poor	8+	5

3. *The Human Touch*

Many business letters sound indifferent, superior, or wooden. The Human Touch refers to the quality of writing that makes your letters sound as though one living, breathing, caring individual is writing to another. Just as you have a distinct tone of voice on the telephone or in person, so you have your own tone in writing. If you get stuck on tone when you try to phrase a letter, stop and rest for a bit. Call up to your mind's eye the image of your best friend, and pretend you're talking to him or her directly, person to person. Remember the words you would use in that happy situation, and write them down. You can't be pompous or wooden when talking to good friends. They won't stand for it! This technique will ensure that your letters display the Human Touch.

You have your own Human Touch. We can't anticipate what it will feel like. However, here are two very different examples of the Human Touch to show you how very differently two people can write when they let their writing style express their personalities.

A Sophisticated Example of the Human Touch >

This first example comes from a highly respected business writer of the more conservative type who is writing to a conservative banking audience. Here he warns against some poor habits of writing. His style is recognizable, distinct, and expresses his gracefully old-fashioned personality:

> The writer will, in his re-reading, harden his heart to his felicitous phrases and his smoothly-flowing paragraphs. He will be alert to censure spiritless sentences, condemn what is rugged and misshapen, draw a line through what is incorrect factually, lop off redundant words and phrases while preserving the virtues of repetition, remove distracting ornament, rearrange what is expressed ambiguously, and throw light upon the parts that are difficult to understand. One needs the sort of hard-hearted determination voiced by Ovid when he said, "When I re-read I blush, for even I perceive enough that ought to be erased, though it was I who wrote the stuff."
>
> – *The Royal Bank Monthly Letter*

Notice that the author writes lengthy sentences, employs a fairly sophisticated level of diction ("felicitous"), and quotes the classical Roman writer Ovid. Therefore, he thinks of his audience as educated and sophisticated. Nevertheless, he speaks sensibly, uses strong action verbs, and makes good points. This passage expresses one extreme of acceptable business writing, where your audience appreciates intricacy of phrasing and reference.

A Colloquial Example of the Human Touch >

Here is a much more colloquial passage from a second writer. Joe Girard is a self-made salesman, with little formal education. His sentences are crisp, purposefully ungrammatical at times ("I made me [myself] a salesman"), but unabashedly express his own enthusiasm and knowledge of selling:

> Somebody once told me that I was a born salesman. Let me tell you that's not true. Some salesmen, maybe even most salesmen, may be born to it. But I was not born a salesman. I made me a salesman, all by myself. And if I could do it, starting from where I did, anybody can. Stay with this story and you'll soon see what I mean.
>
> – Joe Girard, *How to Sell Anything to Anybody.*

Mr. Girard thinks of his audience as relatively uneducated, but full of energy, intention, and purpose. He writes to put them at their ease, and to encourage them, by making them see that they do not require perfect grammar to become successful salespeople.

We don't recommend that you adopt a style as formal as the first, or as informal as the second. However, whatever their drawbacks, both writers have found a gracious or a lively tone that expresses their individuality.

In seeking to develop your own style, try to write with a tone similar to that which you use on the telephone, though more carefully worded and organized. This care is necessary because written messages may undergo a close and lasting scrutiny.

Should You Use Your Reader's Name >

Yes, attempt to use your reader's name in the body of your letter at least once – even when composing form letters. Dale Carnegie often said that the sound of a person's name has a sweet ring to it in his or her own ears. Although sales letters such as those from *Reader's Digest* repeat the reader's name too many times, perhaps, most people like to see their own name in print. Just be sure to spell it correctly! In particular, check to see that if you have used their name in the inside address of your letter, you have also used it in the salutation.

Writing for the Boss >

One of the most difficult tasks you may ever face is to be asked to write a letter for someone else, such as your manager. This is a special talent, like that of a ventriloquist. How do you imitate their Human Touch? Some people can do it easily; others cannot. If you get discouraged trying to write in this way, remember that the letters you write for another person cannot be as comfortably written as those you write for yourself, so simply do your best, and improve by examining and imitating the tone of your manager's corrections.

One new alternative that has received growing acceptance is to write the letter in your own voice, and then type your manager's name underneath the Complimentary Close in the normal way. However, instead of your manager signing the letter, *you* do, underneath the word "by". This approach retains the manager's responsibility for content, while leaving the writer responsible for style. Use of this system demonstrates the manager's confidence in you as a writer.

Example of a Letter Written on Behalf of a Manager

> Ms. S. Buckingham
> 1615 Travis Drive
> Portland, Maine
> 01345
>
> Dear Sue,
>
> Here is the letter you requested from our Director of Financial Services regarding your contract extension.
>
> To confirm our agreement, we have ordered two seminars a week on business writing for twelve weeks, on the dates we selected last Tuesday.
>
> I hope this clarifies our understanding. If you require any additional information over the next three weeks, please contact Sandra Ludwig at 787-1453. She will be handling these matters while I'm away on leave.
>
> Best wishes for a successful completion of our training course.
>
> Yours truly,
>
> Bill Gibson
> Manager, Employee Planning
>
> By: W.O. Simpson
> Staff Development Officer
> Management Development

Here the manager has accepted responsibility for the content of the letter, but the author, W.O. Simpson, has signed it to accept responsibility for the style.

EXERCISE 3

The Human Touch

Write a letter instructing a subordinate how to handle a procedure which you know well, for example, how to run the fax machine. Read the letter aloud, revising to bring the written words closer to your style of conversation over the telephone. In particular, remove all trace of superiority and authoritarianism. Ensure that you use the other person's name at least once.

Check your letter against the version given in the Answer Key. For more practice using the Human Touch, try the exercises on Sincerity in Unit Ten - How to Write With Style.

4.

Summary of Tone

You have studied how to generate good will through the use of the You Attitude, the Positive Approach, and the Human Touch. These qualities will establish a communication context favourable to your message. Congratulations on your hard work! To this point, you know how to write clearly, correctly, and with good will. Here's another challenge: learn how to use an Effective Structure – the topic of Unit Six.

Answer Key

EXERCISE 1
The You Attitude

Underline the words in the following letter which refer to the writer. Then rewrite the letter with the "you" attitude.

> Dear Mr. Winfield:
>
> We are in receipt of your letter requesting permission to franchise our product in Alberta. We always appreciate receiving a letter from agents who wish to handle our soap. We have received more submissions than we can easily handle.
>
> In any case, I am afraid that it is against our policy to sell distributor rights to more than one franchisee in cities of less than 7,000, and as Mr. Hicraft is already open for business in Crow Creek, I regret we cannot authorize another agency.
>
> If we decide to change our marketing policy we will contact you. We will keep your name on file for six months.
>
> Sincerely,
>
> Derek Jones

This letter does not display the "You" attitude. All the underlined words refer to Mr. Jones and his company.

Using the "you" attitude point of view, you might rewrite the letter as follows:

> Dear Mr. Winfield:
>
> Thank you very much for your interest in becoming a franchisee for Super Soap Systems. Your application was most welcome.
>
> To protect Super Soap franchisees, we award only one franchise in cities with a population of less than 7,000. As

> you may know, Mr. Winfield, Mr. Hicraft currently has the rights to the Crow Creek franchise.
>
> However, if you would care to apply for the franchise in Elbow Grease, your application would receive immediate favourable attention. Please let me know if you find this alternative acceptable.
>
> Sincerely,
>
> Derek Jones

To gain more practice changing "we" attitude letters into "you" attitude letters, go on to the Review Exercises.

EXERCISE 2
Identifying Negative Words

The underlined words create a negative tone in the following memo. The only positive word appears in bold print.

> Some couriers have carelessly sent all their undelivered parcels on to the Halifax depot for storage. This has created several problems.
>
> Therefore, supervisors should eradicate any worthless parcels before **forwarding** them. The Halifax depot suffers from the general space problems too. We are not a garbage dump.
>
> Do not hesitate to submit further difficulties to this office for inclusion in our list of problem areas within the organization.

The number of negative words in the above letter gives it an extremely poor tone. Note how the following revision uses positive words to convey the same negative news but in a non-threatening way:

> Some couriers have sent all the undelivered parcels to the Halifax depot for storage. The Halifax depot has not **approved** this action.
>
> Therefore, supervisors should not **forward** undeliverable parcels. The Halifax depot does not have **sufficient** space to store parcels from the **entire** Atlantic region.
>
> **Please call** us or **send** us your **suggestions** about any **improvements** you would like to see in our organization.

For more practice, try the Review Exercises.

EXERCISE 3
The Human Touch

Here's an example of a letter explaining a procedure to a colleague:

> Dear Sally:
>
> In our phone conversation of April 10, you asked me to explain how to operate our new fax machine. You shouldn't have any problems if you just follow these steps:
>
> 1. Place the document printed side down on the machine.
> 2. Key in the telephone number.
> 3. Press "go".
> 4. File the transmission slip in the grey file box above the photocopier.
>
> Call me if you have any questions. Thanks again, Sally, for the reports you sent over last Thursday. I'll phone you Wednesday to make plans for our meeting on Friday.

Your letter will, of course, express your own personality. However, if you just make sure you visualize your reader as a living, breathing person with his or her own set of expectations and needs, you will go a long way towards avoiding stuffiness.

Review Exercises

Test your understanding of Unit Five with the following exercises. Refer to the *Better Business Writing Answer Key* or your instructor for suggested responses.

EXERCISE 1

The You Attitude

Underline the words in the following sentences that refer to the writer and then rewrite the sentences from the "you" point of view.

1. We are afraid that we have to refuse to provide your venture with a $10,000 loan because our policy does not allow us to give loans to companies who have operated for less than 1 year.
2. If we decide to alter our meeting schedule, we will contact all our clients, such as yourself, so they can make the necessary arrangements.
3. Our product should be enjoyed by the type of customers we presume you service.

4. We appreciate receiving your letter telling us about what happened with one of our company's sales representatives.
5. We believe that the number of credit obligations you have at present will seriously hamper our chances of receiving prompt payment of our loan.

EXERCISE 2

Negative and Positive Words

Underline the negative words in the following sentences and then use positive words to rewrite the sentences, keeping the same message.

1. We regret to inform you that your application for a loan has been rejected.
2. I fail to understand how you can do much of anything to prevent the reports you carelessly mixed up from being a total mess.
3. Your employment here will be immediately terminated if you refuse to curtail your chronic absences.
4. We are sorry if our late submission of your tax return caused you terrible inconvenience and problems.
5. Your complaint about the defective product you purchased from our company will be dealt with without delay.

UNIT SIX

How To Structure Your Letters Effectively

Now that you have a good understanding of how to take your reader's needs and feelings into account, you need to learn how to how to write letters that have an effective structure. Here's what you'll learn in Unit Six:

1. Psychological Layout of Letters: Yes and No Letters
2. Physical Layout of Letters
3. Gender Neutral Language.

After working through Unit Six, you will review the first six units of *Better Business Writing* in Unit Seven and then go on to study how to write different types of letters such as sales letters and application letters.

O *Introduction*

To become a really effective letter writer, you will need to apply the You Attitude, the Positive Approach, and the Human Touch; in addition, you should *structure* your letters for maximum clarity and efficiency. To do this, you need to take into consideration the following two components:

1 Psychological layout,
2 Physical layout.

You should also choose gender neutral words and phrases that reflect a sensitivity to all your readers. To start off, we'll look at psychological layout.

1. *Psychological Layout: Yes and No Letters*

The structure of a letter will vary depending on the psychological thrust of the communication – whether you're asking the reader to accept good or bad news. Psychologists have found that you should sequence messages differently depending on whether they contain information that will strike the reader as welcome ("good" news) or unwelcome ("bad" news). For this learning session, we will term "good" news letters "YES" letters, and "bad" news letters "NO" letters.

The YES Letter >

The YES letter either gives good news *or* provides information that moves business matters forward.

Macro Hint:

Consider all informational memos and letters as YES letters for the purpose of structuring.

The most effective order for the YES letter is as follows:

1. Say YES.
2. Supply necessary details.
3. Close in a friendly way.

Let's take a look at the reasoning behind this structure, keeping in mind the realization that it is normal human behaviour to say "yes" last – not first. Many letter writers feel that if they say "yes" first the reader will not finish reading the letter they have laboured over. However, it is not in your best interest to make your reader anxious before receiving welcome news. You will serve your reader's interests best by providing a positive response as soon as possible – usually in the first paragraph. As with the "You" attitude, you determine your reader's interests when you try to see things from your reader's point of view.

Example of the YES Letter >

February 28, 19–

Mr. G.L. Hammersham
4342 Maryland Way
New York, New York
04345

Dear Mr. Hammersham,

Yes

Thank you for your letter of February 14, requesting "a replacement steering wheel for a 1990 Buick Electra." Our factory shipped your wheel to you today.

Details

Your letter did not specify whether you wanted the tan or the ivory edging. I have shipped the tan selection, which was the colour of the original part. If you require ivory, please return the tan edging for replacement.

Positive Close

You should receive your part within five working days. Please let me know if I can be of further help. Our toll-free line is 1-800-555-6789, and you can order by phone seven days a week.

Sincerely,

Jim Foster
Shipping Facilitator

EXERCISE 1

The Yes Letter

Follow the YES letter structure to write a letter that offers a refund. Identify the three stages of your letter, and write the name of each stage (YES, details, close) in the margin.

For more YES letter exercises, refer to the Review Exercises.

The NO Letter >

You could define the NO letter as any letter which either imparts unwelcome news, or which slows business activity. Complaint letters, rejection letters, and "Sorry, we're out of it" letters fall into this category.

Because people do not like to write these letters, those who write them skillfully are extremely valuable to an organization. To succeed, remember that you can often *assist* people by saying "No." For example, when you receive a request for credit from an applicant you know could not handle it properly, you would be doing the applicant a favour by saying No. Similarly, you provide assistance when you refuse a job application from someone not suited to the work.

Remember that in this kind of NO letter the three elements of good tone – the You Attitude, the Positive Approach, and the Human Touch – are even more useful than in the YES letter. This is worth repeating: Keep No letters positive in tone, speak with the You Attitude, and maintain your Human Touch. If you can do all this, even your NO letter will leave a good impression.

The NO Structure

The most effective sequence for the NO letter is as follows:

1. Say Thank You for the request.
2. State the context governing the decision so the reader is prepared for the conclusion.
3. Say NO graciously (or clearly infer it).
4. Provide a positive alternative where possible.
5. Close in a friendly, businesslike way.

As you can see, this sequence avoids saying NO first. Inexperienced writers say NO first – and then provide the explanation or context, when the reader may feel too emotionally downcast to listen to reasonable explanations. Attempt to have readers reach the conclusion before you state it, so that by the time you say No, they are thinking, "Well, I already knew that." This delay gives readers time to protect their egos and is particularly important in cases where readers have invested a great deal in a positive response from your organization.

How to Say NO

To establish your method of saying NO in letters, carefully weigh these considerations:

1. Always make it clear that you are rejecting an idea or a proposal or a single element of a person's experience, and *not* the applicant personally. For example, instead of saying, "There were several applicants who were more suitable than you," say, "There were several applicants whose *credentials* in marketing exceeded yours." Here you are talking about only one aspect of a person: credentials in marketing. In short, always refer to *isolated qualities* rather than *people* in NO letters.

2. Always speak as though the position applied for – rather than you as a person – requires certain characteristics that the unsuccessful applicant lacks. Say, "This *position* requires an expert in financial planning," rather than "*We* require an expert in financial planning" or "*I* require an expert in financial planning." In this way, you make it clear that you have not rejected the person due to any personal disapproval.

3. Give only the single main reason for rejection, and – where possible – have it apply to the area in which the person could most usefully improve. For example, in a case where an otherwise qualified and suitable applicant has had a number of poor references, say, "*One* of the main things this position requires is an excellent job history," rather than, "Job history, academic credentials, and length of service are the *three* main things we look for in applicants." Listing only one deficiency is called the "rifle" approach, as opposed to the "shotgun" approach, where you list a multitude of deficiencies.

Where negative news is involved, the reader will scan your list outlining his or her shortcomings. If they find that one item on this list is not completely correct, they will discount your entire letter as prejudiced. This can lead to costly appeals of your decisions when awarding jobs or contracts, for example. On the other hand, if you mention only one key element your letter will gain acceptance more quickly – and may result in personal improvement that will benefit everyone.

4 Keep the wording positive. Say, "Mr. Elton, your application was one of many we received from *extremely qualified* people," rather than "Mr. Elton, your application was one of hundreds we received." Say, "The *successful* applicant's credentials were *extremely impressive*," rather than, "Your credentials were *comparatively poor*." Positive wording counts greatly in this kind of letter.

***Example of the NO Letter* >**

Ms. Esmerelda Somerset
1704 Mainstream Avenue
Chicago, Illinois
64980

Dear Ms. Somerset:

Buffer

Thank you for your application for a position as an agency representative within our firm.

Context Details

As you may know, this position requires a great deal of experience in dealing with people who can be extremely aggressive. Consequently, applications from those who have handled similar positions in the past have a distinct advantage.

No

In the case of this opening, we have selected a candidate with several years of experience in a similar position.

Positive Alternative

However, your application impressed the selection panel strongly. They have asked me to suggest that you submit another application after a further year's experience.

Positive Close

Ms. Somerset, thank you for your excellent application. I wish you good luck with your career development, and hope to hear from you in one year.

Sincerely,

T.L. Champion
Vice President, Marketing

EXERCISE 2

The No Letter

Hint

Write a NO letter that refuses to extend credit to a customer. Use the correct structure, keep the proper tone, and include all the elements mentioned above. Identify each of the 5 stages in the letter by using brackets in the margin. Refer to the Answer Key for a sample version.

Revise to ensure that the wording is neither negative *nor neutral*, but as sincere and positive – though never saccharine – as you can make it.

2. *Physical Layout*

Once you understand the psychological effect of tone and structure, you need to format your letters correctly on the page and to use salutations and complimentary closes correctly. As with spelling, educated readers often judge writers on the basis of their knowledge of forms and layout.

Letter Format

You can choose from a number of formats for business letters. Each format is designed to present the message clearly and attractively. Here are two major ones: the *full block style* with no paragraph indentations and the *modified block style* with paragraph indentations.

A traditional argument in favour of eliminating indentions (full block) is that it saves typing time, and therefore costs less. However, the effect on the reader is not as pleasing as the modified block: the eye likes the breaks from full lines of print provided by paragraph indentions. Choose the format appropriate for your purpose and audience.

The following letter uses the Full Block format to convey a NO message. Note that the tone of this letter is extremely poor.

Full Block Layout

Date	April 5, 19–
Three or more blank lines	
Inside address	Clean Construction Inc. 1819 Turnstile Place North Carolina, 24544
Att'n line	Att'n: T. Whitehead
Subject line	Account Number: 333-45622-35889 Previous Balance: $1,344.65 Credits: .00 Balance Due: $1,344.65
Salutation	Dear Cardmember:
Body	We are writing to notify you that your account is overdue. You owe us $1,344.65. Our records show that although you have been a Cardmember for less than one year, your payments have frequently been received late. This is unacceptable to us. The United Payment Card is a charge card, not a credit card. Our terms call for payment in full upon receipt of each monthly statement. This requirement was clearly indicated to you in the Cardmember Agreement which you received with the Card. The United Payment Card is not for everyone. Charges are approved based on your past spending and payment record. We value you as a Cardmember but, if your late payments continue, we will consider suspending your charge privileges. Please mail your cheque today for the full balance due. If it is in the mail, thank you.
Complimentary Close	Sincerely,
Corporate Name	UNITED PAYMENT CARDS LIMITED
Signature	
Typed name Business title of writer	M. Reid Card Account Services
Ref. initials	MR:aak

The second example uses the Modified Block format for a YES letter. Note the excellent tone.

Semi-block Layout

Date	August 25, 19–
Three or more blank lines	
Inside address	Rosalind McCloud 1818 Greenhill Avenue South Hills, Ontario N7B 8X5
Salutation	Dear Rosalind:
Body	We received your letter letting us know you want to stop being in the Financial Family, and have adjusted our records accordingly. Enclosed are tax receipts for your contributions in the fiscal year just ended. As the person on staff responsible for our communications, I was particularly interested in your comments about the "depersonalization" you have noticed. My commitment is that we always speak person to person, and I would appreciate any specific comments you could make that would point to where we are not doing so. Rosalind, your stand for the end of hunger is clear in your letter and in your support of Families for Children. Your contributions have also made the work of The Hunger Project possible, and I respect the commitment you have made over the years.
Complimentary Close	Yours truly,
Signature	
Typed name Business title of writer	John Boyle Director of Communications

Salutations and Complimentary Closes

Within the format you choose, whether Full Block, Modified Block, or an in-house style, you have a number of Salutations and Complimentary Closes available. They can be grouped into four levels of descending formality, as follows:

Level	Salutation	Complimentary Close
Very Formal	Sir: Madam:	Very respectfully yours, Yours respectfully, Respectfully,
Formal	Dear Ms. Butterfield: Dear Sir/Madam: [Note: "Madam" is outdated, but no alternative has yet arisen]	Very truly yours, Yours truly, Yours respectfully,
Normal	Dear Peter Johnson, Dear Ms. Spokander, Dear Mr. Hudson, Dear L.Y. Harrison, [Use when the person signs with an initial]	Sincerely yours, Yours sincerely, Sincerely, Yours truly,
Personal or Friendly Business	Dear Mary, Dear Paul, Dear Tom, Dear Client, Dear Customer, Dear Friend, Dear Reader,	Most sincerely, Yours cordially, Cordially, Regards, Best regards, Yours,

3. *Gender Neutral Language*

Good writers take care not to irritate their readers. This means using gender neutral language. Until this usage becomes more common, it may seem a bit awkward, much as the use of "Ms." seemed odd to some writers when it replaced "Mrs." and "Miss" in the 70's. However, your time will be well invested learning this new style – artificial though it may seem at first.

1st Case

Change the third person singular pronoun "he" to the third person plural pronoun "they". Instead of "Ask the client to send in *his* order," say "Ask clients to send in *their* orders."

Caution: Avoid a lack of agreement such as this: "Every student must send in *their* application." Instead, write

"*Students* must send in their applications." Refer to Unit Three – How to Connect Thoughts – to review the correct use of pronouns.

2nd Case

Change the third person singular to the second person singular "you". Instead of "The supervisor is responsible for posting *his* time schedule monthly," say "*You* are responsible for posting *your* time schedule monthly."

3rd Case

Change "his" to "his or her". Instead of "Each writer has *his* own style," say "Each writer has *his* or *her* own style."

4th Case

When writing job descriptions, replace "he" and "his" with a series of phrases which do not require subjects. Traditionally a job description might read like this: "The administrator will be responsible for setting *his* department's policy, coordinating public statements, administering *his* budget effectively, and codifying *his* hiring procedures." Simply rewrite this sentence in a series of phrases:

The administrator will be responsible for the following:

1. Setting department policy
2. Coordinating public statements
3 Administering the budget effectively
4. Codifying hiring procedures.

5th Case

Change job titles where appropriate. "Salesman" becomes "Sales Representative," "Mailman" = "Letter Carrier", "Stewardess" = "Flight Attendant," "Chairman" = "Chair."

As with every major change in language, these new usages may seem awkward for awhile; however, the principle of writing in a gender neutral way has been gaining broad public acceptance more quickly than many people once believed possible. By adopting this new style graciously, you will demonstrate your respect for all your readers.

4. *Review: Units Five and Six*

You have seen how certain techniques of tone and structure can help you become a better letter writer. As with any skill, however, the spirit with which you undertake your task counts infinitely more than the precise adherence to rules. Always fine-tune the general recommendations about tone, in order to match your personality and suit your reader's needs.

All things excellent
are as difficult as
they are rare.
– *Spinoza*

We are confident that your use of the You Attitude, the Positive Approach, and the Human Touch will improve the quality of your communication with all your readers. When you add the proper psychological and physical layout, your messages will be extremely effective. Now it's up to you to put this knowledge to work!

✓

Answer Key

EXERCISE 1
The Yes Letter

Follow the YES letter structure to write a letter that offers a refund. Identify the three stages of your letter, and write the name of each stage (YES, details, close) in the margin.

Dear Mr. Baudet:

YES

Thank you for informing us of your experience at the Tropicana Hotel in Mazatlan. You should receive your refund of $118.98 for one night's accommodation by August 31.

Details

Please contact us immediately if your refund does not arrive on time. We would like to settle this matter to your satisfaction as quickly as possible.

Complimentary Close

Thank you again for informing us that you did not enjoy a pleasant night's stay at the Tropicana. Your comments will help improve our service to everyone who travels with Sun Tours, Inc.

Sincerely,

Don Warren
President

EXERCISE 2
The No Letter

Write a NO letter that refuses to extend credit to a customer. Identify each of the 5 stages in the letter by using brackets in the margin.

Dear Ms. Green:

Say Thank You

Thank you for your application of June 15 requesting a loan of $3000 to take a vacation to Hawaii.

Provide the Context Governing Decision

You may have already read our Loan Brochure and noticed that we generally consider loan applications from customers who have been dealing with the bank for more than 12 months. This policy allows us to offer very competitive rates.

Say NO graciously

Ms. Green, I understand you have been a customer of

Pacific Savings and Loan for eight months. For this reason, I cannot yet approve your loan application.

Provide Alternative

However, I suggest that you re-apply in four months, at which time I would be pleased to review your request.

Close positively

Thank you for thinking of Pacific Savings and Loan. We look forward to serving you in the future.

Sincerely,

Ellen Banks
Loans Officer

Notice how this letter avoids negative words such as "regret" or "refuse". For more practice with the "no" format, try the Review Exercises.

Review Exercises

Test your understanding of Unit Six with the following exercises. Refer to the *Better Business Writing Answer Key* or your instructor for suggested responses.

EXERCISE 1

Rewriting the Yes Letter

Use the "Yes" letter format, positive words, and the "you" attitude to rewrite the following letter.

Mr. A. Harding
66 No. 10 Road
West River, AB
H2T 8YR

Dear Mr. Harding:

The West River School prides itself on hiring only the most qualified and dedicated teachers available. To this end, we use a rigorous screening system that weeds out those applicants who do not conform to our uncompromising standards.

You applied to teach high school level English. Rarely do openings in your area of expertise occur. However, this term we have a temporary position open for an English teacher with qualifications such as yours.

Please reply, in writing, before April 25 indicating if you plan to take advantage of this opportunity. The West River School's policy is that all teaching assignments for the following September must be confirmed no later than June 1.

Sincerely,

George Cador
District Superintendent

EXERCISE 2

"NO" Letter Structure

Place the paragraphs in the following letter into the correct "no" letter format.

Dear Ms. Smith:

Paragraph 1:

You state that you need a refund because you have started a new job and cannot go on your holiday as planned. While we sympathize with your situation, we have to uphold our company's policy as described above.

Paragraph 2:

Thank you for your letter of August 15, outlining why you feel Dream Vacations should refund the deposit you made on a trip to Hawaii. Your description of why you need a refund certainly requires close consideration.

Paragraph 3:

You may wish to consider applying the deposit to another trip at a more convenient time. We are prepared to offer you that option, although normally Dream Vacations does not transfer a deposit from one trip time to another.

Paragraph 4:

Please give me a call at 867-2215 to discuss your plans for another vacation time. I hope you find your new job satisfying and decide to resume your travel plans when convenient.

Paragraph 5:

Our company's policy states that deposit refunds are made only in medical emergencies supported by a letter from a physician. Very occasionally, we grant refunds in cases of family death. This policy allows us to offer the lowest excursion fares possible.

Prove It To Yourself

Congratulations! If you've attempted all the exercises so far, you've accomplished a great deal already. Now you can test your understanding of what you have learned in Units One to Six with the following Review Exercises. Your ability to complete these exercises correctly will show you how much you've learned and provide an important review. To check your answers, refer to the *Better Business Writing Answer Key* or your instructor.

EXERCISE 1

Subject and Object Nouns

Underline the true subject nouns (the "doers" of the action) and double underline the true object nouns (the "receivers" of the action) in the following sentences.

1. John owns his own business.
2. The university occupies a park-like campus near the city.
3. Housing prices rose to a median cost of $300,000 last year.
4. My report was read by the Board of Directors.
5. The company publishes three brochures detailing how to set up and run a home based business.
6. After working on the proposal for several months, Joan discovered a serious research problem.
7. A lack of communication resulted in a problem that would not disappear.
8. Cultivate the ability to adapt to unexpected demands on your time.
9. The box of business cards balanced precariously on the edge of the desk.
10. The fax machine was repaired by the technician.

EXERCISE 2

Changing Linking Verbs to Action Verbs

Underline the Linking Verbs. Rewrite the sentences, replacing the Linking Verbs with Action Verbs. Notice that you may need to change the order of the nouns in some sentences to use an Action Verb.

1. The meeting is too long.
2. All employees are responsible for complying with the company's policy regarding appropriate footwear.
3. Documentation of unusual incidents is the responsibility of the Administrative Assistant.
4. The new supervisor is unable to make up work schedules for the employees she manages.
5. Your sales record is up to our company's expectations.
6. Sally is certain that the new client appreciates her efforts.
7. This report will be useful to the company.
8. He is available for consultation from 9 a.m. to 5 p.m. daily.
9. The Sales Department will not be attending the seminar.
10. We are hopeful of completing our evaluation by next Wednesday.

EXERCISE 3

Rewriting in the Active Voice

Using the 3-step procedure outlined in the section on the Active Voice, underline the grammatical subject in each of these sentences; then rewrite each sentence, if necessary, in the Active Voice pattern.

1. The staff bulletin board may be used only by full-time employees.
2. All requests for printing services must be initialed by the Administrative Secretary.
3. Pay cheques are issued by the Business Office on the last Friday of each month.
4. Jane was reimbursed by the company for her business trip to Toronto.

5. Allison Miles submitted a detailed summary of the June meeting to the Executive Committee.
6. Requests for references regarding company employees are handled by the Personnel Department.
7. The plan adopted by the Union representatives will not be accepted by Management.
8. The minimum acceptable notice required by resigning employees is outlined in the Company's Policy and Procedure Manual.
9. Special leave may be granted to regular full-time and part-time employees by the Administrator.
10. The letter is proofread by the secretary.

EXERCISE 4

Changing the Passive to the Active Voice

Circle the grammatical subject-nouns in the following sentences, where present. Underline the objects. Double-underline the verbs. Provide a subject-noun if needed, and use action verbs to rewrite all the sentences in subject–verb–object order.

1. Managers are expected to schedule medical and dental appointments outside of working hours.
2. Payment for overtime is made by the company to employees who work more than forty hours in any given week.
3. The annual staff luncheon will be attended by all employees.
4. Some method must be found to cope with the excess paperwork.
5. Telephone requests for work performance references are referred to the Personnel Supervisor.
6. Your application for employment has been carefully considered.
7. The laser printer must not be used to print work not directly related to company business.
8. Peter rejected the new contract and left the company.

9. An excellent proposal has been submitted.
10. Vacation times are chosen according to the employee's length of service with the company.

EXERCISE 5

Writing the Power Sentence

Turn the following passive voice sentences into Power Sentences. Note that you may have to supply a subject for those sentences written in the Divine Passive. Follow the format provided for the first sentence.

1. The proposal was discussed by the committee members.

   Notice that the subject, verb, and object are all umbrella words. Provide specific replacements to successfully rewrite the sentence.

S	V	O

   1 ____

   2 ____
   action verb

   3 ____
   specific subject *specific verb* *specific object*

2. The executive was hired by the company.
3. This report was not written with sufficient details.
4. Your sales presentation for the product was rejected by the client.
5. All employees are required to submit their vacation requests.
6. This program was made to answer all your questions about tax returns.
7. Your request for a loan has been denied by the bank.
8. A big profit was made in the third quarter by the company.
9. A great many mistakes are made by Mr. Saunders in his reports.
10. The office is cleaned regularly.

EXERCISE 6

Paragraphs

Write a paragraph describing why your company should buy Brand A rather than Brand B of a certain product. You choose a product and supply the necessary details to compare the two brands. Product ideas include: photocopiers, computers, fax machines, coffee makers, felt tip pens, etc.

After you have written your paragraph, underline each transitional marker you use and define its category (i.e. comparison, contrast, time, etc.).

EXERCISE 7

Pronoun Agreement

Underline the incorrectly used pronouns in the following sentences and then replace all linking verbs with action verbs and rewrite the sentences so that each pronoun agrees with its antecedent in person, number, and gender. If possible, you may wish to rephrase some of the sentences to avoid using pronouns or to avoid sexist connotations (see gender neutral language in Unit Six). Note also that in some cases you may have to change the form of the verb to agree with the correct pronoun.

1. Either the legal assistant or the secretary is certain to make himself available to take on the extra work.
2. Neither Mr. Smith nor the accountants could agree about his plans for setting up an audit.
3. If there are extenuating circumstances for your absences which I am unaware of, I would be glad to meet with you to discuss it.
4. The Records Department must maintain a record of all personnel and update them as required.
5. After you check each sales invoice, file them in the Accounts Payable folder.
6. Jack needs to finish the contract for ACM Industries by Wednesday so they can be promoted to vice-president.
7. Every book and computer disk in the office was assigned their proper place.
8. The speaker asked each woman at the conference to give their opinion of Joan Daniel's book.

9. Both of the girls needed to revise her letters.

10. Neither the accountants nor the vice-president could complete their work on time.

EXERCISE 8

Pronoun Reference

Underline the pronouns in the following sentences and then replace all linking verbs with action verbs and rewrite the sentences to remove any ambiguous pronoun references.

1. The currently existing Client Referral Centre, with a usage rate of 400 clients per year, may be able to increase their volume substantially if more supervisors and/or consultants were available to make follow-up calls.

2. Colin prevented the group from discussing the issues because he refused to agree with their opinions.

3. Your actions have restricted the Sales Department with the result that a 15% decrease in sales has occurred since this began.

4. Mr. Albertson should be given free reign to train the new employee as long as he does not compromise company policy.

5. Sally Chu believes she needs a company car to experience the increase in sales her Department must achieve by year-end.

6. Although the purchase of computers will increase our budget this year, they save time and labour in the long run.

7. At present, we have advertisements prepared to run in both daily newspapers. This will cost $200 for two days.

8. Space alterations resulting from the renovation of our offices should commence as soon as possible for they require that all employees reorganize their workstations.

9. The vice-president is pleased with your recent progress as Supervisor and is considering giving you a raise if it continues.

10. If you have a solution to our current financial difficulty that you feel will lower our debt to the bank, please bring it to my attention.

EXERCISE 9

Subject-verb Agreement

Underline the verbs in the following sentences and then replace all linking verbs with action verbs and rewrite the sentences so that the subjects and verbs agree.

1. Neither the current telephone system nor the photocopier adequately satisfy our needs.
2. While making our employees happy is a priority, satisfying the demands of our customers are our top priority.
3. The expense of purchasing three new computer terminals for the use of our accountants have been justified by the recent reduction in outstanding accounts receivables.
4. Neither the employees nor the company want to relocate to another city.
5. The Customer Action Group, as well as its affiliated societies, were pleased with the new Better Business Handbook.
6. Also covered by the policies was a note about safety and a checklist regarding earthquakes.
7. The merger of the two giant corporations have resulted in increased salaries for all employees involved.
8. Either Ms. Morgan or her assistant were responsible for the breakdown in communications that occurred last week.
9. The committee is asking questions, reading the reports, and voting on the issues presented.
10. The meeting, consisting of representatives from every company involved in the takeovers, have adjourned until further notice.

EXERCISE 10

Point of View

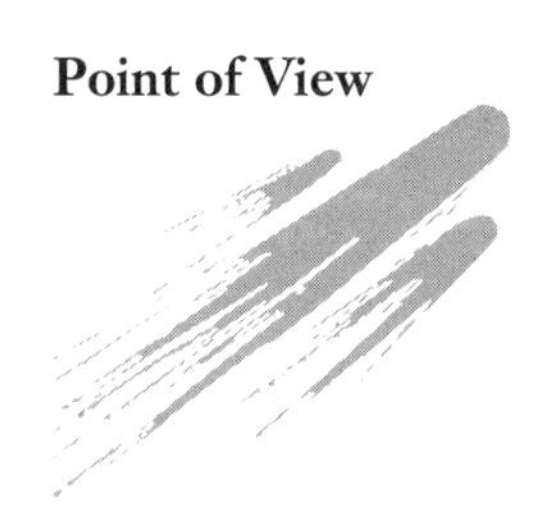

Replace all linking verbs with action verbs and correct the point of view errors in the following sentences.

1. Please send us $132.98 to cover the cost of your new software package and it would be appreciated if a self-addressed stamped envelope was also included.
2. If you wish to secure a worthwhile position in business, one should obtain the necessary qualifications.
3. A vote was taken and every person at the seminar decided to stay an extra two hours.
4. As you can appreciate, this is a problem that you cannot ignore without a solution being found.
5. Alice, you have been with Superior Corporation for 18 years and until this matter surfaced, your record had been excellent.
6. I recommend that you schedule a meeting with Mr. Davis so that he can be informed of your position on the issue.
7. To increase efficiency and employee loyalty, we must make employees more directly responsible for their actions through some sort of profit sharing plan being set up.
8. Perhaps you have an explanation for your failure to complete your report on time, but no reasons were given to the company.
9. The Bank Manager carefully studied our report and then rejects it.
10. I feel that if our Department had its own secretary, it would be able to sell more automobiles and our company's profits would be increased.

EXERCISE 11

Parallelism

Replace all linking verbs with action verbs and rewrite the following sentences to eliminate errors in parallel structure.

1. Phase 3 of the Office Development Plan provides full-time employees with new options in the development of work schedules and offering alternate, more appropriate options to part-time employees.

2. Our reports have shown an unacceptable decrease in sales of both furniture and accessories because clients complain that communication with the Sales Department was becoming increasingly difficult.

3. Phone messages are being misplaced, files are not being sorted properly, and the overall effort of our employees is unacceptably low.

4. Shawn cannot deal with the additional work from the Accounting Department as well as servicing the rest of the company.

5. These factors are affecting your insurance rates and action needs to be taken to rectify the problem.

6. Your present policy covers you if you have an accident, miss your flight, or your money is lost.

7. The company was efficient, gave good service, was people-oriented, and answered all complaints promptly.

8. We need to implement changes in the following areas: hire a new Administrative Assistant, purchase three computer terminals, printing room reorganization, renovate the staff lunchroom, and setting up of a client referral process.

9. After much deliberation we have decided to secure a loan of $20,000 from the bank, to expand our services, relocate, and to find a new distributor.

10. The Committee decided it should discuss Joe Watson's grievances and he should be offered a leave of absence for three weeks.

EXERCISE 12

Coordination and Subordination

Replace all linking verbs with action verbs and rewrite the following sentences to make them logical and grammatically consistent.

1. I recommend we place our advertisment in the Morning Sun as it is a well read newspaper and we need results as quickly as possible.
2. The present system is very inefficient as we are losing approximately twenty hours per week total and this should be spent with our customers or they will soon go elsewhere.
3. The recent rise in the number of customer complaints we receive is a result of disorganized delivery schedules and this affects the whole company.
4. Employees are not very committed to their jobs, which is causing problems that range from inadequate filing systems to phone calls being left unanswered, annoying our valuable customers.
5. Although Best Industries employs only one secretary, to keep costs down, I believe employing an additional secretary for the Sales Department will enable the company to become more cost efficient.
6. The number of sales Jake made in 1990 far exceeded the number of sales made by his colleagues but this wasn't enough to excuse his failure to declare all his expenses.
7. Our current printing costs could be lowered if we bought a photocopier and our employees would appreciate not having to walk to the printshop every day.
8. We accepted his proposal. It clearly expressed why we should hire him. He would do a good job of redecorating the office. He has an excellent sense of style.
9. The level of participation in this year's conference was more extensive.
10. You may feel you require assistance. Maybe your problem is personal or professional. Either way, we can meet. Call me to set a time.

EXERCISE **13**

Usage

Underline and then correct the usage errors in the following sentences.

1. WXE Financial Group, that was comprised of employees from every major bank, met for an annual meeting on April 10.

2. Another aspect of this proposal is that it recommends we sell most of our assets and move into smaller offices.

3. If you are so unorganized that you loose the key to your locker, you will forfeit you're $10.00 deposit.

4. Due to the fact that we have less than nine children in attendance today, I have decided to close the school irregardless of the policy stated by the School Board.

5. I do not feel the seminar leader sufficiently orientated us to the requirements of the course.

6. This presentation provided us with a real different view of the events which led to the bankruptcy of TTT Inc.

7. Ms. Swale choose to reject the company's plan to hire a new vice president to run all it's Alberta franchises.

8. The Relief Society was comprised of a variety of charitable organizations which donated their time and money to help homeless persons.

9. Its important to note the affect of increased sales on employee morale.

10. The company employees that needed extra time off were referred to the Personnel Department.

EXERCISE 14

Spelling

Place a tick next to the correctly spelled words and rewrite the incorrectly spelled words.

1. definately ____________
2. productivity ____________
3. occasionally ____________
4. excellence ____________
5. unmanagable ____________
6. circumstances ____________
7. detremental ____________
8. absenses ____________
9. confermation ____________
10. disatisfied ____________
11. personnel ____________
12. concurrent ____________
13. reduction ____________
14. facilitate ____________
15. controling ____________
16. enhancement ____________
17. insentive ____________
18. managment ____________
19. unecessary ____________
20. privatly ____________
21. benefited ____________
22. apreciate ____________
23. supercede ____________
24. accidently ____________
25. similiar ____________
26. sensible ____________
27. recomend ____________
28. committee ____________

EXERCISE 15

Punctuation

Apply the rules of punctuation to correctly punctuate the following sentences.

1. After I finished photocopying the vice-president asked me to type a letter.
2. Mr. Anderson stated I disagree with your conclusions.
3. To ensure you handle your money efficiently you should hire a Financial Advisor.
4. Give your writing the 3S treatment strength sincerity and simplicity.
5. The Committee's decision to revoke holiday pay made the entire organization angry particularly the employees on an hourly wage scale.
6. These improvements will amount to an additional $10,000 but I believe that increased efficiency will offset this cost.
7. Firstly our staff does not seem committed, they seem to have no idea what roles they play in our organization.
8. Ms. Johnson our only secretary is unable to keep up with the paperwork she has too many duties to perform.
9. I would also like to discuss an alternative arrangement that may help you that is enrolling in a course on Business Management.
10. The takeover bid failed to meet our requirements therefore we decided to maintain control of PTU Inc.

EXERCISE 16

The You Attitude

Underline the words in the letter that refer to the writer and then rewrite the letter using the You attitude.

Mr. George Allen
4489 Ring Road
Victoria, BC
V7Y 4R8

Dear Mr. Allen:

We received your letter complaining about the quality of our salespeople. We usually don't receive complaints because we carefully screen our salespeople to ensure they do not reflect poorly on our company.

However, we are prepared to acknowledge the problems which occurred when one of our salespeople mistakenly refused to provide the service contract asked for. We will make sure this never happens again.

To show our good will, please find enclosed a service contract which specifies the items requested.

Sincerely,

J.L. MacDonnell
Customer Service Representative

EXERCISE 17

Negative and Positive Words

Underline the negative words in the following sentences and then use positive words to rewrite the sentences, keeping the same message.

1. We are unable to recover from the loss incurred by your company's insufficient attempts to pay us the money we are owed.
2. Submit your application form without delay if you wish to avoid missing the deadline.
3. Although your qualifications do not lack promise, we regret to inform you that you would be unsuited for the position of Office Manager.
4. Unfortunately, Joe Small, a member of your clerical staff, has made some serious mistakes in photocopying the Chandler account.
5. You are liable both for all errors made by your staff and for any instance of slovenly conduct that may jeopardize the status of this company.

EXERCISE 18

The Yes Letter

You are a manager of a clothing store (or any other kind of retail operation) and a customer has written to complain about one of your products. Use the Yes letter format to promise the client that your company will offer a refund or some other compensation (you decide, e.g. two free shirts, etc.).

EXERCISE 19

The No Letter

Use the "No" letter format, positive words and the active voice to rewrite the following letter.

Mr. G. Fredericks
4589 Central Road
Toronto, ON
M8H 7QJ

Dear Mr. Fredericks:

We received your application of January 25 for a $25,000 loan to purchase a late model Corvette. After close examination of your banking and loan history, some important acknowledgements were made and your loan was rejected.

At present you are making about $3,000 per month before expenses. As you support a family of five, your financial burden must already be heavy. In addition, last year you acquired a 30 year mortgage at 10% for $150,000 from the Bank of Montreal for the purchase of the house in which you are presently residing. The monthly mortgage payments are $1,370. On March 15 of this year, you received a $5,000 loan to help start your consulting business. The payments from this loan amount to $450 per month for the next 12 months.

Perhaps you should consider paying off your current debts and increasing your business revenues before planning to buy a luxury car. Your loan application would be gladly reconsidered in a year when your business loan is paid off.

Sorry about refusing your loan, but we hope to talk with you again in 12 months.

Sincerely,

Doug Halston
Loans Officer

How To Be An All-Purpose Correspondent

O Introduction

Now that you've completed the first half of this course, it's time to take on the larger issues in business writing – different types of letters and reports. You can adapt the principles of the "yes" and "no" layouts to all types of business letters and memos. While each type of letter contains different kinds of information, you can better transmit this information if you first organize your letter to take into account its psychological impact on your reader. The following sections discuss how you should present the specific kinds of information required for a memo and the following five types of business letters: the sales letter, the collection letter, the complaint letter, the letter requesting a service or product, and the application letter.

1. Memos

The word "memorandum" comes from the Latin "it is to be remembered". You send a memo to remind someone of an event, idea, or procedure. Because you generally use memos to communicate with people within your organization, you can adopt a more familiar tone than you would when writing a letter to a new customer or the president of a rival company. Of course, you want to apply the Human Touch to all your business writing, but with a memo you can dispense altogether with any kind of formality.

Two principal requirements apply to memo writing:

1 A friendly tone,
2 Brevity.

Communicate the message as directly as possible so that your reader can get back to work. For example, avoid starting your memo with this kind of long-winded introduction:

> In accordance with the decisions made at the Management Committee meeting held last Wednesday at 10 a.m., this memo plans to summarize those decisions and discuss how they impact on each employee's working day.

You can safely delete this entire first sentence when you use a set format and get to the point quickly. Look at how the following memo gets the information across clearly and succinctly.

Example of a Memo

MEMORANDUM

To: All Employees

Date: March 18, 199-

From: Alice Martin, Personnel Manager

Re: Four Recommendations Regarding Employee Conduct

The Management Committee meeting on April 10 made four recommendations regarding the conduct of all employees. Please note the following requirements, which were unanimously agreed on:

1. *Identification Tags:* Please ensure that your identification tag is visible at all times when you deal with customers.
2. *Lunch Breaks:* Please take your lunch break either between 11 a.m. and noon or noon and 1 p.m.
3. *Tardiness:* Those arriving late more than once per month without sufficient reason will have 5% of their salary deducted from their cheques.
4. *Dental/Medical Appointments:* Please obtain permission from your Supervisor before you make a dental or medical appointment during working hours.

If you have any questions or concerns, give me a call at Local 451.

This memo doesn't include unnecessary background discussion. Staff having questions know whom to contact. Many organizations could save a great deal of time if they encouraged such conciseness.

Memo Rules >

To ensure your memos get read, apply the following rules:

1. Opening

Get right to the point. Don't begin with a wordy preamble that just gives background information. For example:

> I've noticed that your department's productivity has declined in recent weeks.

Instead, state the reason for the memo:

> Because productivity in your department has not maintained a satisfactory level in recent weeks, I suggest the following actions:...

Then list the actions required, preferably in order of importance.

2. Tone

Remember the Human Touch! Be friendly and professional and avoid using negative words and making threats, especially if the memo requests the improvement of an employee's performance. You will not get optimum results if you write:

> Should you wish to remain employed at our company, you must immediately prevent the productivity level in your Department from dropping any further.

But your memo's results will improve if you write:

> I feel confident that you will soon raise the productivity level in your Department and so maintain your good standing with our company.

The second sentence *implies* that a failure to act will result in serious consequences. However, it gives the reader the benefit of the doubt by appealing to his or her desire to do a good job. People generally respond to a show of confidence more readily than to a parental slap on the wrist.

3. Information

Back up your statements with the relevant facts and figures, or indicate where the reader can obtain more detailed information. Don't write:

> I've analyzed the expense we would incur by acquiring a new photocopier and concluded it is justified.

Specify the amount of money involved and briefly summarize why you feel the money should be spent:

> A new photocopier would cost the company $6,000. We currently spend $10,000 a year to send our copying to an outside printer. Even with the addition of approximately $2,000 to cover annual maintenance and paper costs, we would save $2,000 in the first year by making the purchase now.

4. Ending

Ask for some kind of immediate action and give a date and time, if possible. Don't write:

> Let's meet and talk this matter over.

Be specific:

> Could we meet at 3 p.m. on Wednesday to discuss the progress you have made? Call me at Local 311 to confirm.

Memo Review >

To write a memo quickly and efficiently, use the following format:

1. Begin with a short statement that provides the necessary context for the message.
2. Provide the required information in as brief a form as possible.
3. Close with a specific request for action.

Strive for brevity while you cultivate a tone of *good will.* The Human Touch can enliven even the most mundane of messages. Employees who receive memos written with consideration and humour will respond more willingly than employees who receive a list of orders. For example, you could say "Get those reports to me by 3 p.m. today". Your reader will no doubt comply with your request, but with how much eagerness? Don't make the mistake of using brevity as an excuse for brusqueness. Pretend you will receive the memo yourself and write it accordingly. For example, "Could you hand me your report by 3 p.m. today?" gets the message across in a respectful and pleasant way.

2. *Sales Letters*

You may be surprised to learn that, in terms of psychological layout, the sales letter has more in common with the "no" letter format than the "yes" letter format. You must gain the reader's confidence at the beginning of the letter, provide details in the middle of the letter, and then gently lead the reader to *want* to buy your product, just as in the "no" letter you gently lead the reader to accept your "no". The key to success lies with your ability to prompt the reader to say "yes" to your product before you even ask.

Before you write your sales letters, establish who your audience will be and use a set format.

Sales Letter Audience

Above all, remember that a sales letter cannot *make* anyone buy anything. It simply exists to let people who want to buy know what products are available.

However, one sales letter will not serve the needs of all the types of clients you wish to reach. Therefore, *tailor* your sales letter to a particular group of readers. For example, you will probably write one type of sales letter to appeal to small business owners and another type of letter to large corporations.

The more you know about each individual who reads your sales letter, the more likely you will be to make a sale. People like to hear about what concerns *them*. Always paint an image of your likely reader in your mind as you begin to write. One proven method is to picture your best friend.

Sales Letter Structure

Once you determine your audience, use the following five-paragraph structure to present your information:

1	Generate interest.
2	Provide options OR discuss the client's needs.
3	Describe your product or service in terms of how it will help your reader.
4	Give the financial details.
5	Request action.

Note that you can use Paragraph 2 to provide the options you've set up in Paragraph 1 or to discuss the client's needs further.

Generate Interest

Paragraph 1:

You must *interest* your readers in your product and *encourage* them to find out how to obtain it. You do not want to alienate your readers by insulting their intelligence with such opening gambits as "This is your lucky day, Mr. Jones" or "Don't get me wrong – I'm not trying to sell you anything – yet." Who would not be affronted by an approach like that? Instead, start off with common ground – something you think your reader will agree with. Here's the opening line of a sales letter asking small business owners to contract their paperwork out to a word processing service:

> As you know, business letters and reports must be accurately typed and attractively presented if they are to attract attention and get results.

This opening appeals to the reader's desire to make sure any letter or report he or she sends out is indeed "accurately typed and attractively presented". However, you also want to stress that your service will not only supply attractive documents but will save your reader time and money. Continue your opening paragraph by appealing to your reader's desire to save time and money:

> To get these results without spending too much time or money, you can make at least three choices about how to handle the letters and reports your business generates.

At this point – the end of paragraph one – your readers should be intrigued enough to find out the nature of these three choices. In paragraph one, therefore, you appeal to what your readers already know and then provide some reason why they should continue reading.

Provide Options OR Discuss the Client's Needs

Paragraph 2:

If your first paragraph has succeeded in gaining the attention of your readers, your second paragraph should reward that attention with some hard facts. Here's the second paragraph of the word processing letter:

> Choice 1: You can type your letters and reports yourself. If you choose this option, you may spend so much time working on your documents that you have little time left to work on marketing your business.
>
> Choice 2: You can hire a secretary. Certainly you will wish to consider this choice when your business is making solid profits. But what do you do during those periods when business falls off?

Choice 3: You can contract your paperwork out to a word processing service that guarantees fast, accurate results at short notice.

Notice how the use of indented paragraphs to present the choices breaks up the monotony of the traditional letter format. By providing a great deal of white space, this technique opens up the letter and makes it attractive. The reader can quickly scan the three choices, make a decision regarding their relevance, and possibly agree with Choice 3 immediately.

If your product or service does not fit an option format, you can use the second paragraph to expand on the client's needs. Discuss what a person such as your client probably looks for when he or she wants to buy a product or service like the one you offer. Here's the second paragraph of a sales letter promoting a gardening service:

> As the crocuses start to bloom at the beginning of each spring, you may walk around your garden and wonder how you can turn it into a lush paradise by mid-summer. Maybe you want a vegetable plot over in the corner and a few new shrubs to perk up the front entrance to your house. But how can you guarantee the results you want if you don't have hours to spend planting, weeding, and watering?

After a second paragraph such as this, you can easily swing into a description of your services in paragraph three.

Describe Your Product or Service

Paragraph 3:

By paragraph three, your readers already know what you will ask for. You don't want to ask yet, however. You want first to describe your product or service in terms of how it will satisfy a need that your opening paragraphs and your readers have already identified. Here's the third paragraph of the letter promoting the word processing service:

> If choice #3 appeals to you, take a quick look through the enclosed brochure that details the many services my company, *Coral Word Services*, can offer you. In addition to professionally typing all your documents on an IBM compatible computer supported by a laser printer, *Coral Word Services* will personalize your form letters by merging them with your client lists, use graphics to add reader interest to your reports, generate labels, correct grammat-

> ical errors, and much more. You provide us with the rough work and *Coral Word Services* will do the rest!

Continue to think about your reader when you start describing your product or service. Always relate what you do in terms of how it will help your reader. Remember the "you" attitude!

Provide Financial Details

Paragraph 4:

Provide your reader with the financial details of your service or product. Don't use catch phrases such as "all this at the incredibly low price of $9.99". Your readers will likely have a pretty good idea what a service or product such as you offer should cost. Preserve the trust you've tried to establish: don't try to make your readers believe they will get something for nothing.

> When you compare the cost of either doing your paperwork yourself or hiring a secretary with the $25.00 per hour rate charged by *Coral Word Services*, I'm sure you'll agree that contracting your work out will often make good financial sense. A job involving the typing and printing of three one page letters, for example, will cost you approximately $30.00. That's only $10.00 per letter! And for a small additional charge, *Coral Word Services* will pick up your work and deliver it back to you – usually within one working day.

You may also include in paragraph four any relevant details regarding discounts, payment options, ordering requirements, etc. Whatever information you include, avoid expressing it in "hype" terms. You can certainly imply that you offer a good deal, but you don't want to turn your readers off with phrases such as "you'll never get a deal like this anywhere else", or "I offer you the lowest price in town".

Request Action

Paragraph 5:

You've interested your readers, given them three options, described what you have to offer, and given price details. Now you want your readers to act. Of course, you really hope they will buy your product or service. However, you can't just write "come on in and buy my product". Instead, inform your readers what your next step will be and give them one or two alternatives. For example:

I will call you next week to discuss how *Coral Word Services* may help increase the productivity of (insert client's business name). If you have some work you need completed right now, please give me a call at 242-8876. We provide prompt, accurate and reliable help – even at short notice. Thank you for your attention. I look forward to serving you soon.

Sales Letter Length

Try to keep your sales letter to one page. You want to establish friendly contact with your readers – not make them wade through pages of closely typed text. Use one inch margins and a semi-block layout that attractively breaks up the space.

Sales Letter Examples

Sample Sales Letter 1

April 20, 199-

Ms. Donna Parker
Vice-President
Ajax Marketing
1187 Principal Street
Knoxville, Tennessee
56891

Dear Ms. Parker:

Generate Interest

As you know, a business such as Ajax Marketing needs to transfer information rapidly in order to meet the demands of a competitive economy. You can now choose from a number of options that each allow you to send and receive information with varying degrees of reliability and quickness.

Provide Options

Choice 1: You can contract a courier service to pick up and deliver your documents – usually within a few hours. Over time, the cost of this option can become very high.

Choice 2: You can purchase one of many fax machines on the market that transfers your information with speed and accuracy.

Choice 3: You can invest in a new type of fax machine – the Fax-O-Matic – that not only sends and receives information, but provides full colour graphics and a two year guarantee.

Describe Your Product

If choice #3 appeals to you, take a quick look through the enclosed brochure that details the many options available on the Fax-O-Matic. In addition to transferring and receiving information through the telephone lines, you can hook the Fax-O-Matic directly into your computer system to process and then print computer generated materials. The Fax-O-Matic also leads the market in graphics quality and colour printing.

Give Financial Details

When you compare the cost of either using a courier service or purchasing a standard fax machine with the $2000.00 cost of a Fax-O-Matic, I'm sure you'll agree that the many new features offered by the Fax-O-Matic make its price very affordable for a high volume business such as Ajax Marketing. And if you purchase your Fax-O-Matic before June 15, you will receive a 25% discount off our regular price – making your new machine only $1,500!

Request Action

I will call you next week to discuss how Fax-O-Matic may help increase the productivity of Ajax Marketing. If you have any questions or would like to have the Fax-O-Matic demonstrated in your office, please give me a call at 293-6645. Thank you for your attention; I look forward to serving you soon.

Sincerely,

Kathy P. Kwan
President

Encl.

Sample Sales Letter 2

January 19, 199-

Mr. and Mrs. Anderson
2387 East Street
Helena, Montana
45789

Dear Mr. and Mrs. Anderson:

Generate Interest

Your garden can and should reflect the same high level of taste and care you give to the interior of your home. When you choose trees, shrubs, and flowers that complement the architectural features of your house, you increase the value of your property and add hours of pleasure to your home life.

Discuss the Client's Needs

But as the crocuses start to bloom at the beginning of each spring, you may walk around your garden and wonder how you can turn it into a lush paradise by mid-summer. Maybe you want a vegetable plot over in the corner and a few new shrubs to perk up the front entrance to your house. How can you guarantee the results you want if you don't have hours to spend planting, weeding, and watering?

Describe your Product or Service

GreenArt Gardeners can help you design and maintain a garden that meets both your practical and aesthetic needs. Here's what we offer:

- Weekly maintenance: lawn cutting, pruning, watering
- Landscaping advice
- Flowers and vegetable planting
- Fall clean-up.

Provide Financial Details

You will find our rates competitive and reasonable. A weekly maintenance contract for a city-size lot, for example, will cost you approximately $150 per month. And think of the time you will have saved that you can use to *enjoy* your garden rather than be a slave to it. For landscaping planning and planting, you would pay $40 per hour – we can landscape most lots for under $1000.

Request Action

Mr. and Mrs. Anderson, if you contact GreenArt Gardeners before the end of March, you can take advantage of our Spring Package: $300 to set out all your bedding plants and plan your vegetable garden. Please call us at 454-8891 to set up an appointment time. Your garden can only benefit!

Sincerely,

Jack Tarsan
President
GREENART GARDENERS

3. Collection Letters

Money is like muck, not good except it be spread.

– Francis Bacon

The overwhelming majority of people want to pay their bills on time. Keep this fact in mind when you approach the task of writing to a customer who has not paid an invoice you sent in good faith. Ask yourself: "Why hasn't this customer paid?" Most of the time, the answer will be "because he or she does not have the money right now."

But what can you, the collection letter writer, do to get money out of people who don't have any? You can actually do a great deal if you take the time to apply a bit of elementary psychology.

Collection Letter Psychology

Let's think of a typical non-paying customer – we'll call her Ms. Watkins. First off, give Ms. Watkins the benefit of the doubt. Probably when she purchased your product or service she fully intended to pay you when she received your invoice. So what happened? Ms. Watkins probably ran out of money. Therefore, when she receives your first letter reminding her that she hasn't yet paid her invoice, how do you think she feels? Impatient? Insulted? Infuriated? Stop a minute. How would *you* feel if you received an overdue notice when you did not have enough money to pay it? That's right – you would probably feel embarrassed. No one, including our Ms. Watkins, likes to admit to a lack of money.

If it isn't the sheriff, it's the finance company. I've got more attachments on me than a vacuum cleaner.

– John Barrymore

But what can you do? Ms. Watkins ignores your first collection letter, probably because she hasn't any money and feels embarrassed. It helps to understand her position, but you still need to be paid. Take this maxim to heart:

> **Try to convince the customer to pay your company first.**

It's a pretty safe bet that Ms. Watkins owes money to more creditors than just your company. If she's low on funds, she probably receives her fair share of collection letters. But the time will come (usually) when Ms. Watkins finally regains her earning power. If she doesn't have sufficient money to pay all her creditors, she is likely to pay first the company that wrote her the most understanding and humane collection letters.

What About Threats?

You may disagree and maintain that Ms. Watkins will first pay the company who sent her the most effective threats.

You may be right – on one level. Ms. Watkins may well respond to a threatening letter, but will she ever want to deal with your company again? Worse, will she tell all her business associates about your heavy handed approach and then convince *them* never to deal with your company? Remember, you are in business to get and keep customers, not to lose them unnecessarily.

Escalating Urgency

Conventional wisdom has long stated that the tone of urgency you use in each of a series of collection letters to the same customer must escalate in proportion to the customer's increasing "delinquency". We don't find that this approach yields the best results in the modern world of customer relations. Certainly, your final attempt will be extremely firm, but it should also remain helpful, sympathetic and understanding – particularly when you have to assign the debt to a collection agency.

Collection Letter Structure >

Regardless of what stage in the collective process you are at, you can structure all collection letters in four paragraphs as follows:

1 Specify the problem.
2 Provide positive alternatives.
3 Imply the consequences of non-payment as you would to a friend. Do not threaten.
4 Close positively.

Collection Letter Sttyle and Tone >

Odd as it may seem, writing collection letters can be satisfying, if done positively. Keep the following points in mind as you choose your words:

1 Apply the *3S* treatment: Strength, Sincerity and Simplicity (see Unit 10).

2 Avoid negative words: "Did you remember?" rather than "You have forgotten."

3 Choose positive words: "encourage", "please", "hope", "your behalf".

4 Write in the first person: you want the customer to relate to you as a real person rather than your corporate identity.

Rebuke with soft words and hard arguments.
– *Proverb*

5 Do not issue a reprimand: this makes you seem as unattractive to deal with as a parent scolding a child. Remember the collection letter psychology discussed above. Most customers don't meet a payment date because they lack the necessary funds, not because they deliberately want to cheat your company. Under 4% of customers will never pay – don't risk alienating the more important 96% by using the wrong tone.

6 Apply the Human Touch: appeal to the customer's sense of fair play by indicating that payment will positively affect not just an impersonal company but a human being – you, the Collector.

7 Be firm, but don't threaten. Simply explain the consequences from a supportive point of view. Do not let the customer think you will back down if you don't receive payment.

8 Refer often to the customer's situation: try to make the customer understand what it feels like when invoices remain unpaid.

9 Emphasize sales and service: remind the customer of what he or she paid for and indicate that you would like to continue the business relationship with future sales.

Collection Letter Stages

Although you may write up to five or more letters before you assign the account to a collection agency, the following three letters cover a range of intensity from mild to serious.

Letter 1

In Stage 1, you write a gentle reminder letter – always giving the customer the benefit of the doubt. You avoid all negative words, use the You attitude, and add the Human Touch in four short paragraphs.

September 24, 199-

Mark Vaughn
President
HT Inc.
348 West Street
Albany, NY
98054

Dear Mr. Vaughn:

Specify the Problem

You may wish to check your records for the invoice we mailed to you on August 1 for $356.78. Have you already sent a cheque?

Provide Alternatives

If this account remains unpaid, please use the enclosed self-addressed envelope to send the $356.78. Alternatively, you may wish to consider sending a cheque for a portion of your account – perhaps one third for a total of $118.93? We can then work out a payment schedule for the balance.

Imply Consequences

I need to receive your payment before I can authorize our Sales Department to provide you with further services. Since you have just started doing business with us, I hope I can encourage you to keep your account current so that we may continue to maintain the plumbing facilities at HT Inc.

Close Positively

Thank you for your payment, Mr. Vaughn. We look forward to supplying you with plumbing services in the future.

Sincerely,

Joe Pleasant
Credit Manager

Letter 2

When your early attempts to obtain payment do not bring any response, you have to present your case more energetically while still maintaining a polite and respectful tone and You attitude. Use the four paragraph format and choose words that convey more urgency than the words used for the Stage 1 letter.

October 31, 199-

Mark Vaughn
President
HT Inc.
348 West Street
Albany, NY
98054

Dear Mr. Vaughn:

Specify the Problem

Your payment of $356.89 has not yet reached us. You'll remember, I'm sure, that you agreed to pay your account in full on receipt of our invoice on August 1 for the services you contracted in July. Your account really must be paid as soon as possible – we can't afford to carry an invoice for almost three months without receiving some kind of payment.

Provide Alternatives

In my letter of September 24, I suggested that you pay one third of your account and then establish a payment schedule for the balance. I am more than willing to explore this option – but I need to hear from you!

Imply Consequences

As you know, our Sales Department cannot help HT Inc. with its plumbing maintenance until I receive your payment. Also, I may have to send your account to our Collection Agency if I don't receive payment for a portion of your account by November 15. I understand that a new business such as yours makes many demands on your time and your cheque book. Still, I hope you will help us out so that we can continue to help you. If you can find the time to phone me to discuss how you would like to handle this, I'd greatly appreciate it.

Close Positively

Mr. Vaughn, thank you for making a payment and I look forward to hearing about the continued success of HT Inc.

Sincerely,

Joe Pleasant
Credit Manager

Letter 3

The final letter in the collection process must specify that time has run out. The customer must either pay, deal with a collection agency, or face legal proceedings. Even at this stage, however, the tone should remain positive and "human" – possibly even unconventional.

> November 15, 199-
>
> Mark Vaughn
> President
> HT Inc.
> 348 West Street
> Albany, NY
> 98054
>
> Dear Mr. Vaughn:
>
> *Specify the Problem*
>
> Help! I have not yet received your payment of $356.89, due last August 1, and here we are almost ready to haul out the Christmas decorations.
>
> *Provide Alternatives*
>
> On October 31, I asked you to send me just a portion of the $346.89. Where is it? Please dash off a cheque now so that I can move your account out of our receivables file.
>
> *Imply Consequences*
>
> Your account is scheduled to go to Acme Collection Agency on November 30 unless we receive payment by November 29. Surely you would prefer to protect HT Inc. from such a proceeding.
>
> *Close Positively*
>
> Mr. Vaughn, I hope to hear from you before November 29.
>
> Sincerely,
>
> Joe Pleasant
> Credit Manager

The Creative Approach >

The above letters use the You attitude and the Human Touch, but they remain relatively conventional. You can try a more creative approach. You may be surprised at how well customers respond to something a bit out of the ordinary. Here's an example of another way to write the final collection letter:

Final Collection Letter

November 15, 199-

Mark Vaughn
President
HT Inc.
348 West Street
Albany, NY
98054

Dear Mr. Vaughn:

Please indicate which of the following situations applies to you regarding your outstanding invoice for $356.89, due last August 1:

1. You are flat broke, but expect some cheques to come soon. YES ☐
2. You have some money, but are worried we won't accept part payment. YES ☐
3. You have enough money to pay a few bills, but can't understand our statement. YES ☐
4. You don't ever want to pay us. YES ☐

Could you send this letter back as soon as possible? I have to forward your account to the collection agency if I don't get some reply within ten days.

Thanks for helping me out.

Sincerely,

Joe Pleasant

Note the completely non-threatening tone of this letter. Mr. Pleasant merely wishes to determine Mr. Vaughn's situation – no reprimand, no condescension. Mr. Vaughn would have to be a hard case indeed if he failed to respond to such an appeal; however, at this stage, it's unlikely any approach would have better results.

4. *Complaint Letters*

A consumer is a shopper who is sore about something.

– *Harold Coffin*

If possible, most of us would prefer never to have to write or receive a letter of complaint. However, think of the complaint letter as a service letter rather than a vehicle to express your irritation or anger. When you write a complaint letter, you want your reader to take some action. You do NOT want to antagonize your reader. When you answer a complaint letter, you want your reader to think well of you and your product or service. You do NOT want your reader running around town grumbling about your company. Rather than concentrate on your *emotional* reactions, focus on the reason *why* you write or answer a complaint letter – to obtain full or partial payment, and to avoid customer ill will.

Writing the Complaint Letter >

No one likes to be criticized. Keep this fact in mind when you write your complaint letter – no matter how angry you feel. Think how you would react if you received a letter complaining, in rude and vindictive terms, about one of your products. Rather than wanting to grant the complainer what he or she asks for, you would more likely feel hostile, abused, and ultimately, defensive. People who are put on the defensive generally do not give in easily.

Rather than picturing your reader as a faceless corporation that only wants to take advantage of you, imagine your best friend receiving the letter. What kind of complaint letter would win his or her sympathy and inspire positive action? Probably one that presented a solution that struck you as reasonable, don't you think?

Complaint Letter Format >

1. Give precise details regarding your purchase of the defective product or service.
2. Describe the problem.
3. Request agreement to a specific, realistic solution and close positively.

Complaint Letter Tone >

1. Use neutral words to describe the situation – avoid emotional words such as "inexcusable" or "disgraceful".
2. Take the position that the defective product or service was a mistake, NOT deliberate. Assume that the company will *want* to reimburse you.
3. Apply the Human Touch – write to a person, not a corporation.

Example of a Complaint Letter >

June 15, 199-

Mr. Alex Hawkins
President
Vacations Unlimited
3367 West Street
Los Angeles, California
97866

Dear Mr. Hawkins:

Give Precise Details of the Purchase

On May 15 I arrived at the Oasis Hotel in Baja, California for a one week vacation that one of your agents, Ms. Dawes, booked for me in March. You should know that the service and facilities at the Oasis Hotel did not live up to your advertisement.

Specify the Problem

Your brochure described the Oasis Hotel as "a brand new resort complex located on the beach". In addition, it listed swimming pools, a 24 hour restaurant, and complimentary coffee among the services available and published a picture of a "typical" room. This description did not at all resemble what I discovered. My experience of the Oasis Hotel was as follows:

1. Because the hotel was still under construction, my room lacked hot water, curtains, and complimentary coffee. The staff did not seem very concerned with my disappointment.
2. Both swimming pools were out of order.
3. The restaurant did not serve food after 4 p.m.
4. The hotel was located two hot miles from the beach.

Request Action and Close Positively

Mr. Hawkins, I'm sure you understand how I feel after paying $1,500 for a vacation that did not match its advertised value. I request compensation – a 50% refund would seem fair. I look forward to receiving your cheque for $750.

Sincerely,

Ms. R.A. Sunburnt

Answering the Complaint Letter >

When you answer a complaint letter directed at your service or product you have two obligations:

1 To resolve the customer's problem,

2 To encourage the customer to buy again.

You have to strike a fine balance between taking responsibility for the problem and maintaining your company's integrity.

Complaint Answer Format >

The answer to the complaint letter uses the "yes" letter format:

1	Say yes.
2	Supply necessary details.
3	Close in a friendly way.

Complaint Answer Tone >

1 You certainly do not want to grovel, nor do you want to sound as if you are conferring a favour by even answering the complaint.

2 Avoid negative words such as "problem" or "defect".

3 Do not remind the customer how much he or she suffered as a result of the complaint.

4 Concentrate on solving the problem in a positive way that maintains the customer's good will.

Example of a Complaint Letter Answer

June 30, 199-

Ms. R.A. Sunburnt
2268 14th Street
Pasadena, California
57881

Dear Ms. Sunburnt:

Say Yes

Thank you for your letter of June 15 describing your experiences at the Oasis Hotel in Baja, California. I certainly agree that you did not receive the level of treatment you deserve as our guest. I am pleased to enclose a voucher for a 50% discount on the next vacation you book with Vacations Unlimited. Alternatively, you may enjoy staying as our guest for two nights at the Pasadena Resort Hotel.

Supply Necessary Details

You may wish to come into the office next week to discuss when you would like to apply the voucher. In September, we have a special one week package at the Hawaiian Gala Hotel described in the enclosed brochure. With your 50% discount, this package would cost you only $500. *Travel Time Magazine* recently ranked the Gala as one of the top ten hotels in the Hawaiian Islands.

Close in a Friendly Way

Ms. Sunburnt, thank you again for your helpful comments, which I greatly appreciate. I look forward to discussing plans for your Hawaiian vacation.

Sincerely,

Alex Hawkins
President
Vacations Unlimited

Notice how the above letter does not actually give the customer what she asked for – a 50% refund. However, the writer makes what he does offer sound like a reasonable compromise. If this answer encourages the customer to accept a discount instead of a refund, then the writer has accomplished two important objectives – satisfying the customer and generating new business.

5.

Letters Requesting a Service or Product

Use the "yes" letter structure for any letter requesting a service or product. You don't want to waste your reader's time with a long preamble. Your reader should understand your request after reading your first paragraph.

A high percentage of the business letters you write will be some type of request letter. Here's a partial list of reasons for making requests:

- To obtain information: prices, specifications, product availability, etc.
- To make or confirm travel arrangements.
- To obtain brochures, price lists, catalogs, etc.
- To order products.
- To secure a favour, invitation, or endorsement.
- To contract the services of another business.

Strike a balance between providing too much and not enough information. You want your reader to be able to fulfill your request without having to contact you for clarification. Now that the fax machine makes communication almost instantaneous, try to write request letters that your reader can absorb quickly. Your reader should then be able perform the required action, and fax you a reply by the end of the day.

Request Letter Format

1 State your request politely – get to the point quickly. For example:

> Please send me the most recent catalogue of your outdoor recreation equipment. I would also appreciate receiving any additional information about tents and climbing gear.

2 Supply all the necessary details. For example:

> I plan to place orders for a varied selection of high altitude tents and rock climbing equipment by the beginning of March. Could you deliver the products by April?

3 Close positively. For example:

> Thank you for your attention to my request. I look forward to seeing your new catalog.

Study the following sample Request Letter and then try writing your own version in the Review Exercises provided in Unit Nine.

Example of a Letter Requesting Service or Product >

September 10, 199-

Service Manager
ARCO Toys Inc.
458 East Street
Montreal, PQ
M5T 2W4

Dear Sir/Madam:

State the Request

Please send me 16 dozen Big Block sets at your advertised price of $5.67 per set.

Supply Necessary Details

Could you send the sets Priority Post so that I receive them by September 30? I have a large order to fill by October 15. Please invoice me for the sets and delivery charges, if applicable.

Close Positively

Your service in the past has always been first-rate. I look forward to continuing a steady relationship with ARCO Toys.

Sincerely,

Raymond Rowan
Purchasing Agent
Toys Galore

6. Application Letters

A wise man will make more opportunities than he finds.

– *Francis Bacon*

When you write a letter applying for a job or any type of favor, approval, or grant, you present yourself as you would your product in a sales letter. The distinguishing point of an application letter is that you place your request in the first paragraph.

Application Letter Format >

Apply the following format to write your application letter:

1 State your purpose and refer to the circumstances that led you to make the application, for example, a newspaper advertisement.

2 Describe your qualifications briefly. Emphasize the qualifications of particular interest to the position.

3 Detail your expectations (why you want the job, salary requirements, availability, etc.).

4 Request an interview and close in a friendly way.

Application Letter Tone >

In an application letter, you sell yourself with words. You want to *attract* your employer's attention and *convince* him or her to grant you an interview. To be effective, your application letter should employ three techniques: summarize the facts, satisfy your reader's needs, and emphasize your personal strengths.

Summarize The Facts

Don't make vague claims about your qualifications – be precise, strong, and selective. Your resume already lists all your qualifications and experience. You want to summarize the main points of your resume without needless repetition. To do this, concentrate on what you *did* at one or two of your past jobs, rather than what your position was. For example, if you have two year's experience as a manager of a small retail store, provide details as follows:

> As manager of the Craft Boutique for two years, I ordered all stock, wrote sales letters and advertisements, and handled all the bookkeeping.

Try to present a high percentage of facts in proportion to the number of words you use.

Satisfy Your Reader's Needs

Visualize the person who will read your letter – what does he or she need? How can you satisfy that need? By concentrating on the reader of your letter, you minimize the tendency to just "blow your own horn" rather than show what you can offer your potential employer.

Don't think about *your* need for a job; think about the *employer's* need for the best possible employee. For example, relate a statement about your academic qualifications to the requirements of the position:

> The marketing courses I took as part of my Bachelor of Commerce degree gave me the training to determine a target market for your products and then develop an appropriate marketing strategy.

Make it a rule not to include any facts about your background and qualifications that do not *directly* relate to the position you are applying for. Your reader wants to find the best person for the job. Show how you should be that person.

Emphasize Your Personal Strengths

Once you have summarized your qualifications and shown how they can help your reader, concentrate on describing how your *personality* suits you for the position. Stress your willingness to develop your skills and your enthusiasm for the type of work you're applying for. Without boasting, state one or two strong points, such as good communication skills or an ability to work well with people. You can also state what you hope to accomplish. For example:

> I enjoy the challenge of working with a new company to increase sales and give good customer support.

By emphasizing your personal strengths, you try to show how you differ from the other applicants. Make your reader feel that you have the confidence to do a good job.

Example of an Application Letter >

November 12, 199-

Ms. Darlene Velasquez
President
A-1 Communications
Suite 45 - 2289 North Street
Halifax, NS
H4R 7AT

Dear Ms. Velasquez:

State Your Purpose

I would like to apply for the position of Sales Manager at A-1 Communications as advertised in the *Halifax Gazette* of Saturday, November 10. Enclosed is my resume detailing my qualifications and experience.

Describe Your Qualifications

I recently graduated from the University of Toronto with a Bachelor of Commerce degree. In my final year, I concentrated on Marketing and Business Communications courses for small businesses. I am especially interested in applying my skills to find a target market for your products and to develop an appropriate marketing strategy. I have also worked part-time for three years as the Assistant Sales Manager for Best Printing Co. where I developed a successful advertising campaign for their line of stationery.

Detail Your Expectations

Because of my experience in advertising and technical writing, I particularly wish to become involved in a company such as A-1 Communications. I enjoy the challenge of providing effective customer support with a product I can believe in. My salary expectations are in the $30,000+ range and I could start work immediately.

Request An Interview and Close Positively

I would like very much, Ms. Velasquez, to meet with you to discuss how I could apply my skills to benefit A-1 Communications. You can reach me at 876-2377. Thank you for your attention to my application. I look forward to hearing from you.

Sincerely,

Madelaine McDonald

Encl.

Notice how the writer of the above letter uses a confident tone without bragging about her skills. She implies that she has lots of ideas that could help the company and projects an enthusiastic image. Try to use a natural style and clear sentences that will have a positive effect on your reader.

Finally, consider researching the company you are writing to before mailing your application. Such research shows the organization you have rare initiative, and will give you a good idea of exactly where you might fit in. This kind of letter gets far better results than a generalized, mindless mailout. Trade quantity of applications for quality!

7. *Types of Letters: Review*

To summarize, here are the formats for each of the five types of letters we discussed.

Sales Letter:
1. Generate interest.
2. Provide options OR discuss the client's needs.
3. Describe your product or service in terms of how it will help your reader.
4. Give the financial details.
5. Request action.

Collection Letter:
1. Specify the problem.
2. Provide positive alternatives.
3. Imply the consequences of non-payment.
4. Close positively.

Complaint Letter:
1. Give precise details regarding your purchase of the defective product or service.
2. Describe the problem.
3. Request agreement to a specific, realistic solution and close positively.

Complaint Letter Answer (YES Letter Format):
1. Say yes.
2. Supply necessary details.
3. Close in a friendly way.

Request Letter:
1. State your request politely.
2. Supply all the necessary details.
3. Close positively.

Application Letter:

1 State your purpose.
2 Describe your qualifications.
3 Detail your expectations.
4 Request an interview and close positively.

When you use one of the formats described above to write your business letters, you free yourself from indecision about *what* to write. Now you can concentrate on *how* to write – the subject of Unit Ten. But first, practice using the letter formats by rewriting the letters given in Unit Nine - Practice Your Letter Writing Skills. You will find that one of the most efficient ways to improve your own writing is to edit someone else's. The pressure of the blank page disappears when you have a piece of writing to work with. All you have to do is decide how to improve a poorly constructed sentence - a much easier task than trying to think up an original sentence.

Before you rewrite each letter in Unit Nine, determine what the letter *should* say and then shift the sentences and words to communicate the message in the clearest and most sincere way possible. Experiment with different ways of saying the same thing until you find a style that suits your personality.

UNIT NINE Practice Your Letter Writing Skills

Practice what you have learned about letter writing in Units Six, Eight and Nine by rewriting the different types of letters in the following exercises. For suggested responses, refer to the *Better Business Writing Answer Key* or your instructor.

EXERCISE 1

Rewriting the Memo

Correct all grammar and usage errors, eliminate unnecessary words and phrases, and apply the Human Touch to revise the following three memos.

Memo 1

To: Joe Brown
From: Alice Smith
Re: Decreased Sales due to Absence

Since being promoted to sales manager, your numerous absenses are being far too frequent. As a result, sales has decreased considerably.

If you are having health problems, then this must be discused with me. Or you workload maybe way too demanding. In any case, your absences have got to stop, sales is the most integral department of our company

If this situation will continues and sales are not immediately improved, both you and your sales department will be dealt severely with by the president.

Memo 2

To: George Flynn
From: Sally Yuan
Re: Secretarial Help

The Sales Department has an escalating amount of paperwork to deal with on a daily basis. As a consequence, productivity is declining.

A reasonable response to this problem would be the hiring of an additional secretary. I've analyzed the expense associated with hiring a new secretary and concluded that the benefits of increased clerical support would outweigh the costs.

Could we get together and discuss this concern as soon as is mutually convenient?

Memo 3

To: Simon Battersea
From: Charles Tidball
Re: Possible efficiency improvements

Having time recently to review the status of our office operation, I have located areas in which I believe improvements could be made, improving efficiency considerably.

Some adjustments would be easy to execute resulting in marked improvements immediately. Others would take somewhat longer and would require the participation and encouragement of upper management.

There is a slight urgency concerning some of these matters and therefore I would request a meeting soon, if at all possible.

EXERCISE 2

Rewriting the Sales Letter

Use the correct sales letter format and an appropriate tone to rewrite the following two sales letters.

Sales Letter 1

Ms. Sally Feinstein
President
Feinstein Interior Designs
4389 West 1st Ave.
Chicago, Illinois
54789

Dear Ms. Feinstein:

How would you like the chance to take your work wherever you want to go? You can finish a report on the airplane, plan your day while riding the bus, or work half the night in bed.

I understand from our sales representative, who deals regularly with your company, that you do a great deal of travelling but do not have a laptop computer. You may not be aware of it, Ms. Feinstein, but Small Computers Inc. is the third largest laptop computer maker.

I'm sure you have heard about the benefits of owning a laptop computer when you have a busy work schedule. To provide you with still more information, I am enclosing a brochure of our latest product - the Laptop 24Z0AK. You will be amazed by the features of the 24Z0AK. It's an incredible little bundle of power.

Should you need more information about the Laptop 24Z0AK or any of our other wonderful products, I would be glad to meet with you. Better yet, I will call you in several days to see if you would like me to show you how the Laptop 24Z0AK can help you be a better business person.

Sincerely,

John Warner
District Sales Director

Sales Letter 2

Mr. Bob Torqual
The PeachTree Restaurant
548 South Street
Palm Springs, CA
98771

Dear Mr. Torqual:

Have you been in to see our latest selection of chinaware? We at Fine Dining Ware know you will be entranced by the new designs we have in stock.

The other day I ate lunch at the PeachTree and was, I'm sorry to say, not pleased by the quality of the plates and cups. My salad plate was chipped and the pattern on my coffee cup did not match the pattern on my entree plate. I think you may want to consider buying a completely new set of chinaware.

At the moment, we have a good sale on. You can get 30% off our regular price. Come down to our show room and we'll talk about how we can best equip the PeachTree with the very finest and most reasonably priced dinnerware to be found in any restaurant in the Palm Springs area.

Thanks for your attention. I'll call you soon - and by the way, my lunch was excellent! Keep up the good work.

Sincerely,

Don March
Vice-President: Sales

EXERCISE 3

Rewriting the Collection Letter

Use the correct Collection letter format and an appropriate tone to rewrite the following two collection letters.

Collection Letter 1 (Stage 2: Medium Pressure)

Mr. Harold Markham
Western Sun Inc.
785 East Street
Honolulu, Hawaii
87796

Dear Mr. Markham:

While we are well aware that times are tough for small businesses such as yours, we still have to insist that you pay at least a portion of the money you owe us.

We've been waiting for your cheque for 3 months now and can't wait much longer. I'm sure that business must be picking up for you now that the winter tourist season is well under way.

Thanks for your cooperation.

Sincerely,

Cindy Yarrow

Collection Letter 2 (Final Stage)

Ms. Antonia Rosselli
66 West 9th Street
Bowling Green, Kentucky
78834

Dear Ms. Rosselli:

Your account has been delinquent for 5 months. Certainly you have been given ample time to settle this indebtedness. Any longer delay cannot be accepted.

In order to avoid further embarrassment to you and additional communication, I suggest this bill be paid while there is still time.

If you pay within the next 10 days, you can avoid legal action. Govern yourself accordingly.

Sincerely,

Adam Prentiss
Collections Supervisor

EXERCISE 4

Rewriting the Answer to a Complaint Letter

Use the correct format and a good tone to rewrite the following two answers to complaint letters.

Complaint Answer Letter 1

Ms. Grace Allenby
44 West 4th Street
Minneapolis, MN
78655

Dear Ms. Allenby:

Thank you for your informative letter of October 30 regarding your dissatisfaction with one of my salespeople, Mrs. R. Sanderson. I would like to apologize for the treatment you received and try to make up for some of your inconvenience.

It has always been my intention to provide a medium for you the customer to view our vacuum cleaners without feeling pressured to buy. What better place than in your own home?

The tactics employed by Mrs. Sanderson were unacceptable and thanks to you, it has finally come to my attention. Steps have since been taken to ensure that this sort of situation does not occur again.

Once again, Ms. Allenby, I must apologize for all of the inconvenience you have suffered. Please accept this complimentary set of vacuum-cleaner bags as a small token of my appreciation for all your time and effort.

Sincerely,

Harold Watkins
President

Complaint Answer Letter 2

Mr. D. King
889 E. 54th Street
Calgary, Alberta
T5Y 9RE

Dear Ms. King:

Sorry for any inconvenience that may have been caused due to the fact that we placed the wrong washing instructions on your purchase from our store.

We at Good Clothes Inc. take great pride in our service and product quality and will fully cooperate if you feel you must exchange or refund your purchase.

When you return to Good Clothes Inc., ask for me, Mr. Saunders, and I will expedite your service personally. Once again, I wish to apologize for the annoyance this mistake may have caused you.

Sincerely,

John Saunders
Customer Service Supervisor

EXERCISE 5

Rewriting the Request Letter

Use the correct Request Letter format and an appropriate tone to rewrite the following two request letters.

Request Letter 1

Ms. T.W. Johannsen
Seminar Division
Corporate Management Ltd.
669 West Street
San Francisco, 91509

Dear Ms. Johannsen:

Could you possibly send me the various organizational materials I'll need to prepare the workshop I'm giving in six weeks time on the first of March? I am hoping that you have enough material to help round out what I already have.

You should perhaps note that I particularly need Section "B" of the published proceedings from last year's conference. Your library should have a copy of these proceedings — they are filed in a large binder with the proceedings from the past 10 years. Unfortunately, they are not filed by year.

I will continue to be out of the country for about a month. If you have any questions, Don Harlen will be looking after my various and sundry responsibilities in the meantime.

Please also send me a signed copy of your letter of agreement. I'm really sure this will be a good workshop. I want to thank you for having given me the opportunity and I look forward to meeting with you when I get to San Francisco in six weeks.

Yours very truly,

Gordon Ralston

Request Letter 2

Sales Manager
AXON Computers Ltd.
348 New Street
Montreal, PQ
H7Y 4ET

Dear Sir/Madam:

I'm thinking about buying a new laser printer quite soon. I run a small company that would like to upgrade its image by giving all our documents the professional look possible with a laser printer.

I heard from a colleague that your company stocks numerous laser printers. Could you tell me which one I should buy and how much?

Thanks for your help.

Sincerely,

Donna Webb
Office Manager

EXERCISE 6

Rewriting the Application Letter

Use the correct Application Letter format and an appropriate tone to rewrite the following two letters of application.

Application Letter 1

Ms. Daniela G. Mowat
Director of Personnel
SeaScan Leisure
Suite 1189 - 335 Main Street
Toronto, ON
M5F 1AH

Dear Ms. Mowat:

Having just graduated from university with excellent grades, I would like to apply for the position of Assistant Sales Manager which you advertised in the *Morning Star* last Saturday.

With my Bachelor of Commerce degree, I feel well qualified to fulfill the requirements of the position you advertised. I also have lots of experience working part-time at Nickel's Department store for 5 years. I was promoted three times while at Nickel's — my last position was Assistant Supervisor of Men's Wear. I learned all about how to order stock, write promotional materials, etc.

At university, I excelled in my Marketing courses. I am confident that, with my enthusiasm and sincere desire to do well, I will make a great Assistant Sales Manager. I am also really interested in the outdoors and the kinds of products your company sells.

Thank you for reading the enclosed resume. I would appreciate coming in for an interview - how about next Wednesday at 10 a.m.? I look forward to hearing from you.

Sincerely,

Carey Donaldson

Application Letter 2

District Support Manager
Service Operations
Computers Canada Inc.
1190 Standard Street
Winnipeg, Manitoba
T7J 2K2

Dear Sir/Madam:

Re: Job Application for Customer Support Representative

I graduated a few years ago from the University of Manitoba and have worked since then as Sales Representative for an Electronics company. In response to your company's January 9 advertisement in the *Winnipeg Chronicle*, I am writing to apply for the position of Customer Support Representative or any other similar job opening. My resume is enclosed.

I have a wide range of experience with electrical, optical and mechanical systems. I have extensive experience in Public Relations, Customer Service, Direct Sales, Management, and Training, excellent communication skills, and a natural ability to work well with others. I am confident that I can do a good job for Computers Canada Inc.

I would be pleased to provide complete details of my experience and qualifications during a personal interview at your earliest convenience. My telephone number is (604) 980-9748. Thank you for reading this letter and I look forward to meeting with you at your earliest convenience.

Sincerely,

Brent Ewasiuk

How To Write With Style

In the first nine units of *Better Business Writing*, you have learned how to write Power Sentences and Paragraphs, connect your thoughts grammatically, avoid common writing errors, focus on your reader, and write a variety of effectively structured letters. You have also done numerous exercises to help you develop your skills. All that practice will pay off in Unit Ten where you will turn your attention to developing an effective style. At the end of Unit Ten, you can test your learning with more Review Exercises. In Unit Eleven, you will tackle the business writer's most complex task – how to write a report that gets results.

0 *Introduction*

Read over your compositions and, when you meet a passage which you think is particularly fine, strike it out.
–Samuel Johnson

To communicate with your readers effectively, you need to make your writing vigorous and easy to read. By cultivating a sensitivity to how words interact with each other, you can develop a clear, animated style that makes readers feel you not only care about what you write but that you also care about what your readers think.

Your use of Power Sentences and the Active Voice, combined with correct grammar, already energizes your writing. To take the final steps toward achieving a dynamic style, give your writing the *3S* treatment: Strength, Sincerity, and Simplicity.

1. *Strength*

Style is effectiveness of assertion.
– George Bernard Shaw

Would you buy an umbrella from the writer of the following sentence?

> Our company's umbrellas are of the very best quality and should be of service for many years to come.

Three stylistic problems drain this sentence of the power to motivate readers.

1 The writer uses two linking verbs to describe the umbrellas: "*are*" and "*should be*".

2 The customer never appears – perhaps the writer doesn't see the customer as very important.

3 The words used to describe the umbrella appear so frequently in advertising as to be virtually meaningless.

Remember the three steps to the Power Sentence? These steps add strength to your writing style. Look at the difference specific words and action verbs make to the sentence at hand:

> The Designer Umbrella collapses into a small enough package to fit into your purse or back pocket!

Instead of extolling the umbrella's high quality and great service record, this sentence describes one of the main attributes of the umbrella: its size. Do not *tell* your reader that your product is good; *show* your reader what your product does. You want to use words that make a picture pop into your reader's mind so that he or she can immediately grasp your meaning and act upon it.

Be not simply good; be good for something.
– *Henry David Thoreau*

To strengthen your writing, choose action verbs that *exactly* express the activity engaged in by the subject. For example:

> The accountant *scrutinized* the records.

This sentence describes the situation more vividly than "The accountant *looked* at the records" or "The accountant *studied* the records." The verb "scrutinized" provides readers with a clear picture of a person who not only looks at the records but intends to find the smallest error. How differently you would react if your accountant scrutinized your records rather than merely looked at them! You would make sure your records were in good shape.

Consider the action verb "provide". Depending on the context of the sentence, "provide" could mean contribute, dispense, allocate, disburse, designate, give, distribute, supply, equip, award, furnish, outfit, grant, assign, etc. Think how much stronger your sentences would be if you chose the precise meaning of the verb provide. For example:

> The secretary *provided* the committee members with copies of the minutes.

This sentence elicits a much hazier picture than "The secretary *distributed* copies of the minutes to the committee members". In the latter sentence, you can visualize the secretary sending out the minutes. But you get an even stronger image if you use a verb that specifies *how* the secretary distributed the minutes: "The secretary *faxed* copies of the minutes..." or "The secretary *mailed* copies..." or "The secretary *handed out* copies..." You can see that the action verb does not need to be fancy – only precise.

Note how the first sentence in each of the following pairs conveys a weaker image than the second sentence.

Weak	1.	This report *gives us* reasons why we should get new office furniture.
Strong	1.	This report *explains* why we should purchase new office furniture.
Weak	2.	The technician *looked* at the copier for signs of misuse.
Strong	2.	The technician *inspected* the copier for signs of misuse.
Weak	3.	We *thought* his speech was too long.
Strong	3.	The length of his speech *exhausted* us.
Weak	4.	I *will take care* of the process of hiring a new salesperson.
Strong	4.	I *will screen* and *interview* candidates for the salesperson position.
Weak	5.	In spite of the fact that our costs went up by 14% of gross sales, we still *managed* to go over last year's record by 5%.
Strong	5.	Although costs climbed to 14% of gross sales this year, our profits *surpassed* last year's record by 5%.

EXERCISE 1

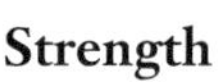

Strength

Replace all linking verbs with specific action verbs and use clear images to pump strength into the following weak sentences.

1. I am assured that you will agree the future benefits of taking on more personnel to handle this new contract will far outweigh the extra costs we'll have to pay.
2. Mr. Aiken, our only word processing operator, is

slowly falling behind in relaying sales orders, as he has many other tasks to perform, and having them confirmed on time so as to achieve our delivery goals.

3. Because our company has grown greatly in the last few years, the production department is creating a lot of paperwork.

4. It is proposed that to take advantage of the Contract System we work at encouraging everyone involved to increase their contribution to the company in a way which is reinforcing the Contract System and is increasing the profitability of the company.

5. Being new to the company, I have noticed that staff are not committed to their jobs, filing systems are disorganized, and clients are annoyed.

Check your answers with the suggested versions in the Answer Key.

2. *Sincerity*

Style has no fixed laws; it is changed by the usage of the people, never the same for any length of time.

– *Seneca*

You have probably received many business letters that overflow with phrases such as "it has come to my attention that" or "please be informed" or "we make it our business to" or "pursuant to your recent inquiry". Writers who use these phrases apparently want to project a total lack of personality – as if business writing must be void of all humanity. In the section on the Human Touch in Unit Five, you learned how to write letters in a personal style. In this section on Sincerity, we will look at the role of diction. To help make your style sincere, you should avoid jargon, "big" words, and stock phrases.

Jargon >

The business world abounds with specialized words developed to accommodate the computer revolution and sociological changes. Writers may wish to impress readers with words such as "interface", "access", "timeline", "timeframe", "bottom line", "infrastructure", "personage", "input/output", etc. because such words signify a kind of "hipness" to contemporary thought. No one wants to run the risk of sounding uninformed. Unfortunately, the use of jargon limits the writer to a particular time – like calling something "groovy" nowadays instead of "totally awesome". You would not dream of using such slang in business writing, unless very sparingly to achieve a particular effect.

Similarly, the use of contemporary jargon diminishes the impact of your writing because it can become quickly dated and pegs you as someone who eagerly follows trends rather than sticks to clear and thoughtful modes of expression.

Note how the reliance on jargon words in the following sentence makes the message superficial:

> It is vital that we get motivated to formulate the parameters of this company's expansion venture so as to capitalize on some meaningful feedback and instigate a viable dialogue in the final analysis regarding the bottom line case scenarios in our sector before escalating on-stream contacts with prospective worthwhile clientele.

What? Say that again! Even if you recognize all the words in the above sentence, you have to work hard to decipher what the writer wants to tell you. After a few minutes of thought, you may decide the sentence means:

> We must discuss our company's plans for expansion before we approach new clients.

Unfortunately, most readers would not take the trouble to find a clear meaning. They would put aside the jargon-filled document and get on with some important work. You certainly don't want your reports and letters to meet such a fate.

Be on the alert for seemingly innocent words like "access", "cope" or "connection" that work perfectly well in some situations but may be "jargonized" all too easily. For example:

> The managers discussed the instances of personnel absences in connection with the reduced rate of production.

In this sentence, jargon words and phrases such as "in connection with", "instances" and "reduced rate of production" add excess verbiage but contribute little to meaning. Cut the jargon out:

> The managers discussed the connection between personnel absences and the drop in production.

"Big" Words

Armed with a university degree or two and a heightened sense of importance, some writers insist on sprinkling their documents with obscure words that drive their readers into their dictionaries. Business writing should produce business results – not provide a podium for the writer to air his or her grasp of diction. While you would probably not use a word such as "confabulate" when you mean discuss, you might be tempted to throw in words such as "quandary" for problem, "felicitations" for best wishes, "demonstrate" for show, or "expedite" for advance. If possible, try to use a familiar word instead of a longer synonym.

Remember, as a reader of business documents you want fast results. You certainly don't want to have to stop to ponder the meaning of an unfamiliar word. Your readers also want results quickly. While you can occasionally choose a less common word for the sake of precision, you generally want to avoid frustrating or intimidating your readers by using the simpler versions of the following "big" words:

accede.......................................agree
accordingly...............................so
acquiesce ....agree, consent
admonish..................................warn, caution
affirmative ....yes
aggregate..................................total
allay ....calm, ease
alleviate ....reduce, ease
allocate ....assign
append......................................add
ascertain ....determine
attain ....gain
authenticate ....prove, confirm
avert ....prevent
categorize.................................arrange
cognizant..................................aware
commence ....start, begin
concurrent.................................parallel, similar
consolidate ....join
constitute ....make up, form
contribute ....give
counterpart ....copy, match
curtail ....shorten
defer ....postpone
definitive ....final

deliberation .... review

delineate .... outline

devise .... make

discontinue .... stop

disseminate .... distribute

divergent .... separate, different

effect, effected .... take, taken

elucidate .... clarify

endeavour .... try

entail .... involve

enumerate .... list

equitable .... fair

erroneous .... wrong, not right

exhort .... urge

facilitate .... assist, ease

fundamental .... basic

furnish .... supply

gauge .... measure

hereabouts .... here

illustrate .... explain

impacts on (as verb) .... affects

impart .... tell

initiate .... start

intelligible .... clear

juncture .... (do not use to mean "point")

liaise .... connect

manifest .... show, reveal

market .... sell

modicum .... bit

modify .... change

necessitate .... require

optimum .... best

paramount .... chief

parity .... equality

penchant .... aptitude, ability

peripheral .... outer

permutation .... change

perusal .... study

preamble .... introduction

predicated .... based

predilection .... preference

present .... show

prior to .... before

procure .... buy, purchase

promulgate .... promote

ramification .... result

rationale .... reason

recapitulate .... review, summarize

relinquish ....give up
remunerate................................pay
repercussion ....effect
sanction ....approve
stipend.......................................wage, payment
terminate...................................end
utilize ....use
viable ....workable, practical

Stock Phrases >

As with jargon and big words, the use of stock phrases drains business writing of sincerity. When you read a letter full of phrases such as "due to the fact that", "in the case of", "for the reason that", "from the point of view that", "enclosed herewith", "as per your request", etc., you feel a sense of detachment. You may even perceive the writer as someone who merely copied some "business" sounding phrases without any thought to how they will affect you, the reader. For example:

> Due to the fact that our company can no longer sustain the loss incurred by your failure to make payments in the amount of $300 per month, this is to acknowledge that your credit privileges have been discontinued, effective immediately.

This sentence *distances* the writer from the reader because it uses stock phrases to excess: "due to the fact that", "can no longer sustain", "loss incurred", "make payments", "in the amount of", "this is to acknowledge that", and "effective immediately". You can write the same message without stock phrases and with a lot fewer words:

> We cannot continue to offer you credit until we receive your $300 monthly payments.

Notice how the condescending tone disappears with the elimination of stock phrases. You may not like the message, but at least you get the truth without the addition of meaningless phrases designed only to place the company high above you – the customer. Here's another example:

> It has come to my attention that you find it absolutely essential to immediately acquire additional stock for the

purpose of expanding your place of business in the near future.

Due to the large quantity of business transacted by the city council, we most respectfully request that anyone wishing to insult the council please limit himself to 15 minutes or to 15 insults, whichever is shorter.

– Sign in office of Mayor Travis LaRue, Austin, Texas

This sounds as if the company hired a robot to write its letters. Try to avoid phrases such as "it has come to my attention" – it has been used so frequently that it lacks any power to catch a reader's interest. Cut out the stock phrases:

> I understand you need to purchase more stock right away so you can expand your company.

After writing a sentence such as this, you can offer your assistance in a friendly and sincere manner.

You can either substitute a short and sincere equivalent for a stock phrase or delete the stock phrase altogether. Here's a list of stock phrases to either delete or replace:

after much careful analysis, we decided	we decided
as a consequence of	because of…
as per our recent conversation	as we discussed on (date)
at the present time	now
at this point in time	now
come to a mutually satisfactory solution	agree
corrective action	(specify)
I am writing to inform you	(just give the message)
I have reason to believe	I believe
I will await your further instructions	(delete)
I would like to take this opportunity	I will
if it is agreed upon	if you agree
if this is not the case	if not
in as short a time as possible	as soon as possible
in consideration of your immediate reply	when you reply
in keeping with	consistent with
in light of the fact that	because
in point of fact	therefore
increasingly difficult	more difficult
it is quite evident that	(avoid)
it has been noted	(just give the message)
it has come to our/my attention	(just give the message)
more than happy	happy
much needed	appreciated, needed
mutually satisfactory	satisfactory, acceptable
needless to say	(so don't say it!)
nowhere to be seen	nowhere

on your behalf..for you
please be informed.................................(just give the message)
please feel free ....(just give the message)
pursuant to your recent inquiry ....as you requested...
rectify the situation................................(be specific)
utmost importance ....important
very near future ....soon
vital importance.....................................important
we are in receipt of your letter...............(obvious: delete)
we are not disposed to ....we will not
your earliest convenience ....(avoid)

EXERCISE 2

Sincerity

Replace linking verbs with action verbs and revise the following sentences to eliminate stock phrases, jargon and "big" words.

1. I would like to take the opportunity to meet with you at your earliest convenience so that we can discuss the problem and come to a mutually satisfactory solution.
2. Please be informed of a new product being brought on the market by our company.
3. I wish to address how the less than optimum operation of our business negatively impacts on our relations with customers and threatens to affect the level of our current output.
4. I conjecture that the enhancement of two-way communication between employees and management can lead to an augmented mutual understanding and a concurrent rise in overall productivity.
5. The downside to going forward with the renovations entails having to revamp our current filing system to accommodate the influx of materials from the other departments.

Refer to the Answer Key for suggested responses.

3. Simplicity

Proper words in proper places, make the true definition of style.
– *Jonathan Swift*

Difficult concepts require simple expression. A good writer slashes superfluous words to make even the most complex technical instructions easy to understand. You've already reduced your chances of slipping in superfluous words by striving to make your writing sincere. To achieve maximum simplicity, analyze each sentence you write to determine how you can use fewer words with more punch.

Repetition >

Use repetition very sparingly and only to make an important point. Do not waste your reader's time with sentences such as this:

> In consideration of your long and continuing service, I would like to bestow the award of this plaque on you to express my appreciation and gratitude.

Delete either "long" or "continuing" – they both mean virtually the same thing in this context. You can then replace the phrase "bestow an award" with "to award" because the verb "bestow" implies the giving of something and so sounds repetitious when combined with "award" and then "plaque". Finally, eliminate either "appreciation" or "gratitude". The sentence does not suffer from the removal of repetitious words:

> In consideration of your long service, I would like to award you this plaque to express my gratitude.

Now just turn the sentence around to remove the redundant phrase "in consideration of" (the award is obviously made for a reason):

> I would like to award you this plaque to express my gratitude for your long service.

You can avoid repetition by going easy on the adjectives and descriptive nouns. Use an adjective or descriptive noun if necessary, but don't over-qualify. For example:

> His skill and expertise gave the RRSP Department the inspiration and motivation it needed to increase its sales to an all time high.

"Skill and expertise" and "inspiration" and "motivation" have similar meanings. You don't need to describe the subject's qualifications with four words when two words will give the same meaning with more impact. By cutting out repetitive words and being specific, you can reduce this sentence from 23 words to 11 words:

> His expertise motivated the RRSP Department to increase sales by 39%.

If you find yourself writing one word and then following it closely by its synonym, stop and cut!

Expendable Words >

> Words are not crystal, transparent, and unchanged; they are the skin of living thoughts, and may vary greatly in color and content according to the circumstances and time in which they are used.
>
> – *Oliver Wendell Holmes*

You can easily remove expendable words by avoiding the stock phrases discussed in the section on Sincerity. Even if you succeed in deleting just one word per sentence in a two page letter, you have shortened your letter by approximately twenty words. Business readers will thank you. Here's an example of a sentence packed with expendable words:

> At the present time, we wish to inform you that our Customer Service Department is in the process of upgrading its capabilities to better serve your every need.

You can safely delete "at the present time" because it adds no information. The phrase "we wish to inform you" also adds little to the sentence – after all why say you plan to inform your reader? Just give the message. You can go on to cut out the padding words "is in the process of" and finish by slashing the word "every". No Customer Service Department can satisfy its customers' **every** need so why bother saying so? Here's the cut version:

> Our Customer Service Department is upgrading its capabilities to better serve your needs.

So far, the sentence has been reduced from 28 words to 13 words. Still more cutting is possible by substituting an action verb for the verb phrase "is upgrading" and turning the sentence around:

> The upgrading of the Customer Service Department will better serve your needs.

12 words. The sentence is clear and simple, but lacks punch. It requires specific details – the term upgrading means very little and "needs" is vague. How about:

> Our Customer Service Department now accepts your credit application at three new locations.

The sentence finally says something worth reading. Compare the revised version to the original:

> At the present time, we wish to inform you that our Customer Service Department is in the process of upgrading its capabilities to better serve your every need.

Which version would you rather read?

Be merciless with expendable words. If a word does not add meaning to a sentence, amputate! Your writing will improve and your readers will be grateful.

Note how the first sentence in each of the following pairs is long winded and woolly-minded compared with the concise sentence:

Expendable Words 1. Please be advised that your marketing strategy has met with considerable interest from the Committee members (16 words).

Simple Words 1. Your marketing strategy interested the Committee (6 words).

Expendable Words 2. Enclosed please find the information you required from us with regard to your proposed plan to prepare an analysis of the Carter account (23 words).

Simple Words 2. Here is the information you need to analyze the Carter account (11 words).

Expendable Words 3. Inasmuch as we appreciate the manner in which you approached the subject at hand, please be advised that your investigation does not meet our requirements at this time (28 words).

Simple Words 3. While we appreciate your approach, we cannot approve your investigation (10 words).

EXERCISE 3

Simplicity

The following sentences contain too many unnecessary words. Cut each sentence down to the word number specified.

1. The position of sales manager requires making the most effective use of your time during working hours by contributing to the maintenance of current sales and the diversification of new sales (31 words). Cut to *20* words or less.

   Sample Answer: As sales manager, you must effectively manage your time to maintain current sales and develop new sales (17 words).

2. The dates that we have you down for attending the seminar do not seem to correspond with when you indicated you were available when we talked last week (28 words). Cut to *18* words or less.

3. The kind of work that needs to be done in the Accounting Department is not complex but is very time consuming work, and since these tasks are not very complex, we could easily hire someone straight out of school to fill the position (43 words). Cut to *28* words or less.

4. The object of this newly formulated productivity system is to improve the productivity of the Production Department and to create increased profitability by improving the overall performance of the assembly line operators, the assembly line machinery maintenance operators, the training of all workers, and the implementation of Quality Control measures designed to improve the overall quality of the products currently being produced (62 words). Cut to *35* words or less.

5. At the present time, the Production Department is failing to operate at full capacity due to an inability on the part of the supervisors to effectively make sure employees arrive at their work on time (35 words). Cut to *24* words or less.

Refer to the Answer Key for sample responses.

4. *Elements of Style Review*

A good style must, first of all, be clear. It must not be mean or above the dignity of the subject. It must be appropriate.

– Aristotle

To develop a clear and pleasing style, decide exactly what you wish to say and then say it as concisely as possible. No one should be impressed by big words and long, complicated sentence structure.

Apply the **3S** treatment to your writing as follows:

Strength: Use action verbs and specific words. Do not make generalized statements such as "The seminar was interesting" if you wish to interest readers in your reports and letters. Instead, be concrete: "The Time Management seminar taught me how to schedule my day effectively."

Sincerity: Do not try to sound "business-like" by using stock phrases, jargon, and "big" words. Just as you would reject a phrase such as "I remain your most humble and obedient servant" because it is antiquated, so you should be wary of phrases such as "it has come to my attention" or "facilitate bringing this timeframe on line". If you cannot be sure of the meaning of a word or stock phrase, do not use it. Remember that your readers deserve clarity – not a vocabulary test.

Simplicity: Use as few words as possible to convey your meaning. You don't have to be abrupt, but you do want to avoid verbiage. For example, "I would like to say that I think we should take this opportunity to meet together to talk about strategies for upgrading our current unit of sales" uses 27 words to say: "Let's meet at 3 p.m. to talk about sales" (10 words). You can almost always find words to cut when you revise your documents. Think what your reader needs to know, not what you think you should write.

To develop your style further, go on to the Review Exercises.

Answer Key

EXERCISE 1
Strength

Replace all linking verbs with specific action verbs and use clear images to pump strength into the following weak sentences.

1. I am assured that you will agree the future benefits of taking on more personnel to handle this new contract will far outweigh the extra costs we'll have to pay.

   By spending approximately $50,000 per year for two new accountants to handle the Mason contract, we will gross an additional $350,000 over three years, and be able to accept more large contracts.

2. Mr. Aiken, our only word processing operator, is slowly falling behind in relaying sales orders, as he has many other tasks to perform, and having them confirmed on time so as to achieve our delivery goals.

   Mr. Aiken does not have time to relay sales orders and confirm them for delivery because he handles word processing for the whole company.

3. Because our company has grown greatly in the last few years, the production department is creating a lot of paperwork.

   The 45% growth in production since 1987 has resulted in a 60% increase in the amount of paperwork the production department must complete each year.

4. It is proposed that to take advantage of the Contract System we work at encouraging everyone involved to increase their contribution to the company in a way which is reinforcing the Contract System and is increasing the profitability of the company.

   We must encourage all employees to produce 20% more than last year to reinforce the Contract System and increase the company's profits.

5. Being new to the company, I have noticed that staff are not committed to their jobs, filing systems are disorganized, and clients are annoyed.

   Note: Give *specific* examples:

   As a new employee, I have noticed that staff take long coffee breaks, the filing systems do not contain last year's Financial Statements, and clients complain about constantly busy phones.

EXERCISE 2
Sincerity

Replace linking verbs with action verbs and revise the following sentences to eliminate stock phrases, jargon and "big" words.

1. I would like to take the opportunity to meet with you at your earliest convenience so that we can discuss the problem and come to a mutually satisfactory solution.

   Could we meet at 10 a.m. on Monday to discuss a solution to our cash flow problems?

2. Please be informed of a new product being brought on the market by our company.

   Take a look at our new Centaur Cellular Phone [or any specific product of your choice].

3. I wish to address how the less than optimum operation of our business negatively impacts on our relations with customers and threatens to affect the level of our current output.

   Note: Determine a situation that *demonstrates* what is wrong with the company. For example:

   One Sales Representative cannot handle all our customers and still give a high level of service.

4. I conjecture that the enhancement of two-way communication between employees and management can lead to an augmented mutual understanding and a concurrent rise in overall productivity.

   If employees and management discuss their mutual concerns, productivity will probably increase.

5. The downside to going forward with the renovations entails having to revamp our current filing system to accommodate the influx of materials from the other departments.

   If we continue the renovations, we must re-organize our filing system to include materials from the other departments.

EXERCISE 3
Simplicity

The following sentences contain too many unnecessary words. Cut each sentence down to the word number specified.

1. The position of sales manager requires making the most effective use of your time during working hours by contributing to the maintenance of current sales and the diversification of new sales (31 words). Cut to *20* words or less.

   Sample Answer: *As sales manager, you must effectively manage your time to maintain current sales and develop new sales* (17 words).

2. The dates that we have you down for attending the seminar do not seem to correspond with when you indicated you were available when we talked last week (28 words). Cut to *18* words or less.

   Please confirm your availability for either the March 18-24 seminar or the April 10-16 seminar (17 words).

3. The kind of work that needs to be done in the Accounting Department is not complex but is very time consuming work, and since these tasks are not very complex, we could easily hire someone straight out of school to fill the position (43 words). Cut to *30* words or less.

   Because the tasks required to fill the position of Junior Clerk in the Accounting Department are simple but time consuming, we could hire a recent high school graduate (28 words).

4. The object of this newly formulated productivity system is to improve the productivity of the Production Department and to create increased profitability by improving the overall performance of the assembly line operators, the assembly line machinery maintenance operators, the training of all workers, and the implementation of Quality Control measures designed to improve the overall quality of the products currently being produced (62 words). Cut to *35* words or less.

   The new productivity system will increase profits by improving the performance of the assembly line and machinery maintenance operators, training all workers, and implementing Quality Control measures to monitor production (30 words).

5. At the present time, the Production Department is failing to operate at full capacity due to an inability on the part of the supervisors to effectively make sure employees arrive at their work on time (35 words). Cut to *24* words or less.

   The Production Department operates at less than full capacity because the supervisors do not ensure employees arrive at work on time (21 words).

Review Exercises

Test your understanding of Unit Ten with the following exercises. Refer to the *Better Business Writing Answer Key* or your instructor for sample responses.

EXERCISE 1

Strength

Replace all linking verbs with specific action verbs and use clear images to strengthen the following weak sentences.

1. You will find our new "Rainpulse" showerhead gives you great showers and lets you save money on hot water.
2. A concern has been expressed to me that you have been absent without reason on far too many occasions.
3. Where additional staffing is needed, the Personnel Department will be permitted by the administrator to allow temporary increased staffing to help with the increase of the workload.
4. Very many of the less efficient companies went out of business and there was a lot of unemployment.
5. One of the things which we find missing in your system is strong and clear direction from management of what they want done.
6. By hiring a new secretary, our paperwork will be completed quicker, enabling more accurate and up to date accounting records to be kept.
7. The financial statements gave some indication of being important for deciding how to carry on in the future.
8. As you stated in your letter, you had some kind of problem with one of our products.
9. The most interesting thing about our new line of camping gear is that they really stand up to lots of wear and tear.
10. The Administrative Assistant talked about the proposal at the meeting.

11. Because the fax machine isn't working very well, we aren't getting some of our letters out on time.

12. The new schedule is easy to follow so that Staff are now able to work in a productive manner by using the new schedule which is so easy to follow.

13. We are hoping you will find our new line of ski wear to be of high quality and easy to wear.

14. There are many ways in which we could think of approaching the issue of whether or not we should be handling more new business.

15. The vice-president has given his opinion to the committee regarding what he thinks should be done about hiring a new accountant.

16. After looking for two days at my proposal about how we should increase our services, the Accounts Manager is sure that it will help get more clients.

17. Although you are unable to attend the conference at this time, I am hoping that you will be able to come to the next conference and present your paper on Effective Management.

18. There is a feeling among the employees that our company should be making more of an effort to make available access to a nearby day care facility.

19. I am finding it is difficult to settle how my company should be proceeding regarding its setting up of a new franchise operation in your area.

20. While you are qualified for the advertised position, I have to turn down your application at this time.

EXERCISE 2

Sincerity

Replace all linking verbs with action verbs and revise the following sentences to eliminate stock phrases, jargon and "big" words.

1. In keeping with our resolutions regarding the initiation of strategies to elevate employee efficiency, we have decided that appropriate systems and frameworks will be instituted to find ways in which we can utilize technological developments in the interests

of better promulgating the service and standards our company is justly famous for.

2. I would be willing to use some of my time to liaise with the printing company to maximize the securing of a cost-efficient contract and, in order to ensure we get the contract onstream in the immediate future, I would be willing to work a reasonable amount of overtime hours.

3. I would be more than happy to discuss the recent downturn in sales with you as soon as is convenient.

4. As per our recent phone conversation, I thank you for considering Vacations Unlimited as the travel agent of choice to satisfy all your needs.

5. Should you be obliged to continue as the sales manager of 5 Star Inc., I look forward to meeting with you on September 30 to review the improvements your presence will have made within sales.

6. Over the remaining three weeks of our work to be completed on the Connor account, Max Turner and I will firm up our recommendations for the coming year and ascertain the equipment which we require to fulfill our obligations at the present time.

7. The Multi Corporation Declaration on Productivity resolved that the current productivity drive should be accelerated with greater dynamism and perseverance based on the principles of cost control maintenance and modifying current procurement methods.

8. Globalization of human cooperation for the attainment of technological solutions to environmental concerns should be promoted to ensure the efficient world-wide cross-fertilization of ways and means.

9. The several years of work-related experience I have been fortunate enough to obtain through my liaison with charity groups has given me cause to reflect upon my current commitment to the parameters of my current employment situation.

10. George Walen proposed that we reconsider our commitment to realizing a meaningful dialogue with our employees in light of the fact that they

have expressly refused to schedule their meeting to come online with our expressed timeframe.

11. With regard to public perception of our company, I truly believe that implementation of the recommendations contained herein will ensure the enhancement of our prominence in leading the competition as the company most determined to confront and surmount the challenges of the future.

12. At this point in time, I am more than willing to consider any reasonable rationalizations you can offer that may appear to justify the current marginal performance with respect to your ability to encourage a meaningful dialogue with the relevant personages regarding their approval of our project.

13. I am writing to you to ascertain if it is quite evident that the aggregate sum of our losses at this juncture necessitates corrective action in the very near future.

14. I suggest that we allocate a modicum of funds to canvassing clients who do not sufficiently utilize our services at this point in time.

15. Mr. Jones has acceded to the proposal that it would be most equitable if he was remunerated with a stipend of $10,000 per week.

16. I will endeavour to disseminate the required information in as short a time as possible.

17. The new Accounts Manager has a penchant for making modifications that will consolidate the Accounting and Sales Departments.

18. We will take great pains to fill your order so as to allay any concerns you may feel regarding our current dearth of funds.

19. We have noted that your answer in the affirmative indicates your definitive opinion with regards to our procurement of a new office tower.

20. If you do not shortly curtail your frequent tardiness, we will have to sanction severe repercussions and may even terminate your employment.

EXERCISE 3

Simplicity

The following sentences contain too many unnecessary words. Cut each sentence down to the word number specified.

1. It is recommended that if the measured results show that our proposal has not been adopted by Saltsea Inc., that the proposal be revised and modified (26 words). Cut to *15* words or less.

2. XYZ Company Ltd. has realized very marked success in the field of financial management planning (15 words). Cut to *10* words or less.

3. By making the addition of more clerical staff to our company, I am sure that you will take notice of the increased efficiency brought about by better organization of the office (31 words). Cut to *10* words or less.

4. The first and foremost reason why we need a new full-time secretary is that the clerical work in my department is not being completed (25 words). Cut to *15* words or less.

5. Unfortunately, I am not totally clear what the status of the extra paper requirements is in the current ordering situation (21 words). Cut to *12* words or less.

6. Where we do have a problem is that we lack those items which you specified ordering last year and which I understand you have just requested again through Purchasing, namely those items marked with an asterisk on the Requisition #129 (40 words). Cut to *15* words or less.

7. It is most essential that we spend as much time as is possible going over the financial statements to determine if we are able to think in terms of expanding our company in the fiscal year that is approaching (39 words). Cut to *20* words or less.

8. The new vice-president made his proposal for taking advantage of the upcoming seminar on November 10 to present not only the value of our current time-management programs but also the need our

clients have expressed for wanting proper grounding in the necessary management-related skills and the use of management systems (53 words). Cut to *30* words or less.

9. The concept of corporate responsibility means corporations have a much more comprehensive responsibility for their actions than individual employees of a company in any capacity such as that of a director, manager, accountant, secretary, or janitor have for their actions (40 words). Cut to *20* words or less.

10. It has been brought to my attention that you have been requesting a refund for a total of $35.00 for an item you purchased from us sometime in the past three weeks (33 words). Cut to *18* words or less.

11. With respect to the well-being of our company, it is in our best interest to make progress in the following areas: updating the filing system used at the present time, motivating staff members to increase the unit of their productivity, and purchase a new telephone system to replace the one we are currently using (55 words). Cut to *25* words or less.

12. In consideration of the research I have attempted with regards to the subject matter of the report contained herein, I would first like to state that I had a few problems regarding how I was to structure the data so as to relay the maximum amount while still keeping the report more or less ten pages in length (58 words). Cut to *30* words or less.

13. If every individual on the staff is specifically provided with certain tasks to perform, each person could concentrate on his own responsibility, and thus increase efficiency and productivity; however, if overlapping duties were to occur, not only would it decrease productivity and efficiency, overall frustration among the staff over "what to do" and "how to do it" would increase conflict among the employees which then could also affect the way clients are handled (74 words). Cut to *30* words or less.

14. A variety of your customers will appreciate being able to take advantage of this incredible and out-

standing offer of three brand new calculators for the low low price of only two calculators, which comes to $44.95 plus tax (42 words). Cut to *25* words or less.

15. In view of the fact that you have not made any payments on your account for over three months since March 17, I am now in the position to inform you that you will be required to pay the amount of $36.87 by June 10 or else your delinquent and seriously overdue account will be forwarded to a collection agency (61 words). Cut to *25* words or less.

16. The computer revolution has had repercussions all the way from the small business based in the home to the large and powerful corporation which may purchase hundreds, maybe even thousands, of computers each and every year as new technological advancements and improvements continue to come up with ways of using computers to better enhance the performance and productivity of employees and managers alike (63 words). Cut to *30* words or less.

17. I wish to propose in this report that XYZ Company consider possibly making the purchase of a small, but compact manufacturing plant that manufactures bicycle parts in order to augment the company's current levels of inventory by ensuring a constant supply of bicycle parts (44 words). Cut to *25* words or less.

18. Moreover, it is to be expected that there are a multitude of options to be considered when starting a business such as ours in deference to the fact that there is currently intense and strong competition that at present is threatening to overwhelm all our many attempts to secure a corner of the computer repair market as it now stands (60 words). Cut to *20* words or less.

19. I'm very much afraid that I am required to question the recommendations you made in your recent report on the need to expand our client base because I am more than worried that the products we offer at this point in time will not really appeal to more clients than we are currently servicing (54 words). Cut to *35* words or less.

20. It is my considered opinion that we should very seriously consider making a cost-effective and profitable bid to secure for our company the contract to renovate the local apartment block located in the vicinity of City Park (38 words). Cut to *20* words or less.

UNIT ELEVEN

Organize Your Reports

Unit Eleven will introduce you to the "McKeown (Mac's) Method" of organizing larger-scale writing projects such as procedures manuals and reports. Mac's Method consists of six main steps:

1. Construct the Core Sentence.
2. Write the Outline.
3. Collect information on Cue Cards.
4. Write your first draft without pausing.
5. Perform a final edit of the text.
6. Insert appropriate graphics.

To implement Mac's Method's unique six-step approach to report writing, you must construct a perfect plan *before* you collect data. By making such a plan, you will cut your report writing time dramatically. You will also turn out *perfectly organized* reports – a phenomena seen as rarely as roses in the snow. Once you understand how to *organize* your reports, you can set to work *presenting* your reports in a standard format – the topic of Unit Twelve.

Introduction

Reports range in length from a two-page accident report to a ten-page financial report to a two-thousand page analytical report. Each type of report calls for a different emphasis. If you want comprehensive, detailed information about how to write a particular kind of report, take a look at specialized handbooks such as Ingrid Brunner's *The Technician as Writer: Preparing Technical Reports* (Indianapolis: Bobbs-Merrill, 1983).

Despite their differing lengths, however, all reports require *clear organization*. Finding the right order for an immense amount of data provides the central challenge in most reports. You can easily meet this challenge by using the "systems approach" described in this chapter.

What Is A Report? >

You write a report when you wish to communicate information you have acquired to someone who needs to use that information. You incorporate the following three characteristics into your report:

1 Considerable research,
2 Greater complexity than the letter or memorandum,
3 Meticulous organization.

Your finished report presents and evaluates the *results* of your investigation and research. Your report does **not** merely explore or describe – it accomplishes the *purpose* you establish in the first paragraph.

Of course, you may not know your exact destination when you begin thinking about writing a report. However, by the time you begin to write you must know *exactly* where you will finish. By separating the idea of research from the idea of writing, you can remove all excuses for poor organization of written work. When you know the answer to a question, you can organize your writing to lead your reader clearly to the same conclusion.

An analogy with the growth of a tree may help you to understand the relationship between each of the three preliminary steps in writing a report.

Mac's Method of Report Writing

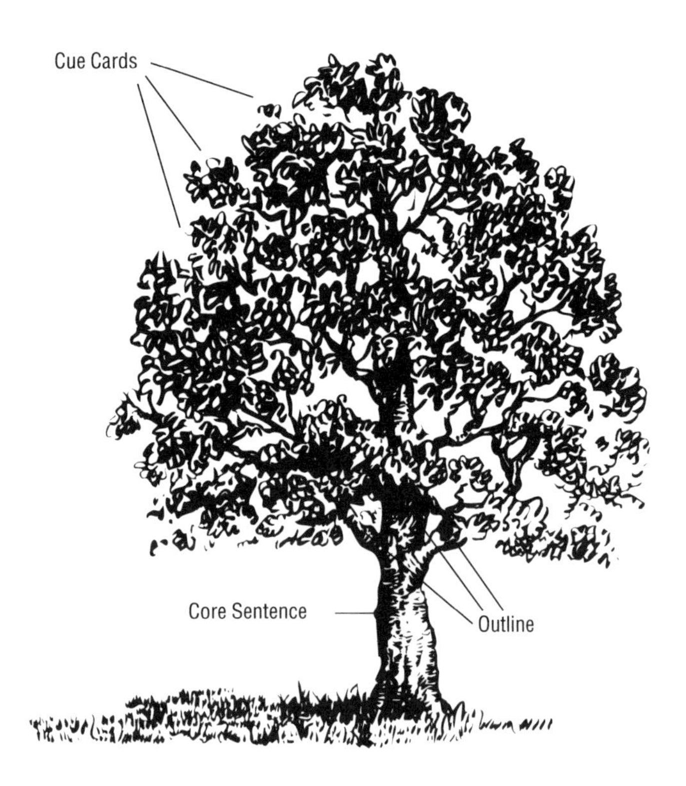

Like the trunk of a tree, the Core Sentence provides the main supporting structure for the report. The Outline, like the major branches of the tree, comes next and determines the direction and the extent of the information covered by the report. Finally, the Cue Cards contain the individual facts clustered under the generalized Outline and resemble the individual leaves on the tree's main branches.

Once you have completed these three stages, your basic organization is complete. The remaining three stages: writing, editing, and inserting graphics, follow quickly and easily. Because the organizational quality of your finished report depends upon the preliminary work, you need to give it your most careful attention.

1. *The Core Sentence*

As a first step in writing any report, Mac's Method requires a Core Sentence. If you write this Core Sentence properly, you will ensure that your report accomplishes exactly what you want it to, and not wander off track. The significance of the Core Sentence lies in the fact that every good report expresses a single major theme or focus. You can express this central intention in a single "one main idea" sentence. Compare the process to focusing a camera carefully *before* you take a picture. The more care you take, the sharper and clearer will be your picture.

Structure of the Core Sentence >

The core sentence presents six carefully sequenced "compartments" in an invariable order:

1 Subject,
2 Verb,
3 Object,
4 A linking phrase,
5 A numeral,
6 The names of the major divisions of the report, in the order in which they will appear in the text.

Here's an example of a core sentence:

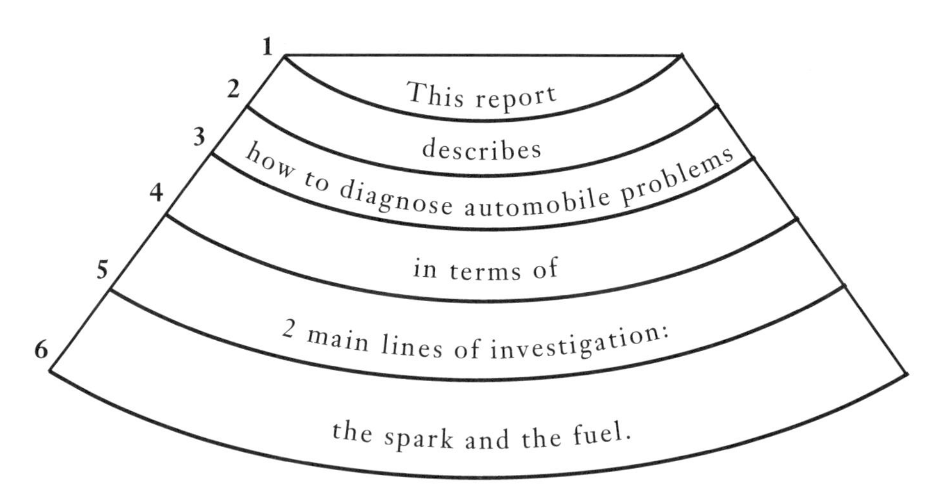

The numbers in the above example correspond to the following components within the core sentence:

1 The *grammatical* subject: "This report".

2 A specific action verb in the present tense: "lists, compares, contrasts, describes". Avoid vague verb phrases such as "is about" or "deals with".

3 An object-noun, or noun-phrase, that describes the general topic of the report: "how to diagnose automobile problems".

4 A linking phrase such as "in terms of," "with regard to," or "composed of".

5 A number (usually 2 or 3 and sometimes 4, 5, or 6) that stands for the number of major divisions covered by the report. Eighty percent of all reports have either two or three major divisions.

6 The names of the major components listed in the order in which they will appear as sections of the report.

If may seem odd to write this core sentence before you have done any research. However, you can find out enough about the topic of your planned research to decide which major components you must cover without running the risk of being submerged by details.

Benefits of the Core Sentence Approach

Writing a core sentence prevents you from wasting time researching material you will never incorporate into your report. Understanding this will save you hundreds of hours of research and is the most valuable lesson you can ever learn about writing reports. Remember, the core sentence guides *you*, not your reader. It focusses your attention on the bull's eye of the target: your report's central idea.

Because of its central importance, be sure to write the core sentence for every report exactly as recommended. If you omit any one of the six categories or change the order of the form or add anything, you depart from the systems approach. The core sentence must be sparse, with no redundant words. It avoids persuasive, advertising language; it shuns humour and ornament. It puts your thinking exactly on target so that you reach your destination (the completed report) as quickly as possible. This approach ensures consistency and excellence.

The core sentence must take time to construct if it is to work. The hardest decisions you make when writing any report are how to organize the material, and what material to exclude. You should spend 25% of the time allotted to writing the report simply writing and testing this one sentence – so experiment until you get it right.

EXERCISE 1

Writing a Core Sentence

Write a core sentence for a report describing entertainment options in your city. Begin with the subject, "This report". Continue with the verb, "describes". Now choose two or three options that you wish to describe in the body of your report.

Refer to the Answer Key for a suggested version.

Other Uses for the Core Sentence

Although the core sentence works well with long, complex reports, you can also use it for other jobs. For example, you can use it to define what you mean to say in a memo. Simply begin:

> This memo lists safety hazards on the plant floor in terms of 4 contributing causes: (list causes).

Also, you can use the core sentence to pre-determine what you intend to say in a letter:

> This letter answers the concern about chemical spills in terms of three safety measures:...

Similarly, use the core sentence to plan a schedule:

> This plan divides Marketing sales targets into three time categories: pre-production, production, and post-production.

The core sentence uses analysis to solve problems: your imagination can apply it to help solve any analytical task.

2. *The Outline*

After writing the core sentence, you create an Outline. The Outline takes up a single sheet of notepaper, and consists of headings and sub-headings which briefly indicate the topic you will write about at each successive stage of the report.

Purpose of the Outline >

The Outline provides an economical guide for your thought and your research. Like the core sentence, it primarily serves the writer of the report – *not* the reader. Its left-brain function is to order thought throughout the report in a logical and natural way. By referring to the outline, you can spot any detour in your thinking *before* you write, rather than *after* you finish the report.

Page Layout for the Outline >

This section demonstrates the kind of outline most commonly used. Notice that the major headings use capital letters, while the sub-headings use only initial capital letters. Notice, too, that the left margin of the sub-headings is indented 5 spaces from the margin of the major headings. This consistent patterning allows you to quickly spot inconsistencies. For example, each heading or sub-heading must have a partner: you cannot usefully divide a section into a single sub-section, since this would not indicate the split of a generalized section into smaller units. Also, such a formalized layout makes it easy to compare headings of the same importance, since they all will have the same left margin. If they exhibit parallelism, you will likely have divided the major section into logical subunits.

***Sample Outline* >**

Here is a sample outline for a report on how to get a job. The core sentence for the report is: *This report describes how to get a job in terms of three principal methods: answering advertisments, making direct calls, and networking with people in related fields*.

From this core sentence, you can generate the following outline before you spend any time on researching:

INTRODUCTION: THE JOB MARKET 1
  Determining Your Field 1
  Understanding Your Qualifications 2

I. ANSWERING ADVERTISEMENTS 3
  A. Sources 3
    1. Newspapers 4
    2. Company Newsletters 4
  B. Suggested Method 4
    1. Application Letter 5
    2. Personal Contact 5

II. MAKING DIRECT CALLS 6
  A. Whom to Call 6
    1. Large Corporations 7
    2. Small Companies 7
  B. Suggested Approach 8
    1. Introducing Yourself 8
    2. Suggesting an Interview 9

III. NETWORKING 10
  A. Sources 10
    1. Networking Organizations 11
    2. Conferences 11
  B. Suggested Approach
    1. Finding the Right People 12
    2. Putting Yourself Forward 13

CONCLUSION 14

The above outline gives you a roadmap. If you follow it carefully, you will avoid making wrong turns that waste time.

Limitations of the Outline >

When arranging major headings, sub-headings, and sub-sub-headings, it is important to know when to stop. In general, even the smallest level of heading indicates that three to six facts can be grouped under it. If you write an outline for one- or two-page reports, you may wish to include single facts as headings. For longer reports, however, you keep splitting categories until you find you have gone far enough for your purpose – then you back up and erase headings until you find a level at which the heading incorporates the required three to six facts.

Other Uses for the Outline >

The major additional advantage to the Outline is that it allows you to gain approval for the extent and coverage of your report before you write it. If your manager approves the purpose of your report as indicated in the core sentence, likes the names and order of the major divisions of the report as they appear in the outline, and approves the sequence of small details as they appear in the sub-headings of the report, then you can write the report in reasonable confidence that its final structure will be approved without revision. Obtain your manager's initialled approval of the draft outline. Make changes at this point and save yourself hours writing a report that will not be approved because it is off-topic, and save your manager countless hours waiting to see your final version.

Other Benefits >

Your Outline serves three other purposes.

1 Use it to write the agenda for meetings – gaining pre-approval in the way mentioned above.

2 Use it to structure in-class essay questions. In this case, you do not use Cue Cards because of time pressures, but the outline will structure your essay and thus give it added quality.

3 Use it to structure essays for outside courses at college or university, such as business management courses. You will find that the outline approach yields superior results.

EXERCISE ***2***

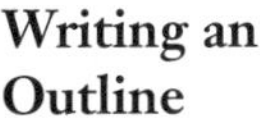

Writing an Outline

Generate an outline for the report described by your core sentence in Exercise 1. Include major headings, sub-headings, and sub-sub-headings. Think carefully about entertainment options in your city and choose only those aspects which you feel would contribute to an interesting and informative report. Check your version with the Answer Key.

3. *Cue Cards*

Cue Cards are 5" x 3" index cards on which you collect your factual information, guided by your outline. They normally include only one fact; in practice, this means one sentence. Under no circumstances write on the back of the card because this practice slows the final ordering.

Example of a Cue Card

Here's a Cue Card that could be written for the report on entertainment options in your city:

> II A 1. Symphony
>
> Our city's Symphony Orchestra performs three times a week from October to April and presents special outdoor concerts during the summer.

Note: The reference numbers in the upper left corner on the cue card correspond to the outline provided in the Answer Key.

> Get your facts first, and then you can distort them as much as you please.
>
> – *Mark Twain*

Leave blank space on the card surrounding the idea; this space acts like the frame on an oil painting, isolating it to aid observation and criticism. If every individual fact passes this scrutiny, your report will be reliable in every detail.

The most tedious part of writing a report is compiling the Cue Cards, so restrict their use to longer reports (over four pages in length), where you cannot expect to hold large numbers of facts in your head for long periods of time. Use 3" x 5" cards rather than cut pieces of paper, for the latter tend to blow away the minute the Office Manager runs past your desk. Pieces of paper also cannot be stored in card files, and will crumple with constant use.

Other Uses for Cue Cards

Cue Cards help create order when you use a dictaphone. They also provide excellent reference materials for short verbal reports to small or large groups. By combining the use of Cue Cards with right-brain techniques you can use pictures instead of words on your cards – as Mark Twain did when lecturing.

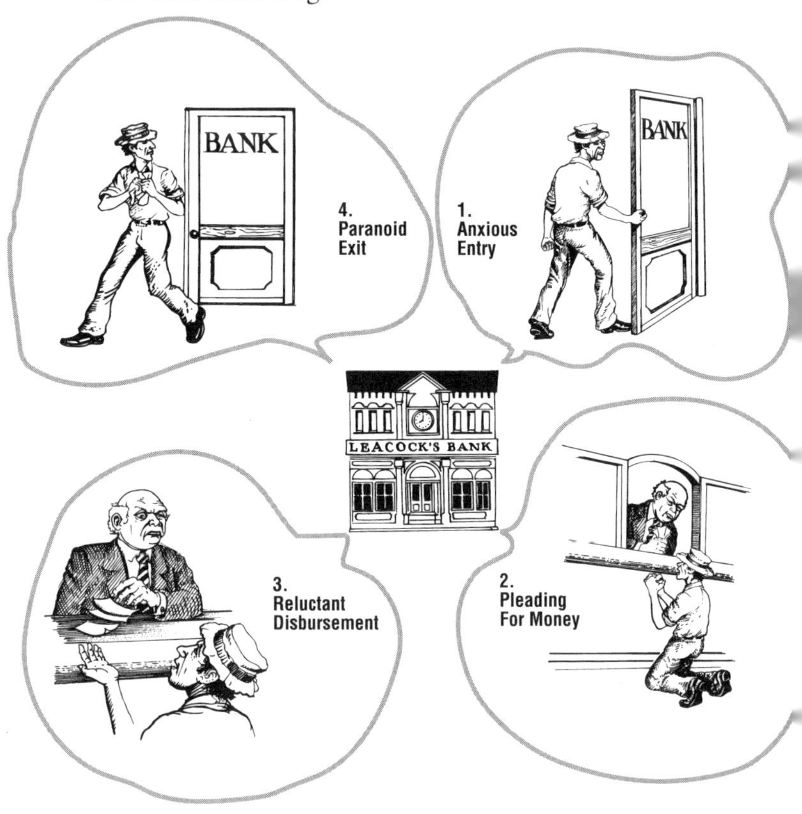

Updating Reports

If you expect to update a report annually, as is the case with performance reports or quality control reports, you will find that your previous year's file of Cue Cards can be re-used, with only minimal updating. In essence, your file provides an individualized encyclopedia that will grow in usefulness as it grows in size. The principle is the same as that of using stock phrases stored on a word processor, except that the phrases express your individual personality and match your own needs.

4. Non-Stop Writing

In composing, as a general rule, run your pen through every other word you have written; you have no idea what vigor it will give to your style.
– *Sydney Smith*

The major problem with the writing stage occurs when, after writing the first paragraph, you go back to revise – and three hours later are still perfecting the first paragraph. This is the stage where you lose most time. Consequently, get in the habit of using the non-stop method of writing. The more challenging you find it, the more you will benefit. Attempt to reach that harmonious flow of ideas which provides coherence and personality to writing. Here is where the labour of compiling Cue Cards repays itself many times over. If you have completed them correctly, you will experience a sense of confidence and elation. Fling the cards off your desk as you write (make sure they're cross-referenced to your outline!) and enjoy the process.

Remember that your practice in writing power sentences and power paragraphs in Units One and Two, your knowledge of grammar and mechanics gained from Units Three and Four, and your style development work in Unit Ten will serve you well when you write your draft. Keep to the active voice, use direct and specific words, apply the *3S* treatment, and strive to make each sentence follow logically from the previous one.

5. Editing

Editing for Grammar >

Make a quick check for clear sentences, specific language, and correct spelling. Of course, if you pre-edited your Cue Cards perfectly, this check will reveal no flaws, except in the case of those transitional markers and phrases that link paragraphs.

Checking Your Conclusions >

Read the entire report, then check to ensure that the introduction and conclusions relate clearly to the body of the report. Remember that conclusions sum up the facts contained in the report, while recommendations provide your ideas for acting on the total meaning of the report. The more solid the facts in your report, the more favourably your readers will look on your recommendations. In Unit Twelve you will learn more about how to present your recommendations and conclusions.

6. *Incorporating Visuals*

Where possible, put graphs and charts next to the text they illustrate. If the visual takes up one fourth of the page or less, consider placing it within the body of the written page. If it is a page in size, put it immediately after the first page of prose referring to it. Put visuals in the appendix *only* if they are merely back-up material, and not useful in clarifying or simplifying information.

You can use a number of different visual components to add style and readability to reports: tables, line charts, bar charts (horizontal and vertical), pie charts, flow charts, schematic diagrams, and pictograms.

Tables >

Tables save time by presenting large blocks of quantitative information in rows and columns, without the connecting threads of prose. Notice that the side captions and figures read sideways to the information in the rows to their right. The headings, however, direct attention to the information in all the lines directly below.

Introduce your table with a short descriptive sentence that informs your readers what to look for.

> Production costs dropped significantly from September to October as follows:

TABLE I

Production Area	*September Costs*	*October Costs*	*Decrease*
Printing	$ 11,659	$ 6,553	$ 5,106
Word Processing	33,962	25,491	8,471
Typesetting	60,591	58,636	1,955
Totals	106,212	90,680	15,532

Line Charts >

Use line charts to plot trends or relationships over time, on an arithmetical grid. Plot time on the horizonal axis; plot the values of the series on the vertical axis.

Take care not to distort the relative proportions of the horizontal and vertical scales. Obviously, by expanding one scale and contracting the other, you can convey incorrect impressions. For example, data plotted on a line chart with time intervals one sixteenth of an inch apart will show more pronounced fluctuations than the same data plotted on a chart with intervals half an inch apart. Also, be careful not to rely solely on colour to distinguish two lines if your report will be duplicated in black ink numerous times – use dashes or dots to individualize lines as well.

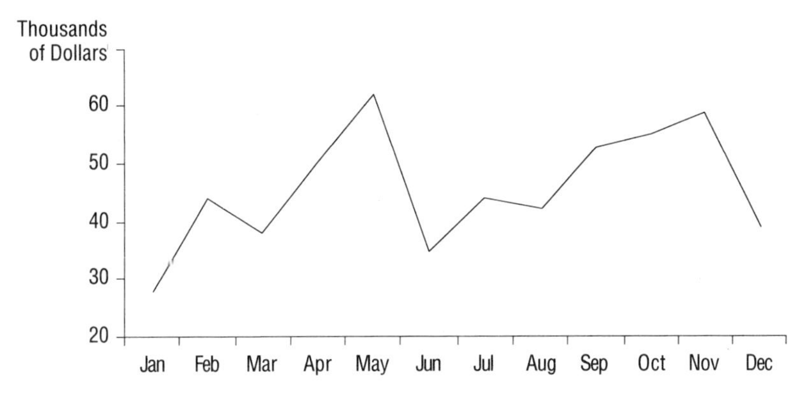

Sales volume, by month, for Jansen Industries, 19X6

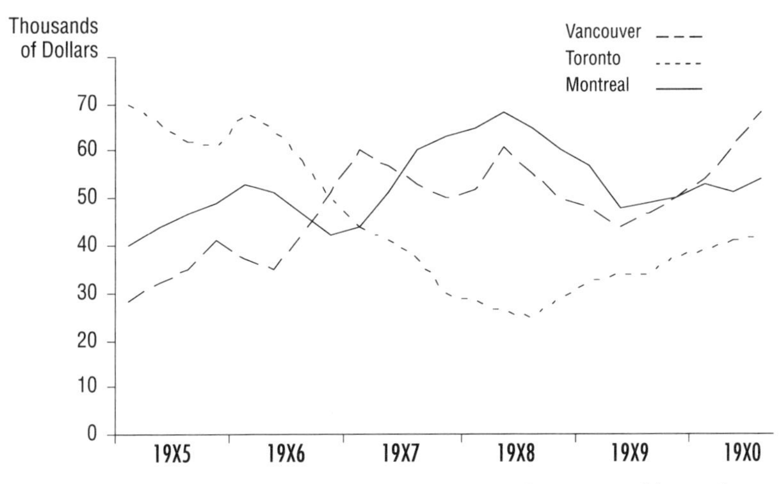

Sales of Vancouver, Toronto and Montreal branches, Jansen Industries, 19X6 to 19X0

Bar Charts

Use horizontal bars to indicate quantities of time, length, or distance. Use vertical bar charts to report numbers, heights, or depths.

December
10,500
November
14,600
October
16,100
September
16,300
August
23,500
0
5,000
10,000
15,000
20,000
25,000

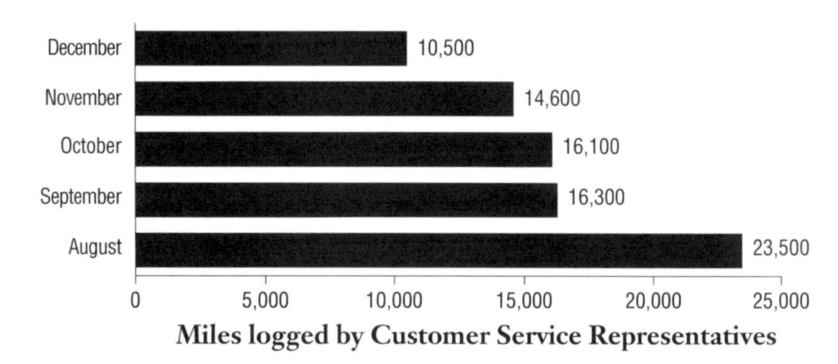

Miles logged by Customer Service Representatives

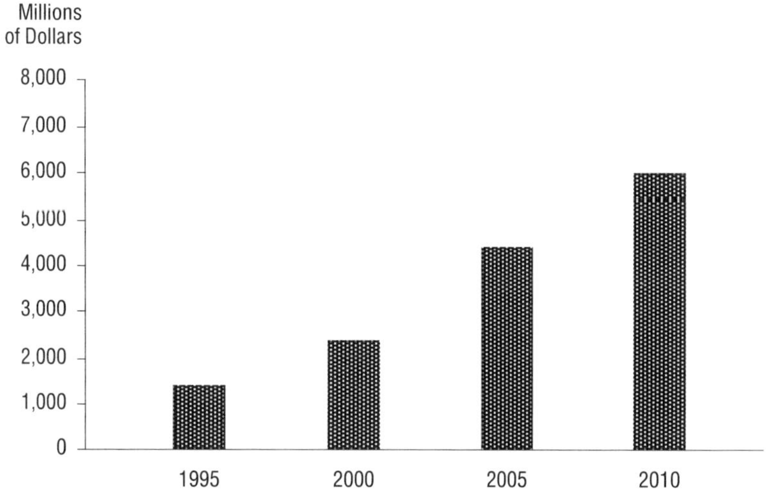

Millions of Dollars
8,000
7,000
6,000
5,000
4,000
3,000
2,000
1,000
0
1995
2000
2005
2010

Projected sales: 1995 to 2010

Pie Charts >

Pie charts show segments as slices sized according to the percentages of the whole: all parts combined make up 100%. Begin at 12:00 o'clock with the largest sector, and subdivide the circle progressively into smaller parts, moving clockwise. Do not use the pie chart for more than six items, because it becomes too difficult to read easily.

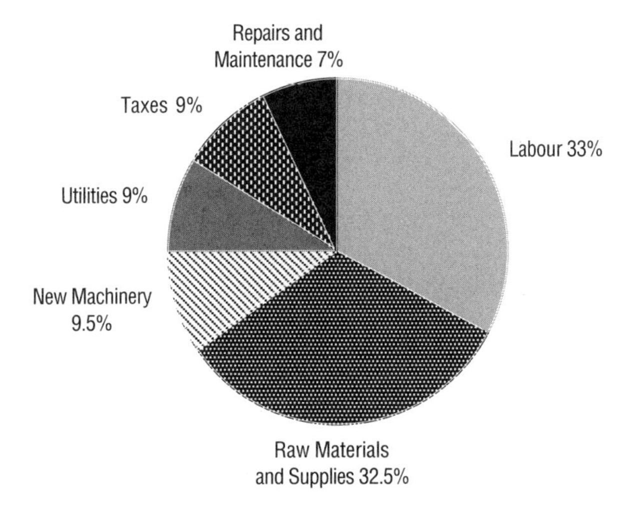

**Operating Costs Breakdown,
New Administrative Centre**

Flow Charts

The flow chart simply indicates movement through time. Rectangles denote actions; diamonds indicate decisions.

Process of Report Writing

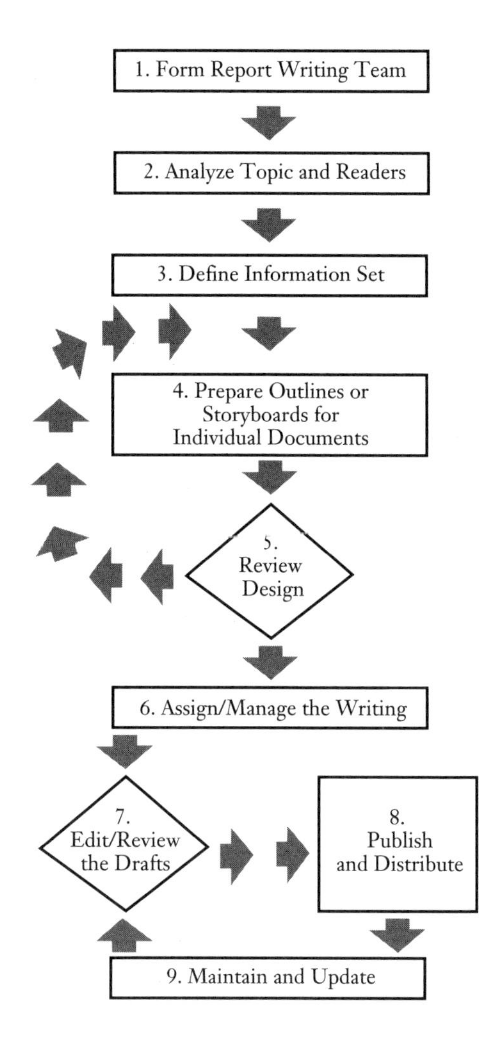

Schematic Diagrams > Clearly label and caption schematic diagrams for maximum usefulness. Put them as close as possible to the text they illustrate, and strive for simplicity.

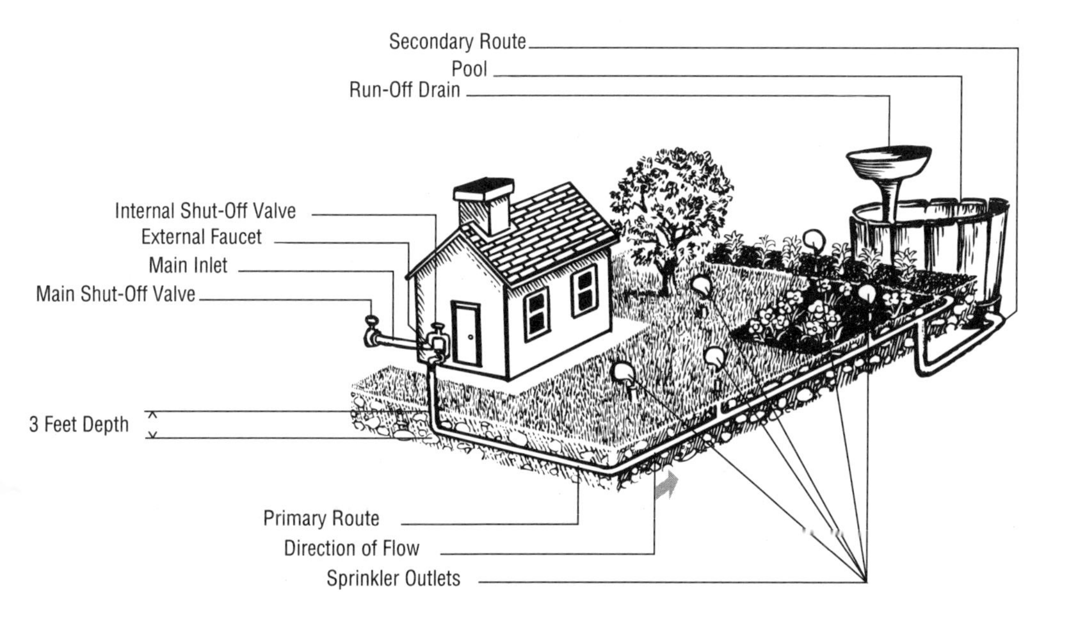

Landscape Design: Sprinkler System

Pictograms

Use pictograms to illustrate numerical relationships in an easy-to-understand format.

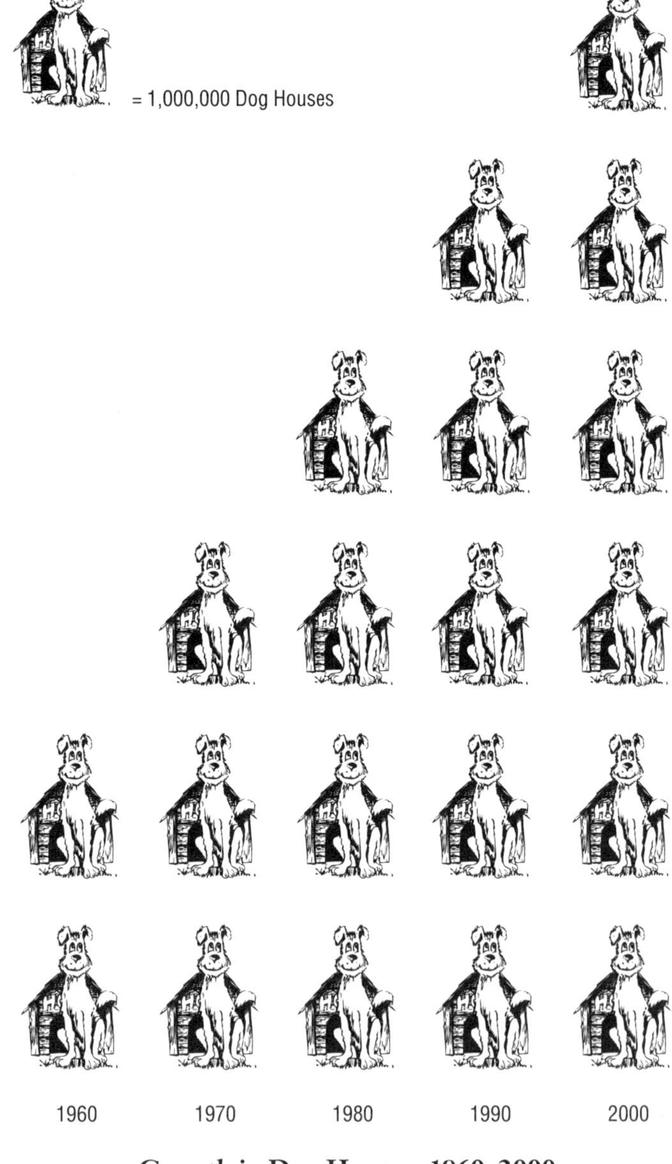

Growth in Dog Houses, 1960–2000.

How To Organize Reports: Review

In Unit Eleven, you learned how to quickly and efficiently organize your report writing tasks. As you progress in your business career, your ability to write a clear report will increase your chances of success. If you remember *first* how to write an effective core sentence and *second* how to develop an efficient outline, you will find the remaining report writing tasks flow smoothly. The important thing is not to be daunted by the prospect of writing a report. Break it into manageable units as discussed in Unit Eleven and you will find much of the anxiety associated with report writing disappears.

Now all you need to learn is how to use an acceptable business format to make your reports look appealing – the topic of Unit Twelve.

Answer Key

EXERCISE 1
The Core Sentence

You were asked to write a core sentence for a report describing entertainment options in your city. Here's a suggested version:

SUBJECT:	This report
VERB:	describes
OBJECT:	entertainment options in Vancouver
LINKING PHRASE:	in terms of
NUMERAL:	two main activities:
NAMES OF MAJOR DIVISIONS:	sports and culture.

EXERCISE 2
Writing an Outline

Using the Core Sentence you generated in Exercise 1, your outline may look something like this:

INTRODUCTION: ENTERTAINMENT OPTIONS
Experience Vancouver

I. SPORTS
- A. DESCRIPTION OF TYPES OF SPORTS ACTIVITIES
  1. Spectator Sports
  2. Public Recreation Centres
  3. Fitness Clubs
- B. BENEFITS
  1. Social Benefits
  2. Physical Benefits

II. CULTURE
- A. DESCRIPTION OF TYPES OF CULTURAL ACTIVITIES
  1. Classical Music: symphony, opera
  2. Theatre
  3. Multi-cultural Festivals
- B. BENEFITS
  1. Social Benefits
  2. Psychological/Intellectual Benefits

SUMMARY
How taking advantage of entertainment options in Vancouver can enrich the visitor's enjoyment of the city.

Review Exercises

EXERCISE 1

Core Sentence

Use the correct format to write a core sentence for each of the following report topics.

1. How to pass exams.
2. The advantages and disadvantages of self-employment.
3. The need for good writing skills in business.
4. Why the college should change from a two semester academic year to a three semester academic year.
5. How to choose a computer system.

EXERCISE 2

Outlining

Write an outline for each of the core sentences you wrote in Exercise 1 above.

Check your answers with the suggested responses in the *Better Business Writing Answer Key* or consult with your instructor.

UNIT TWELVE

How To Make Reports Look Appealing

In Unit Eleven you learned how to write a core sentence, prepare your outline, complete your research, and write your report. In Unit Twelve you will learn how to present your report in a standard format. To do this, you need to understand how to prepare the following three report levels:

1. Preliminary Parts
2. Body of the Report
3. Supplementary Parts.

At the end of Unit Twelve, you will write the components of a typical business report. In Unit Thirteen, you will learn how to use word processing techniques to help you write, and then complete *Better Business Writing* in Unit Fourteen by Checking Your Achievement with a multiple choice test to review all that you have learned.

Introduction

Readers of your report want to know three things:

1 Purpose of your report,

2 Supporting argument,

3 Statistics, details and research materials.

Remember: your readers do not want all the facts. They want to know you have done your homework but not all the detail. Therefore, the first page of your report should provide most readers with everything they need to know to take informed action.

Each business uses a slightly different report format, depending upon the situation, chosen from the following list:

PRELIMINARY PARTS

A. Cover
B. Title Page
C. Letter of Transmittal or Preface
D. Table of Contents
E. Lists of Tables, Charts, Graphs, or Illustrations
F. Executive Summary

BODY OF THE REPORT

A. Introduction
B. Text
C. Conclusions and Recommendations

SUPPLEMENTARY PARTS

A. Appendix
B. Bibliography
C. Index

Not all reports will include every component. You wouldn't include an index, for example, in a report of less than ten pages. However, make life easy for yourself by adopting a format similar to the above.

1. *Preliminary Parts*

Your report should include all of the preliminary parts (except the Lists of Tables, Charts, etc. if your report does not include them). These opening pages provide the reader with the guideposts needed to chart a course through your report.

Cover

Presentation is important in business. The type of cover you choose should establish the seriousness of your intentions as well as protect the pages of your report. Use a simple heavy bond folder in a discreet colour such as grey or brown. If your report runs to more than 20 pages, have it cerlox bound. Although a stylish cover cannot make up for a sloppily written report, it will enhance a good one. Include the title, author, and date on a label affixed to the cover of your report.

Title Page

The title page must look attractive in order to encourage the reader to read on. Three elements govern the effectiveness of a title page.

Appearance

Your title page should consist primarily of white space, with key information clearly laid out.

Title

Choose a brief, effective title. Think of the advertisements you remember. They usually contain fewer than five words. Hook your reader's interest with a short, snappy title.

For example, how keen would you be to read a report entitled:

> The various expansion options available to Datamax regarding the offering of computer training courses to new and existing clients.

Such a title would use up at least four lines on your title page and could well alienate your reader by giving the impression that the rest of the report will be written in the same long-winded style. Cut the title down to seven words:

> Why Datamax Should Offer Computer Training Courses.

This title summarizes the intention of the report and implies that you will make specific recommendations.

Required Information

Once you have decided on a title that focusses directly on the main thrust of your report, include the following components:

1. Prepared for: name of person or company that requested the report.
2. Prepared by: your name, title, and company.
3. Location: e.g., Toronto, Ontario.
4. Date.

That's it! Refer to the sample title page following:

Sample Title Page >

WHY DATAMAX SHOULD OFFER
COMPUTER TRAINING COURSES

Prepared for
Ms. Gail Johnson
President, Datamax Inc.

by
John Morris

President
Morris & Associates
Management Consultants

Vancouver, British Columbia

January 8, 199-

Letter of Transmittal >

You usually clip the letter of transmittal (sometimes called the cover letter) to the front cover of your report. Using normal business letter style, address the letter of transmittal to the person who requested the report and then write three brief paragraphs.

Letter of Transmittal Format

Paragraph 1

State when your reader requested the report. For example:

> Here is the report you requested in your memorandum of September 20th.

Tell the reader the title of the report and provide a very brief description. For example:

> Entitled 'Why Datamax Should Offer Computer Training Courses', the enclosed report examines how Datamax

> can increase its market share by devising a curriculum and hiring instructors to provide clients with training in word processing, database management, and spreadsheets.

Paragraph 2

Imagine you are personally delivering the report to the person who requested it; then, write what you would say. Cover the following points:

- Why you wrote the report: to meet a need, to improve an area of operations, to develop a new direction, etc.
- Any problems you encountered: you were unable to obtain certain research materials essential to your topic, the recommendations in the report cannot be acted upon until certain space requirements are met, etc.
- Any special features the reader should be aware of: the report could be adapted for another company or situation, a particular point should be especially noted, etc.

For example:

> I have assumed that Datamax can acquire an appropriate space in which to offer the courses. As we agreed, the scope of this report purposely excludes research into space options.

Paragraph 3

Make a suggestion regarding future action and then thank the reader for the opportunity to write the report. For example:

> If you would like me to research space requirements for the courses, I would be pleased to meet with you to discuss an additional report. I look forward to hearing your reaction, and thank you for the warm support your staff gave me while I was conducting my research.

Remember to use the same friendly, professional tone to write your letter of transmittal as you would use if you contacted the reader directly. Be as brief as possible – you only want to introduce the report and "touch base" with the reader on a one-to-one level. Save specific recommendations and analyses for the body of your report.

Example of a Letter of Transmittal >

John Morris, President
Morris & Associates
Management Consultants
Ste. 1109 - 1120 W. Georgia St.
Vancouver, BC
V7H 1T3

January 8, 199-

Ms. Gail Johnson
President
Datamax Inc.
4218 W. Broadway
Vancouver, BC
V8H 3E4

Dear Gail:

Here is the report you requested in your letter of August 10th. As we discussed, I've titled the report "Why Datamax Should Offer Computer Training Courses" and examined how Datamax can increase its market share by devising a curriculum and hiring instructors to provide clients with training in word processing, database management, and spreadsheets.

I think you will be pleased with my recommendations regarding how Datamax could add computer training courses to the list of services you already offer your customers. I have assumed that Datamax can acquire an appropriate space in which to offer the courses. As we agreed, however, the scope of this report purposely excludes research into space options.

If you would like me to research space requirements for the courses, I would be pleased to meet with you to discuss an additional report. I look forward to hearing your response to my report and thank you for the warm support your staff gave me while I was conducting my research.

Sincerely,

John Morris
President
JM/ts
Encl.

Table of Contents

You already have your Table of Contents in the form of the outline you used to write your report. Simply add page numbers. Remember to list the major headings and sub-headings and to leave plenty of white space. You want to make your Table of Contents reasonably detailed but not so full of information that it scares off the reader. Avoid listing every single sub-heading of a long report. Limit your Table of Contents to one page or less.

If you have a word processing program that generates a Table of Contents, you can save yourself the trouble of re-typing your outline headings and determining page numbers. Use the Table of Contents feature to mark each of your headings throughout the report, return to a blank page, and then activate the function that brings each of the headings to the screen in the order in which you marked them along with the appropriate page numbers. Here's the Table of Contents for the Datamax Report:

Example of a Table of Contents

TABLE OF CONTENTS

List of Tables, Charts, Graphs or Illustrations

Include a separate list of all your non-text items to help readers quickly find a particular table or illustration. Use your word processing program to generate these lists as well.

Use tables and charts to simplify numerical or written data. Your readers may resent having to interpret endless columns of figures, especially if you provide little or no explanation. Therefore, only use tables and graphs when they express your message better than text alone, and never let a table or graph exist without some textual explanation. In addition, keep your tables brief, with three to ten columns at most. You can always include more detailed information in your appendices. Refer back to Section A for some examples of various types of tables, charts, and visual aids.

Remember that report readers want to know first what you've concluded from your research. They do not necessarily want to see all your data – at least not in the text. Usually you can summarize your data in the body of your report and refer the readers to an appendix if they want to check your figures.

For example, you can state in your report that:

> While 52% of surveyed clients were interested in buying our new product, 32% were not interested and 16% were not sure (refer to Table A in Appendix B for a detailed breakdown of the responses received from 10 client categories).

You do not need to break up your text with the full results of the survey. Give your readers a summary of your data and then quickly move on to describe the *effect* of the data on your conclusions and recommendations.

Executive Summary

You may well perceive the Executive Summary as the main challenge to your report writing ability. Correct! It is the most important page of all and must state, in the fewest possible words, the key argument or recommendation you wish to make.

If your report provides a basis for action, you should have no trouble identifying the what and why in your Executive Summary. Once your readers identify the purpose and recommendations of your report, they can refer to the body of the report to determine exactly how you arrived at your conclusions and how you propose to implement your recommendations.

Apply the principles of simplicity and strength to the Executive Summary because you have to summarize your report in no more than one (double-spaced) page. Ruthlessly eliminate unnecessary words, linking verbs, and passive voice constructions. Directors and senior managers may read only the Executive Summary, so make sure it contains the core of your report. Ideally, a reader who does not have time to read your entire report can receive enough information from the Executive Summary to support the appropriate action.

Include the following components in your Executive Summary:

Purpose of the Report

Your lovingly crafted core sentence establishes both the purpose of your report and the method you use to fulfill this purpose. For example:

> This report describes how Datamax can offer computer training courses in terms of two principal requirements: curriculum and instruction.

Immediately, the reader understands your report's significance as descriptive. It will focus on curriculum and instruction in roughly equal measure. Readers would know right away that the report does not deal with other issues such as office space. A clear and specific core sentence acts as a beacon to readers by leading them forward into clearly charted territory. For example, in the core sentence for the Datamax report, readers can predict that they will have to decide whether or not to offer computer training courses.

Reason for the Report

Here you provide the reason for the report. For example:

> While Datamax leads the competition in its provision of data management services, it must offer computer training courses to maintain its market position.

Methods of Investigation

What methods did you use to obtain your data: interviews? contact with other companies? analysis of financial statements? market surveys? etc. Briefly state your sources:

> The recommendations in this report depend on information from the following sources:
>
> - interviews with companies which offer computer training courses and the instructors who teach the courses
> - contact with Datamax clients to determine the need for such courses
> - cost analysis based on Datamax's current financial position
> - attendance at several computer training courses.

This description of your methods assures the reader right away that you have supported your recommendations and that you've based your report on solid research.

Conclusions and Recommendations

Summarize your main conclusions, then relate them to your recommendations. This portion of your Executive Summary tells readers what you expect them to do about your report. For example:

> By offering computer courses in word processing, database management, and spreadsheets, Datamax could realize a 30% increase in current revenues at a cost easily absorbed by the present operating budget. Datamax should therefore develop course materials and hire one instructor by September.

Your reader now knows precisely what action you recommend.

Sample Executive Summary >

The completed Executive Summary uses only 135 words:

> This report describes how Datamax can offer computer training courses in terms of two principal requirements: curriculum and instruction. While Datamax leads the competition in its provision of data management services, it must offer computer training courses to maintain its market position.
>
> The recommendations in this report depend on information from the following sources:
>
> - interviews with companies which offer computer training courses and the instructors who teach the courses
> - contact with Datamax clients to determine the need for such courses
> - cost analysis based on Datamax's current financial position
> - attendance at several computer training courses.
>
> By offering computer courses in word processing, database management, and spreadsheets, Datamax could achieve a 30% increase in current revenues at a cost easily absorbed by the present operating budget. Datamax should therefore develop course materials and hire one instructor by September.

2. *Body of the Report*

The body of your report contains all the specific information required to support your recommendations. How you structure this information will depend upon how many categories you specified in your Core Sentence. In the Datamax Report, for example, you would discuss two categories (curriculum and instruction). In addition to the "meat and potatoes" information of your categories, the body of your report also includes an introduction and a conclusion.

Introduction >

Your introduction sets the groundwork for the material in your report by providing a relevant context. Begin with a short statement that describes the problem your report sets out to solve (e.g. how to set up computer training courses). Follow this statement with a description of your report's scope. Provide reasons why you leave out certain relevant topics that do not directly relate to your specific problem. For example, in the Datamax report you may explain why you did not include any information on space requirements for the courses (e.g. you cannot research space requirements until you know if the courses will be offered).

Background Information

Your introduction sets out the problem and how you propose to deal with it. In a sub-section entitled Background Information, you describe how the problem developed and what (if any) work has been done in the past to solve the problem. For example, you could describe why Datamax has decided to investigate computer training courses at this time and if they ever conducted a similar investigation in the past. Perhaps they offered a course five years ago that proved unsuccessful. Describe this occurrence and provide reasons why it failed then, but should succeed now.

Identification of Need

Your identification of the need for a solution to your central problem should follow naturally from your discussion of background information. Describe the current situation; then indicate how the information in your report will alter it.

Principal Components >

The principal components of your report will take up the bulk of pages. Here you present your information and show how it relates to your central problem. If you have written an effective outline and kept to it, the body of your report should present no formatting challenges. You already have your major sections and sub-sections. Now just ensure that everything you write relates in some way to the purpose of your report. Present your information in a succinct and readable style. Support it with relevant charts, tables, figures, and illustrations.

Conclusions and Recommendations >

Conclude with a review of the relevant facts and their obvious implications. Then show how these facts lead to your recommendations. Present your recommendations in numbered form. For example:

This report recommends that Datamax proceed as follows to implement computer training courses this year:

1. Offer one course in each of the three subject areas: word processing, database management, and spreadsheets, beginning September 1st.
2. Run the courses concurrently for 10 weeks.
3. Appoint the Research Department to develop course materials in the three subject areas by June 1st.
4. Advertise for a qualified instructor on July 1st.
5. Direct the Personnel Department to screen applicants and appoint an instructor by August 1st.
6. Evaluate the courses in October for possible expansion next January.

3. *Supplementary Parts*

Appendices

You can include in the Appendices all the detailed information that would clutter up the body of your report. Such information includes questionnaires you used in your research, survey results, tables that the reader may wish to refer to but do not need to be included in the text, etc. Keep your appendices short. Your readers don't need access to everything you used to write your report. Select only relevant information.

Bibliography

If you used the work of other writers as the basis for your report, you must list these works in a Bibliography or List of Books Cited. Be sure to include all the relevant information, such as: name of author, title of book or article, publisher, date, and place. For information on how to structure your bibliography, refer to textbooks such as the *MLA Handbook for Writers of Research Papers* by Joseph Gibaldi and Walter S. Achtert, and the Social Sciences and Wall Street Journal *Style Sheets.*

Index

You rarely need to include an index in a report unless it runs for more than 50 pages or uses a great many technical terms. If you do wish to include an index, make it comprehensive. Readers should be able to find a page number quickly for every item covered in the report.

4. *Review: Units Eleven and Twelve*

In Units Eleven and Twelve you learned how to apply Mac's Method to organize your reports, how to present your information in a standard format, and how to write an Executive Summary.

To apply what you have learned about report writing, go on to the Review Exercise at the end of this unit and try the Report Writing Scenario. Before you start, take a minute to think again about the Core Sentence. The most important concept is to *write a clear and concise Core Sentence.* Practise using the six part format to focus your thoughts before you start your research. Here's the Core Sentence format again:

1 **Subject:** This report

2 **Action Verb:** analyzes

3 **Object:** the proposed takeover of Harris Enterprises

4 **Linking Phrase:** in terms of

5 **Numeral:** three requirements:

6 **Names of the Major Divisions:** increasing profits, finding new office space, and hiring additional personnel.

Once you have developed your core sentence, the rest of your report writing task should go smoothly. Just remember to give your readers something to act on.

Review Exercise: Report Writing Scenario

Apply the skills you have learned in Units Eleven and Twelve to complete the report components required in the following practical business situation.

Background Information

You are the new office manager for Jersey Enterprises – a large company that distributes computer components to retail outlets. You have worked for the company for only two months, but you have already written a memo to the vice-president informing her about current office conditions. Filing systems lack organization, staff do not feel very committed to their jobs, telephone calls do not get through, and clients complain about poor service.

The vice-president asks you to write a formal report that describes the office problems and recommends changes. She will present the report to the president and ask for money to implement the improvements your report recommends.

Report Components Required

1. Write a **Core Sentence** for your report. Because you will both describe the problem and present solutions, you may wish to use an action verb such as "analyzes", or "examines", or "evaluates".
2. Write an **Outline** of your report. Include all the headings, sub headings, and sub-sub-headings you will require.
3. Write the **Executive Summary.** Remember to write only one (double-spaced) page and to include all the components described in the section on the Executive Summary above.
4. Write the **Letter of Transmittal**, addressed to the vice-president (you make up the name and address). Remember to mention any limitations of your report.

Suggested Approach

In order to write the report components listed above, you need to make up your own facts and figures regarding the office problems. For example, you may decide that telephone calls do not get through because the existing phone system cannot handle more than two incoming calls at once. Recommend that the company purchase a system with ten lines. Or, you can state that the company loses $4,567 per year because of excess photocopying. Recommend that secretaries only make one copy of each outgoing letter rather than the three copies they make at present.

Get the idea? You can imagine any type of office and any number of different problems. You can then think up possible solutions, based on your knowledge of how an office should operate. Be creative!

Refer to the *Better Business Writing Answer Key* or your instructor for suggested responses.

UNIT THIRTEEN

How To Master the Electronic Pen

You will almost certainly have access to a computer when you work in a business office. Unit Thirteen describes how you can use the word processing program on your computer to help you write. Here's what you will learn:

1. Brainstorming
2. Writing the Draft
3. Final Presentation.

At the end of Unit Thirteen, you'll review what you've learned in *Better Business Writing* to prepare you for the Review questions in Unit Fourteen.

Introduction

Once you learn how to use a word processing program, you will probably shudder at the thought of returning to pen and paper. While some writers maintain that mechanical word processing cannot replace the creative act of writing with pen or paper, most embrace the freedom that creating with a screen and keyboard encourages.

The ability to delete and revise as you write ranks as the most obvious advantage of word processing. However, once you become familiar with your particular word processing program, you will find an abundance of features that put the fun back in the writing process.

After all, writing should be fun – or at least stimulating! Of course, no amount of word processing features can diminish the amount of brain power you must apply to write well. But you can break through the blank paper barrier more easily when you know that whatever you put on your computer screen does not need to stay there unless you want it.

To err is human; to really foul things up requires a computer.
– *Bill Vaughan*

At present, Wordperfect and Microsoft Word are the two main heavyweight contenders. You can use these programs to help you shift around sentences or whole chunks of text, simplify the research process, help you choose just the right words, put itemized lists in order, make global changes to selected words or phrases, and instantly reproduce certain repetitive functions or keystrokes.

1. *Brainstorming*

The successful writer listens to himself. You get a writer's block by being aware that you're putting it out there.
--*Frank Hebert*

How does a blank screen differ from a blank piece of paper? You need the same amount of inspiration for each. You bypass writer's block by using the screen as an erasable notepad that lets you brainstorm. Instead of getting caught up in the act of writing, you type any word you can think of that relates to your topic. Because you can delete any word at the touch of a key, you quickly lose the hesitancy that often accompanies writing with pen and paper. Before long, the words start to coalesce into a pattern. Move the words and phrases around the screen until you find the best arrangement. After sequencing the headings into an outline, the hard work begins: writing lively, coherent sentences.

2. *Writing the Draft*

Simplify, simplify, simplify.
– *Thoreau*

Although no computer program can completely relieve the agony and ecstasy of the writing process, several features of word processing can help you get efficient mileage out of the time you spend writing that all important first draft. Remember, you want to get *something* on screen – preferably as quickly as possible. You can revise later.

Split Screen >

Choose a word processing program that allows you to work with at least two documents at the same time. You can avoid frustration and speed up the writing process by splitting your screen into two parts. Use one half of the screen (called a window in some programs) to write your document and the other half to place your source material or your outline. Imagine yourself writing a report and then suddenly requiring a snippet of information contained in another document you have on file in your hard drive or floppy disk. Find this information as follows:

1 Split your screen horizontally. Your report stays in the top half while the bottom half of the screen remains blank.

2 Retrieve the source document into the bottom half of the screen and find the required information.

3 Copy the information from the document in the bottom half of the screen to the document in the top half.

Instead of using the split screen to retrieve research information, you can place your outline or notes in the bottom screen so that you can refer constantly to it as you write. When you take advantage of the screen splitting capabilities of most word processing programs, you decrease your chances of going off the topic or of missing out important points.

***Thesaurus* >**

If you have a hard drive and a program which includes a thesaurus, you augment your ability to write Power Sentences. For example, you may find yourself using the verb "maintain" too frequently. With a built-in thesaurus, you can instantly look up synonyms for maintain that may better express your idea. Perhaps "support" or "preserve" will project the subtle shade of meaning you require. Use the thesaurus frequently to avoid monotony. Of all the word processing features, the thesaurus ranks as the most valuable to the writer.

***Paragraph Numbering* >**

Most word processing programs allow you to number lists, paragraphs, headings and sub-headings so that if you want to insert a new item between, for example, items 2 and 3, the numbering automatically adjusts: item 3 becomes item 4, and so on. Use this feature to escape the tedious job of re-numbering each item manually. For long business reports in particular, the paragraph numbering feature permits you to add and subtract numbered items at will, thereby freeing you from having to include every item on a first draft. You can always leave a difficult section to work on easier sections, and then return to it without upsetting your numbering pattern.

***Macros* >**

Take time to learn about macros. The macro feature allows you to save a series of keystrokes (such as a commonly used address or company name) under a particular name or letter and then bring the keystrokes back to the screen at any time. By creating macros for phrases you use frequently and for functions such as paragraph numbering, you can save yourself hours of typing time. You can then apply that saved time to your most important task – writing and rewriting your sentences to make them as strong and clear as possible.

Search and Replace

You've just written a 50 page report comparing Product A with Product B. Your supervisor suddenly informs you that Product A's name has changed to Product C. Rather than scroll through your document to find each mention of Product A, you can use the Search and Replace function to almost instantly replace the words "Product A" with "Product C". You can also use the search function to find each instance when you use a linking verb such as "is" or "are". Simply tell the computer to search for "is" and then when the computer finds the first "is", spend some time thinking how you could replace "is" with an action verb. The search function helps improve your writing because you can easily miss linking verbs when you revise. Remember that ultimately you want to try eliminating most linking verbs from your letters and reports.

3. *Final Presentation*

Once you have written and revised your sentences and paragraphs so that they convey as much information in as few words as possible, you can use your word processing program to give your document a professional appearance.

Spell-Check

Use the spell-check function to find any misspelled words that may have crept past your proofreading efforts.

White Space

Arrange your sections and sub-sections so that your reader sees plenty of white space. Nobody likes to read lengthy single-spaced documents with tiny margins. You want your reader to actually read your words – so make it easy by arranging your documents as follows:

1 Clearly define each section with a heading, preferably in larger print or all capitals. Your reader should be able to skim through your document and get the gist of it just from reading the headings and noticing how much information follows each heading.

2 Leave three or four spaces between each section.

3 Indent sub-sections to set them off from main sections.

4 Use tables and statistics sparingly and only when they contain information that your reader can easily understand. Surround your tables and statistics with enough white space to set them off from the main text. Use boxes if possible.

5 Present comparison/contrast items in parallel column form to help your reader easily switch from one item to its counterpart.

6 Place the title of the document and your name or the page number in a "header" that appears at the top of each page.

7 Place the date and page number (if not in the header) in a "footer" that appears at the bottom of each page.

8 Jazz up lists with bullets, asterisks or whatever symbol your printer can accommodate. Don't use just dashes all the time.

9 Search through your document to find full pages of unbroken text. Rearrange these pages with columns, indents, boxed inserts, etc.

10 Use **bold** or *italics* sparingly to highlight important words throughout your document.

By using the above pointers, you help readers to grasp your message quickly. You are aiming for a "reader-friendly" style. So remember the basics: correct spelling, lots of white space, and an appealing format.

Review: Units One to Thirteen

You have now completed the material in *Better Business Writing*. To determine how well you have applied concepts such as the Power Sentence and the You attitude, dig out a letter or report you wrote before you worked through *Better Business Writing* and compare it with some of the letters you have written recently. Check to see if you now use more action verbs and write shorter sentences with more punch. If you have completed many of the Review Exercises in *Better Business Writing*, you should see an improvement in your writing skills. Before you put your feet up and read a good novel, why not take a few moments to review the principal concepts you have learned.

The Power Sentence >

Change from the Passive Voice to the Active Voice

Here is a sentence in the passive voice:

The secretary was hired by the Personnel Officer.

To change this passive voice sentence into an active voice sentence, follow these three steps:

1 Locate the action verb and put it in the present tense.
hire

2 Ask, "Who or what hires?
the Personnel Officer

3 Place the answer to Question 2 at the beginning of the sentence.

Note that the answer to Question 3 *always* provides the true subject of your sentence. Rewrite the sentence in the active voice as follows:

The Personnel Officer hired the secretary.

Write the Power Sentence

Apply this Checklist:

1. Use Subject/Verb/Object order.

   Subject:
   The staff member

   Verb:
   got

   Object:
   several good contracts.

2. Choose an action verb.

   The staff member *secured* several good contracts.

3. Choose a specific subject and object.

   The Vice-President of Sales secured five contracts worth over $3 million each.

The Power Paragraph >

Structure

Key Sentence: The first sentence establishes the core idea.

Illustrations: The next three or four sentences support the key sentence with examples or illustrations.

Concluding Sentence: The final sentence draws the paragraph to an effective close.

Transitional Markers

Lead your reader through your paragraph by using transitional markers as signposts. For example: also, in addition, such as, that is, of course, similarly, on the other hand, but, consequently, then, as soon as, etc.

Grammar Problems

...thou hast men about thee that usually talk of a noun and a verb and such abominable words as no Christian ear can endure to hear.

– *Shakespeare*

Pronouns

Agreement: A pronoun must agree with its antecedent. For example:

> Several unions decided not to ratify its collective agreements.

Rewrite:

> Several unions decided not to ratify *their* collective agreements.

Reference: A pronoun must refer to the correct antecedent. For example:

> The committee approved plans to increase their access to confidential files.

Rewrite:

> The committee approved plans to increase *its* access to confidential files.

Note: You can often avoid pronoun reference problems if you rewrite your sentences to eliminate the pronoun altogether.

Subject–Verb Agreement

The subject must agree with the verb even when extra words come between the subject and the verb. For example:

> Each of the employees at the two companies are hoping for a raise.

Rewrite:

> Each of the employees at the two companies *is* hoping for a raise.

Point of View

Maintain a consistent point of view in each of your sentences:

- Do not use the **active and passive voice** together in the same sentence. For example:

  > I cashed my cheque, and identification was asked for.

  Rewrite:

  > When I cashed a cheque, the clerk *asked* for my identification.

- Use the **same tense** (past, present, future) throughout a sentence. For example:

  As soon as I call a meeting, everybody went home.

  Rewrite:

  As soon as I call a meeting, everybody *goes* home.

- Do not mix together second and third **person references** in one sentence. For example:

  One should obtain an education so that you can secure an interesting job.

  Rewrite:

  You should obtain an education so that you can secure an interesting job.

Parallelism

Make the elements that describe a core idea parallel in structure. For example:

The new manager is very efficient, works independently, and gets along well with staff.

Rewrite:

The new manager *performs* efficiently, works independently, and gets along well with staff.

Coordination and Subordination

Coordination: Show that two ideas in the same sentence carry the same level of importance. Avoid weak coordination by not using "and this". For example:

Jason described why we should expand our operations, and this was not agreed with by the committee.

Rewrite:

The committee did not agree with Jason's description of why we should expand our operations.

Subordination: Show how one idea in a sentence *depends* upon another for completion. *Do not* merely join two ideas with "and" if they do not carry equal weight. For example:

Our sales could be increased if we hired a new Customer Representative and our product line could be expanded.

Rewrite:

We could increase sales if we expanded our product line and hired a new Customer Representative.

Mechanics >

Usage

Determine the correct usage of troublesome words such as principal/principle; complement/compliment; lose/loose; its/it's; that/which; he/him; good/well, etc. For example:

> Candidates who chose to apply for the position of principle, should assure they have performed good on they're exams.

Rewrite:

> Candidates who *choose* to apply for the position of *principal*, should *ensure* they have performed *well* on *their* exams.

Spelling

Make a habit of writing down any word which you frequently misspell. Once you learn how to distinguish an incorrect spelling, you are only a short step from learning the correct spelling. For example:

> Imediately after we arrived at our acommodation, we discovered we had failed to bring our stationary and the money necessary to pay for the conferance.

Rewrite:

> *Immediately* after we arrived at our *accommodation*, we discovered we had failed to bring our *stationery* and the money necessary to pay for the *conference*.

Punctuation

Concentrate particularly on learning to use the comma and semi-colon – the most frequently abused punctuation marks. Remember never to join two complete sentences with only a comma. For example:

> We took the client out to dinner, however he did not enjoy himself.

Rewrite:

> We took the client out to dinner; however, he did not enjoy himself.

Understanding Your Reader >

You Attitude

Avoid using "we" or "I" to start your sentences. Instead, try to use "you" frequently and your reader's name occasionally. Readers respond more readily to letters that take their concerns into consideration rather to letters that seem to come from some superior corporate entity.

Positive Approach

At all times, avoid using negative words such as “regret”, “reject”, “lose”, “lack”, etc. Use a positive word coupled with a “not” to express a negative idea. For example:

> We regret to inform you that we have rejected your loan application.

Rewrite:

> We cannot *grant* you the loan you requested.

Human Touch

Think of your reader as your best friend whom you write to about a business matter. In this way, you will avoid sounding too stiff and formal.

Letter Structure >

Yes Letter Structure

1. Say Yes
2. Supply necessary details.
3. Close positively.

No Letter Structure

1. Thank the writer for the request.
2. State the context of decision *so the reader* anticipates the conclusion.
3. Say NO graciously (or clearly infer it).
4. Provide a positive alternative where possible.
5. Close in a friendly, businesslike manner.

Gender Neutral Writing

Avoid using “he” or “him” when you mean people of both genders. Instead, try to use the second person “you” as much as possible. Alternatively, switch to the plural form “they”. For example:

> A manager must use his discretion when he asks an employee to work harder.

Rewrite:

> *Managers* must use *their* discretion when *they* ask an employee to work harder.

Different Types of Letters

Memorandum

Use a friendly but efficient tone that communicates the message as quickly as possible. Even in short memos, don't forget to apply the You attitude: use "please", "thank you", and positive words.

Sales Letter

Generate interest at the beginning by informing the customer how your product will help them. Focus always on the customer's needs. Use an attractive format and white space to appeal to the customer.

Collection Letter

Remember that the vast majority of customers want to pay your bill, but they usually lack the money. Use a sympathetic approach that will encourage customers to pay you first when they finally have the funds. If necessary, take an unconventional approach (e.g. a questionnaire, cartoons, etc.) when a series of friendly collection letters does not yield results. Most importantly – never threaten.

Complaint Letter

Use positive words to describe a problem – concentrate on preserving your reader's goodwill. You want to achieve results, not hand out reprimands.

Request Letter

Save your reader's time by omitting unnecessary details. Make your point quickly and politely.

Application Letter

Think of your reader's need for an employee rather than your need for a job. Match your personal qualities to the requirements of the position.

Apply the *3S* technique:

Strength

Use action verbs, the active voice, and specific words. If a sentence seems woolly-minded and unclear – cut it out.

Sincerity

Avoid jargon, stock phrases, and "big" words. You want to gain your readers' confidence, rather than impress them with your vocabulary and knowledge of contemporary "in" phrases.

Simplicity

Keep sentences short: an average of 15 words. Remove all redundant words. For example:

> In the event that you find yourself unable to comply with the various requirements listed in the document I've enclosed, you should feel free to give me a call (29 words).

Rewrite:

> If you cannot meet the requirements in the enclosed document, please call me (13 words).

Report Organization > Apply Mac's Method's six-step approach to organize your reports:

1. Construct the Core Sentence.
2. Write the Outline.
3. Collect information on Cue Cards, using single Power Sentences.
4. Write your first draft non-stop.
5. Edit the text; check spelling; add graphics.
6. Write the final version.

Core Sentence

Use the following format:

Subject:	This report
Action Verb:	analyzes
Object:	the relocation of the Toronto office to Vancouver
Linking Phrase:	in terms of
Numeral:	two issues:
Names of divisions:	cost and staffing.

Outline

The outline functions as your roadmap. It guides you through your research to ensure you do not wander off the track. Always make an outline *before* you begin your research.

Report Format

Preliminary Parts

A. Cover
B. Title Page
C. Letter of Transmittal or Preface
D. Table of Contents
E. Lists of Tables, Charts, Graphs, or Illustrations
F. Executive Summary

Body of the Report

A. Introduction
B. Text
C. Conclusions and Recommendations

Supplementary Parts

A. Appendix
B. Bibliography
C. Index

Word Processing

Use your word processing program to help you get over writer's block, to assist you with research, to help you choose just the right words, and to give your document a professional look.

Do you feel you've understood the concepts in *Better Business Writing*? Congratulations! Give yourself a rest and then try the multiple choice questions in Unit Fourteen. If you do well there, you'll know you've mastered the first and most important phase in becoming a skilled business writer. Good luck with our final challenge.

UNIT FOURTEEN

Check Your Achievement

At last – the ultimate challenge! Each of the following sentences contains one grammatical, punctuation, or stylistic error. Underline the error in each sentence and identify it by circling one of the four choices provided. Check your answers with the *Better Business Writing Answer Key* or your instructor.

1. I am concerned about your recent unexplained absences as these absences have resulted in a drop in sales.

A. Spelling
B. Incorrect Conjunction
C. Pronoun Reference
D. Subject-Verb Agreement

2. The Federal Government recognizes the need for affordable housing, therefore, you may wish to contact the Federal Ministry of Housing for financial or legal assistance to build your apartment block.

A. Punctuation
B. Stock phrases
C. Expendable words
D. Lack of parallelism

3. It has come to my attention that you require three days off next week in order to attend your daughter's wedding in Toronto.

A. Active to passive voice
B. Spelling
C. Stock Phrases
D. Pronoun Reference

4. If you spend hours adding up rows and columns of numbers to calculate your monthly expenses, it saves you time to buy a computer.

A. Pronoun Reference
B. Lack of Parallelism
C. Incorrect Conjunction
D. Jargon

5. Don't let sales staff just make a sale, push them to give you information.

A. Stock Phrases
B. Punctuation
C. Expendable Words
D. Pronoun Agreement

6. At the end of each chapter is included exercises to help you apply the material you've just learned.

A. Passive Voice
B. Usage Error
C. Tense Shift
D. Subject-Verb Agreement

7. Usually, the key mistakes include not having an adequate business plan, not finding the right market, and handling cash-flow incorrectly.

A. Tense Shift
B. Faulty Coordination
C. Passive Voice
D. Lack of Parallelism

8. Neither the managers nor the president have made a decision regarding the Butler account.

A. Incorrect Conjunction
B. Tense Shift
C. Subject-Verb Agreement
D. Jargon

9. In consideration of your immediate reply, I will forward the completed contracts.

A. Stock Phrase(s)
B. Passive Voice
C. Punctuation
D. Usage Error

10. We decided to merge with RRR Inc. and the agreement was confirmed.

A. Subject-Verb Agreement
B. Expendable Words
C. Weak Verb(s)
D. Active to Passive Voice

11. It is absolutely essential that we interface with the current market trend in order to complement our business profile.

A. Lack of Parallelism
B. Jargon
C. Usage Error
D. Stock Phrase(s)

12. Overall, I feel convinced that we loose more if we relocate rather than stay in our current offices.

A. Passive Voice
B. Usage Error
C. Tense Shift
D. Subject-Verb Agreement

13. I can't recommend the proposal in light of the fact that we lack sufficient funds.

A. Incorrect Conjunction
B. Spelling
C. Stock Phrase(s)
D. Active to Passive Voice

14. The Committee has voted to retain control of the dental plan in addition to its life insurance package.

A. Weak Verb(s)
B. Pronoun Agreement
C. Tense Shift
D. Pronoun Reference

15. The purchase price of WHT should be reduced to reflect the value of future cash flows in the $4-5 million range.

A. Tense Shift
B. Passive Voice
C. Subject-Verb Agreement
D. Punctuation

16. If assets are purchased, you would obtain a variety of tax benefits.

A. Passive to Active Voice
B. Pronoun Agreement
C. Faulty Coordination
D. Usage Error

17. Renegotiating the contract would result in a delay in the final acquisition date which would allow time to consider the acquisition in the context of your long-range expansion plans.

A. Expendable Words
B. Lack of Subordination
C. Lack of Parallelism
D. Usage Error

18. Greater flexibility is provided as the principal can be repaid at any time.

A. Punctuation
B. Spelling
C. Incorrect Conjunction
D. Tense Shift

19. A lower price, will create more room between the actual debt to equity ratio.

A. Lack of Subordination
B. Subject-Verb Agreement
C. Punctuation
D. Usage Error

20. You should consider other sources of financing so as to avoid using either the bank loan or prefered share possibilities.

A. Spelling
B. Stock Phrases
C. Tense Shift
D. Jargon

21. The analyses is performed using the audited, year-end financial statements of DRQ Inc. and J&C Ltd. for 1990 and 1991.

A. Pronoun Reference
B. Active to Passive Voice
C. Subject-Verb Agreement
D. Tense Shift

22. We should stabilize our operations before any further expansion is undertaken.

A. Spelling
B. Expendable Words
C. Active to Passive
D. Incorrect Conjunction

23. Recommendations were explained and supported and generally flow logically from the analysis.

A. Subject-Verb Agreement
B. Tense Shift
C. Usage Error
D. Stock Phrase(s)

24. To affect the takeover, I recommend that you transfer your common shares to a holding company.

A. Usage Error
B. Weak Verb(s)
C. Passive to Active
D. Punctuation

25. As part of the audit plan, an examination of ETT's market research studies will be undertaken to assess whether the deferred costs relate to marketable products.

A. Spelling
B. Passive Voice
C. Usage Error
D. Punctuation

26. If the criteria is not met, we must write off the development costs.

A. Lack of Subordination
B. Tense Shift
C. Lack of Parallelism
D. Subject-Verb Agreement

27. Each major heading in the two reports I submitted represent a vital stage in the proposed development project.

A. Tense Shift
B. Subject-Verb Agreement
C. Spelling
D. Punctuation

28. The Committee discussed the goals and motives of the company, addressed the limitations of the proposed Cost Schedule, and have indicated the implications of the expansion policy.

A. Faulty Coordination
B. Lack of Parallelism
C. Usage Error
D. Active to Passive

29. References and source materials which every office manager, secretary, and clerical worker needs to have includes postal code directories, dictionaries, and style manuals.

A. Pronoun Reference
B. Subject-Verb Agreement
C. Lack of Parallelism
D. Spelling

30. A filing system works best when records are stored and retrieved according to separate categories or classifications of information.

A. Spelling
B. Passive Voice
C. Tense Shift
D. Incorrect Conjunction

31. Offices which handle a large volume of routine corespondence often use word processing equipment to expedite form letters.

A. Usage Error
B. Weak Verb(s)
C. Spelling
D. Subject-Verb Agreement

32. If you needed to locate several items of related information, you should refer to the table of contents.

A. Lack of Parallelism
B. Usage Error
C. Tense Shift
D. Subject-Verb Agreement

33. When you prepare for the entrance exam, you can gain both time and confidence by recognizing that the goal of the exam is to test the professional capabilities and judgment of candidates.

A. Expendable Words
B. Passive Voice
C. Spelling
D. Punctuation

34. Once you complete the inventory, the process of ordering stock may be initiated.

A. Active to Passive
B. Lack of Parallelism
C. Weak Verb(s)
D. Stock Phrases

35. Their knowledge of the various issues involved in the two tax planning scenarios lack the depth and understanding required of professionals.

A. Expendable Words
B. Incorrect Conjunction
C. Passive Voice
D. Subject-Verb Agreement

36. The president and the vice-president are responsible for keeping records of travel expenses, and he also supervises personnel.

A. Pronoun Agreement
B. Subject-Verb Agreement
C. Usage Error
D. Lack of Parallelism

37. When she requested my assistance with the project, I told her that I am too busy.

A. Punctuation
B. Spelling
C. Tense Shift
D. Pronoun Agreement

38. The courier delivered two bound reports, boxes of computer disks, and a new printer on October 23.

A. Lack of Parallelism
B. Expendable Words
C. Passive Voice
D. Usage Error

39. We should obtain a professional evaluation of our financial situation and we should hire a full-time accountant.

A. Active to Passive Voice
B. Lack of Subordination
C. Subject-Verb Agreement
D. Spelling

40. The meeting was adjourned by the chairperson until more details could be gathered.

A. Passive Voice
B. Tense Shift
C. Punctuation
D. Active to Passive Voice

41. Hoskins & Sons, the acknowledged leader of all the shoe manufacturing companies, welcome your suggestions and concerns.

A. Pronoun Agreement
B. Lack of Subordination
C. Subject-Verb Agreement
D. Tense Shift

42. In response to your letter of August 12 about the proposal, I need more information about their immediate plans.

A. Pronoun Reference
B. Incorrect Conjunction
C. Pronoun Agreement
D. Lack of Parallelism

43. Each of the accountants are hoping to work on the Carter account.

A. Tense Shift
B. Punctuation
C. Expendable Words
D. Subject-Verb Agreement

44. The present system should be replaced as it does not encourage employees to take responsibility for their own actions.

A. Passive Voice
B. Incorrect Conjunction
C. Pronoun Reference
D. Punctuation

45. The recent rise in the number of errors John makes is a result of his poor eyesight and this affects the safety of other workers.

A. Stock Phrases
B. Spelling
C. Faulty Coordination
D. Lack of Parallelism

46. You should base your garden plan on the principle that your not going to want to weed more than a few hours a week.

A. Faulty Coordination
B. Spelling
C. Usage Error
D. Pronoun Reference

47. I hope you respond immediatly to our fund raising campaign.

A. Expendable Words
B. Tense Shift
C. Subject-Verb Agreement
D. Spelling

48. Ms. Adams, our receptionist, cannot handle all the phone calls and she must type all the president's reports.

A. Punctuation
B. Usage Error
C. Lack of Subordination
D. Incorrect Conjunction

49. The restaurant kept us waiting for 2 hours, however, we finally ate a superb dinner.

A. Tense Shift
B. Lack of Subordination
C. Incorrect Conjunction
D. Punctuation

50. We decided to hire a Financial Analyst, move to a suit of offices downtown, and ask for a $300,000 loan from the bank.

A. Usage Error
B. Lack of Parallelism
C. Spelling
D. Stock Phrases

Where Do You Go From Here?

You have learned a great deal about writing effectively by reading *Better Business Writing* and completing the exercises. Continue to develop your skills by attending writing workshops, evaluating the tone and structure of what you read, and practising writing as frequently as possible. Good business writers are not born – they write well because they write often and have learned how to identify errors and correct them.

If you wish to learn more about business writing skills, place a book order, or relay any comments or suggestions about *Better Business Writing*, please contact us at:

Clear Communications Press
1818 Greenock Place
North Vancouver, BC
Canada, V7J 2Z7
Tel: (604) 980-4318
Fax: (604) 980-4665